Anyone Can Create an App

BEGINNING IPHONE AND IPAD PROGRAMMING

WENDY L. WISE

MANNING

SHELTER ISLAND

For online information and ordering of this and other Manning books, please visit
www.manning.com. The publisher offers discounts on this book when ordered in quantity.
For more information, please contact

> Special Sales Department
> Manning Publications Co.
> 20 Baldwin Road
> PO Box 761
> Shelter Island, NY 11964
> Email: orders@manning.com

 Manning Publications Co.
20 Baldwin Road
PO Box 761
Shelter Island, NY 11964

Development editor:	Christina Taylor
Technical development editor:	Robin Dewson
Review editor:	Ozren Harlovic
Project editor:	Tiffany Taylor
Copy editor:	Corbin Collins
Proofreader:	Melody Dolab
Technical proofreader:	Scott Steinman
Typesetter:	Dennis Dalinnik
Cover designer:	Leslie Haimes

ISBN: 9781617292651
Printed in the United States of America
1 2 3 4 5 6 7 8 9 10 – EBM – 22 21 20 19 18 17

To my wife, who so patiently puts up with me.
To my parents, who so patiently put up with me for all those years.
And to the rest of my friends and family, who put up with me,
although sometimes not as patiently as I would like.

contents

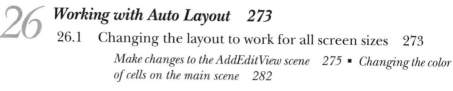

preface

I'm incredibly excited to have finally completed this book. I want to see more people learning to program, but some are intimidated by the enormous world of programming and have trouble finding a good place to start. I hope this book will help.

I didn't major in Computer Science in college, so I probably started my computer career somewhere close to where you are now. I got my first iPhone when they came out in 2007, and I was enamored. I wanted to create my own apps, so I found a local class that taught iOS programming, and away I went. I've been programming on the iPhone in some fashion ever since.

One of the things you'll notice after you begin programming is that your friends will frequently mention that they have a great idea for an app. Then they'll ask if you can create it for them, and they'll promise you a share of what they're sure will be huge profits. I've received so many of these requests that my general response includes telling people they should learn to create the app themselves. They usually follow up with a comment or two about not knowing where to start, not being smart enough, their brain not working like that, or programming being too hard. I constantly deny these things—writing an app isn't rocket science, and I think everyone can do it, given the time and the tools.

I've also been involved in a lot of women's initiatives: specifically, trying to encourage more girls and women to get into science, technology, engineering, and math (STEM) areas. This STEM interest, combined with my friends asking if I could help them create an app, led me to want to write a book for absolute beginner programmers.

This book isn't written just for girls and women, but that was definitely an inspiration when I began.

Why Manning? Well, I had purchased many Manning books in the past, and they were high quality. And many years ago, I volunteered to review draft manuscripts; I've reviewed several, so I was familiar (at a very high level) with the publishing process. As soon as I decided to write the book, I knew it had to be with Manning. I submitted my idea for the book, waited for a few weeks, and then received word that Manning wanted me to write it! Let the panic ensue!

This has been a long, fun journey—one that I wouldn't trade for anything. It's been a labor of love, joy, panic, long nights, stress, and happiness. This is the first book I've ever written, so I appreciate your reading it, and I hope you enjoy it.

Remember: you *are* smart enough, and your brain *will* understand this topic. Be patient—you can do it!

acknowledgments

There are many people to thank for helping make this crazy dream of mine a reality. Thank you to my biggest supporter: my wife, Jocelyn Whitfield. You believed in me, supported me, encouraged me, and picked me up when I was down. I absolutely could not have completed this book without you. Thank you to my parents for also encouraging me, helping me, and, of course, raising me! Thank you to all of my family and friends, as well. You don't know just how much your love and support helped me, especially Clay, Kristine, Nancy, and Ja. I love you all!

I also want to thanks the wonderful people at Manning who made this book possible: publisher Marjan Bace and everyone on the editorial and production teams, including Christina Taylor, Janet Vail, Tiffany Taylor, Corbin Collins, Melody Dolab, Dennis Dallinik, and many others who worked behind the scenes.

I can't thank enough the amazing group of technical peer reviewers led by Ozren Harlovic—Stephen Byrne, Mark Cooper, Igor Delovski, Olivier Ducatteeuw, Laurence Giglio, Pieter Gyselinck, Marius Horga, Jocelyn Jeriah, Kelvin Meeks, Drew Monrad, Jason Pike, and Stuart Woodward—and the talented forum contributors. Their contributions included catching technical mistakes, errors in terminology, and typos, and making topic suggestions. Each pass through the review process and each piece of feedback implemented through the forum topics shaped and molded the manuscript. Special thanks to Robin Dewson, who served as the book's technical editor, and Scott Steinman, who served as the book's technical proofreader.

about this book

I assume you bought this book because you want to learn how to make an iOS app but you've never done any coding before (that, or you know me and want to support me!). Either way, you're going to learn a lot and have fun in the process. The book is meant for people who have never written any code, or who have coded a little something but definitely not an iOS app. It also assumes that you have the patience to read the book, try the examples, and then rework the examples if they didn't work perfectly the first time. That's a lot of what coding is: debugging. Even the best developers miss things, so don't get frustrated when your code doesn't work exactly right the first time. Patience, Grasshopper.

Why iOS apps? If you tell your friends that you're learning iOS (or Swift, or developing for Apple phones), they may say, "Wow, I heard that was pretty hard. Why don't you start with something easier?" Your answer can be, "Well, I have an idea for an app, and I have the patience and willingness to learn. Ergo, I will." People may encourage you to learn something easier, like Hypertext Markup Language (HTML, used in web pages and such). That's all well and good, but you really wanted to learn to create apps for Apple devices (using Swift), so you're reading this book. I'm here to tell you, you can start with iOS, and you can learn to write apps; and with time, patience, and resolve, you can be an expert someday if you want to be.

My goal in this book is to give you just enough of what you need to know to complete the next step, without overwhelming you with a lot of things you don't need to know *right now*. In other words, I'm trying to teach this subject with *just-in-time* learning techniques. This means although there may be pages and pages of stuff you *could* learn about a topic, you don't need to learn all of that up front. I take all of those pages and distill them down into smaller portions of what you *really* need to know in order to get started.

Many people are leery of learning to program. The programming world is huge—there are many languages and many acronyms, and it seems as though some programmers haven't seen the Sun in years. Rest assured, you can get started by learning just the basics, and I'll walk you through the acronyms and the programmer jargon. Think of programming as just another hobby at this point. You can spend as much or as little time on it as you want, but the more time you devote, the better you'll be at it. Imagine me accompanying you on the path—we'll get there together.

Every developer begins slowly, learning the fundamentals. Even the most seasoned programmer had to start somewhere! There isn't a "club" that only allows certain people to be developers. Everyone can do it, including you. Take the time to learn the basics, understand the concepts, and work through the exercises, and soon you'll be an iOS developer, too.

Who is this book is written for?

This book is for absolute programming beginners who've never written a line of code and don't know the underlying concepts for doing so. I make these assumptions:

- You have no development experience.
- You want to learn to make iOS applications.
- You have a Mac on which you can code, or you are willing to purchase a Mac.
- You have patience.

I hope this book proves to be the perfect place for you to begin, because I know you can do it!

Who is this book not written for?

If you're a developer and are already familiar with concepts such as for loops, while loops, and if statements, and you just want to learn about iOS, this probably isn't the book for you. You can find other books that teach the syntax of Swift and differences between mobile development and other platform development, and you'll probably get bored with this book pretty quickly. But if you're a programmer and are only familiar with languages like HTML or COBOL, you can definitely learn something from this book.

Roadmap

The book is broken into three parts:

- *Part 1 (chapters 1–8)*—This is the beginning of your programming career. You'll learn the basics of how programming works, you'll be introduced to Xcode and the Swift Playground, and you'll write a few simple apps to get started.

- *Part 2 (chapters 9-16)*—These chapters will teach you about some additional skills and concepts needed to create apps, including the `while` statement, the `switch` statement, arrays and collections, storyboards, ViewControllers, and tables. Part 2 is more advanced than part 1, so make sure you understand part 1 first.
- *Part 3 (chapters 17-27)*—In these chapters, you'll create a LioN (Like it or Not) app. The LioN app allows the user to add items to a list and rate whether they like those items. When I'm at the store, I can never remember which toothpaste I like; so, I open the LioN app and search for *toothpaste*, and the app shows me which toothpaste I like. The app will serve as a complete example you can follow as you go on to create your own apps.

Source code downloads

You can download all the projects from this book and refer to them anytime. They're available at the Manning website (www.manning.com/books/anyone-can-create-an-app) and on GitHub (https://github.com/wlwise/AnyoneCanCreateAnApp).

Software/hardware requirements

Here's what you need to get started:

- *A Mac computer*—Chapter 1 gives you the basic requirements if you don't have a Mac already.
- *Xcode*—This integrated development environment (IDE) is the primary tool you'll need to create apps. You probably already use a program like Microsoft Word to create documents. Well, Xcode is the application you use to create programs. Appendix A has instructions for installing this free tool, which you'll begin using in chapter 2. I'll also go into more detail about Xcode in chapter 4.
- *A membership in the Apple Developer Program*—Appendix A explains how to join. There are two options: a free membership (which I recommend) and a $99 membership.

Online resources

The resource that will provide you with the most help with this book is the book's website: www.manning.com/books/anyone-can-create-an-app. You can download the examples, ask questions about the exercises in the Author Online forum, and chat with other readers. I'll try to be as responsive as possible and answer your forum questions, and of course you can tell me what you think of this book.

Apple is another great place to explore, including the resources in the Apple Developer Member Center (http://mng.bz/3OjD). You'll need to be a member of the Apple Developer Program; see appendix A for more info. You do *not* need to read these documents to use this book—I'm just providing the location in case you want to learn more about a topic. The Getting Started resources are a good place to start, and the Guides section is another good type of resource is the Guides section.

Stack Overflow (www.stackoverflow.com) is another great place to get answers about specific questions. You can search on your exact need, and it's almost guaranteed that someone has asked the question before and someone else has answered it. Be as specific as possible when searching, or you'll get back an excess of information.

About the author

Wendy Wise has an extensive background in mobile and application development and has worked with several Fortune 500 companies. In her 17-year technical career, Wendy has served as a senior director of software development, a senior product manager for international mobile applications, and a hands-on developer for web and mobile technologies, among many other technical roles. Wendy fully embraces her nerd/geek side, as you'll find out as you read this book. In her spare time, she enjoys beer, coffee, photography, camping, and being outdoors.

Author Online

Purchase of *Anyone Can Create an App* includes free access to a private web forum run by Manning Publications where you can make comments about the book, ask technical questions, and receive help from the author and from other users. To access the forum and subscribe to it, point your web browser to www.manning.com/books/anyone-can-create-an-app. This page provides information on how to get on the forum once you're registered, what kind of help is available, and the rules of conduct on the forum.

Manning's commitment to our readers is to provide a venue where a meaningful dialogue between individual readers and between readers and the author can take place. It's not a commitment to any specific amount of participation on the part of the author, whose contribution to Author Online remains voluntary (and unpaid). We suggest you try asking the author some challenging questions, lest her interest stray! The Author Online forum and the archives of previous discussions will be accessible from the publisher's website as long as the book is in print.

Part 1

Your very first app

Part 1 introduces you to the basic concepts of programming and aims to quickly get your feet wet in the programming world. You'll create your first app in chapter 2 and then in chapter 3 learn more about what you did and why you did it. Chapter 4 walks you through the tool (Xcode) that you use to create apps. You'll go deeper into the programming world in chapters 5–7 by adding buttons and text boxes. Finally, in chapter 8, you'll learn about an exciting tool called the Swift Playground, which allows you to learn and test code quickly and easily.

Getting started
1

This chapter covers

- An overview of creating iPhone and iPad apps
- Learning strategy—what to remember
- What you'll need to create apps for iOS

The world is continuously evolving, and the movement to *mobile-first* is part of that evolution. What is mobile-first? It's the idea that many people use their iPhones or iPads as their main source of information—whether for email, news, social media, the internet, shopping, texting, or phone calls. Because of this, companies are considering how to provide that information on a mobile device (like an iPhone and iPad) first, rather than the old way, which was to make a web page first and then add mobile device applications (apps) to support it.

It's an exciting time for technology growth and evolution, and you're going to be a part of that. This book will teach you what you need to know to get started creating apps for iPhones and iPads. It assumes you have no previous development experience and that this is your first foray into the wonderful world of app creation. If you've developed apps before, some if this information may be familiar because we're starting from the beginning, but everyone can use a refresher every now and then, right?

1.1   *The big picture: iPhone and iPad development*

Creating apps for iPhones and iPads is exciting. I understand that even thinking of creating apps for these powerful devices may seem daunting, but rest assured that we're going to do this together, and you'll complete several applications by the time you're finished with this book. Making apps for iPhones and iPads is complex enough that it has its own vocabulary, which I'll teach you.

Creating an app is known as *developing software*, and by the time you're finished with this book, you'll have developed several apps and will have a beginner's knowledge of software terms and basics. Let's start with the absolute basics to make sure we're on the same page (pun intended).

1.1.1   *Some key terms*

First of all, learning to develop for iPhones and iPads means you'll create apps that can be installed on and run *only* on iPhones and iPads. These applications can't run on any other devices, so make sure you understand what you're getting into. You'll learn to develop applications to run on iOS, which is the operating system (OS) that runs on iPhones and iPads. An *operating system* is the underlying software that runs on machines—like Windows 95 (going old school!), Windows 8.1, or Mac OS X (now macOS). These operating systems do all the hard work of interacting with the electronic components that make up a computer, so you have to interact with the OS instead of trying to tell the computer what you mean when you press a key. The early chapters of this book cover the key concepts of developing for both iPhones and iPads, but the first examples will focus on iPhones. Developing for iPads is not that different, and I'll show you the differences as we move into later chapters.

1.1.2   *Am I developing or programming?*

The term *development* is synonymous with *programming* because you're learning to develop or program apps that will make a computer do stuff. There are many, many programming language options to choose from. A *programming language* is a formally constructed language used to communicate with a machine. When Apple created the iPhone, it created a language called Objective-C (the programming language used before Swift) that, when used by a programmer and *compiled* or *translated* by a compiling program called a *compiler* (more on that later), can be understood and acted upon by the iPhone. Figure 1.1 shows this programming language at work.

As the figure shows, using a programming language to create an app for an iPhone or iPad involves the following steps:

1. You type words on the screen, which are *commands* or *code*.
2. The compiler takes those words, and, if there are no errors in the program, translates them into a language that the machine can understand.

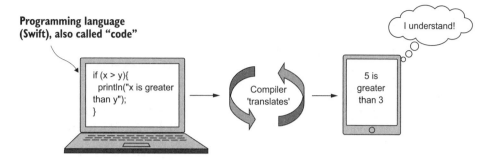

Figure 1.1 The app-creation process (the birds and bees of apps)

Learning to program is much like learning a foreign language. You need to understand the words and their meaning, and then you must put them together in the right order to form sentences.

1.1.3 Objectively Swift

As mentioned, there are many, many programming languages, and they all serve the same purpose of communicating with a machine, which can then act on those programs. For programming iPhones and iPads, there are now two choices of programming languages:

- Objective-C
- Swift

I'm not going to give you the history of the two languages, nor will I attempt to convince you that one is better. Objective-C was used as the first language for programming iPhones and iPads and has been around as long as iPhones have (and even before that). Apple released Swift in 2014, and it's a completely different language from Objective-C. Swift takes a different approach to developing for iPhone and iPad. It simplifies a lot of the complexity that other languages have, making it much easier to learn. I'm not going to focus on the differences or even discuss why Apple created a new language. The bottom line is that you will be learning Swift, and in this book you'll code in Swift.

The good news is that you are starting to learn Swift now, like everyone else. It's a new language, so there aren't people out there with five years of experience in Swift. Think of it: you could be that expert in five years if you want. The coding *syntax* (how you form your commands, or sentences, in the foreign language that we're learning—more on that soon) is easier to learn in Swift than in Objective-C. If you do want to learn more about Objective-C, you can find that information on the Apple Developer site (developer.apple.com).

1.1.4   *Apps you'll create*

This is the exciting part: you're going to create your own apps as you read and work through this book with me. We'll start out with some smaller apps to help you learn the basics, but you'll eventually build the LioN app, which you can download now for free from the App Store. Here's a quick sample of what you'll develop in this book:

- *Hello World*—Every developer's rite of passage in the programming world. The app will launch and display the message "Hello World." It isn't a complex app, but it ensures that you have everything set up correctly and that you know how to create an app.
- *Hello Button*—This app will allow you to press a button and change the text of a label within the app.
- *Textbox*—This app will let you type something into a text box, and then the app will print out the text on the screen.
- *How Many Fingers*—This app will let you play the game where one person (in this case, the app) holds up a certain number of fingers behind their back, and you have to guess how many fingers they're holding up.
- *State Abbreviation Lookups*—This app will let you type in the name of a state, and the app will then display the state's abbreviation.
- *LioN*—A useful app for helping you remember whether you "**Like it or N**ot." I created the app because I tend to forget what brands I like and don't like—take toothpaste, for example. I go to the grocery store and buy one brand because I remember it, but it turns out that I remember it because I don't like it. Now I can open up my LioN app and search for toothpaste, and it tells me that I don't like that brand, but I like this other brand. Quite helpful! The app has a search feature so you can search your LioN items based on the name or description. You'll build the LioN app exactly as it is in the App Store, with the exception of the ads available at the bottom of the screens and the notes.

Before we jump into the Swift language and its syntax, I'll go over some learning strategies that will make programming much easier for you.

1.2   *Learning what you need to remember*

The world of programming is enormous, which you're probably beginning to understand. There is a plethora (I like that word, don't you?) of resources available on the internet, and it's hard to know where to start or what to look for. This book will help distill a lot of that information down into digestible chunks.

The key to learning these concepts is to do the programming exercises in their entirety. You can read through them first if you'd like, but then you need to do the exercises: all of them. There's no better way of learning and understanding than by doing.

When you do the exercises, you will make mistakes. Even the best programmers in the world make mistakes. The key is to have patience and work through those mistakes in order to learn. Make sure you follow the exercises *exactly*, or they may not work the way you expect them to. You won't understand what you type out the first time you do it, but I'll explain as we go, so it will all become clear.

You can always check your work

You can always download the exercises and source code from the book's page at the Manning website (www.manning.com/books/anyone-can-create-an-app) or from GitHub (https://github.com/wlwise/AnyoneCanCreateAnApp) to see how I wrote them and compare them to your work.

1.2.1 Understanding and remembering key concepts

Now, what do you need to remember in this big Wild West of programming? The most important thing is to remember the *concepts* I'm teaching you. It's more important when starting out to remember the underlying concepts than it is to remember the exact syntax (the arrangement of the words and symbols used in programming) of the lines at this point.

Why? You can always write down the syntax or easily look it up online—but if you don't understand the underlying concepts, then you're merely typing words. Learning only the syntax would be similar to me asking you to copy a sentence in German (assuming you don't know German). You can copy it down and memorize it, but it will have no meaning to you unless you *know* German. I'll make it clear as we walk this journey together that some topics are *concept* topics, and some are *syntax* topics. The more you understand the concepts, the better and easier your programming experience will be. Key concepts will be called out in a separate box on the page, whereas syntax topics will look like this: Syntax: example.

1.2.2 Syntax

If you look up the definition for *syntax*, you'll see something along the lines of "the arrangement of words to create well-formed sentences in a language." You're going to learn the syntax of the Swift language—how to write out "sentences" that form code for an iPhone or iPad. As I've said, this is similar to learning a foreign language. In some languages (including English), it's customary to speak or write like this:

- The subject of the sentence first
- Then the verb
- Then the objects

For instance, *I read a book yesterday* is well understood in the English language. If you were to speak or write the same sentence in German (for instance), you would form the sentence as *Ich habe gestern ein Buch gelesen.* (*I have yesterday a book read.*) These are differences in the syntax of the languages.

Each language has syntax rules that make it easy for the writer or speaker to form the sentences, and for the reader or listener to understand the language. Programming languages also have syntax rules that help the computer make sense of what you're trying to do. Being able to write well-formed, syntactically correct code is important when creating apps—but not nearly as important as understanding the underlying concepts. You will begin to remember the syntax the more you code, and remembering your "sentences" will become easier and easier. The underlying concepts I teach in this book are important because they will be the foundation of your programming understanding.

So how do you learn the underlying concepts of programming? I'm so glad you asked.

1.2.3 *The importance of pseudocode*

Programmers have to understand the underlying concepts or plan of what they want to accomplish with any code they create. One way to understand and learn the underlying concepts of a program is to first write your code for whatever you want the program to accomplish in *pseudocode.*

Pseudocode—which for the purposes of this book means "fake code"—is a way to simplify and break down concepts and ideas into a logical progression of steps so they can be more easily understood. The steps you write in pseudocode are for *you* to understand and plan—not for the computer. Think about painting a wall in your house for the first time. You obviously want your work to produce a beautifully painted wall, but where do you start in order to get there? If you start with the end result in mind (the wall is painted) and you try to figure out how to get to the result, you'll need to think about a clear progression of steps in order to get there. Take a moment to think about the steps you would need to make the wall be painted and write them down.

Here are the steps I wrote down:

1 Go to my local hardware store and browse paint sample chips.
2 Select one or more paint samples chips and purchase sample paint.
3 Paint several areas on the wall with the sample paint.
4 Check the painted areas several times during the day to see what it looks like in different light.
5 Pick one of the colors and decide to go with that one.
6 Go back to my local hardware store and purchase more of the selected paint.
7 Get out rollers, drop cloths, paintbrushes, and overalls (I'm pretty messy with paint).
8 Tape the edges of everything.
9 Paint.

You may have fewer steps or more steps than what I've written down, but that doesn't mean that either of our lists is "more correct" or "less correct." You should be clear on the steps needed for painting when you look at your list. Does it make sense to you? Is it complete enough that you can walk through it logically and understand it? Then it's good. You wrote pseudocode for painting. There is no right or wrong pseudocode, unless your end result doesn't produce a beautifully painted wall. You go through the steps as many times as needed to get the result you want.

The steps say, "Get out rollers, drop cloths" and so on. They don't say "Get out rollers, drop cloths, make sure they are clean, set them in the room to paint, take the wrapper off the roller if it is new," and so forth. I've painted so many rooms that I think of this step as part of the "Get out the rollers" step. It makes sense to me. You need to make sure your steps make sense to you. We'll walk through many pseudocode examples for the exercises and code in this book, so you'll have plenty of time to practice and learn. Remember: the key is to list out what it will take to accomplish the steps so it makes sense to you. There is no right or wrong way to do it, as long as the end result is achieved in a logical, ordered way.

Now that you know some of the ways in which you're going to learn, let's talk about what it will take for you to start programming.

1.3   *What you need to create apps for iPhones and iPads*

So, what do you need to get started?

- First of all, you're going to need a Mac computer.
- Xcode, which is an *integrated development environment* (IDE), is the primary tool you'll need to create your apps. You probably already use a program like Microsoft Word to create documents. Well, Xcode is the program you use to create programs. Appendix A has instructions for installing this free tool. You'll begin using it in chapter 2.
- Join the Apple Developer Program. Appendix A explains how to join the program. There are two options to join: the free program (which I recommend) or the $99 program. Check out appendix A for more info.

I'll give you an overview of the Mac and Xcode here, and also talk about some helpful resources, before I send you to appendix A to install Xcode and read more about the Apple Developer Program.

1.3.1   *You're going to need a Mac*

Apple requires that all development for Macs, iPhones, and iPads be done on a Mac. Some ambitious developers have figured out ways around this, but it requires a lot of technical know-how. Trust me on this one—get a Mac if you don't already have one. You don't absolutely need a super-duper, brand-new, high-powered Mac, but it will be easier to write and test code if you have a faster Mac. You need one that has the following:

- Plenty of free disk space on the hard drive.
- At least 8 GB of RAM, but more is better.
- OS X 10.12.x, or Sierra or later (at the time of this writing, macOS Sierra is the latest). It's important that you use a recent version of the Mac OS—it's most compatible with the latest versions of Xcode and will support the latest iPhone features.

You can usually pick up some pretty good Macs on sites like Craigslist or eBay, but make sure you know what you're getting before you buy. I recommend getting the serial number of the Mac you're going to buy (if it isn't new) from the seller and checking the Apple website to make sure it's legitimate and to see if it's still under warranty (CheckCoverage.Apple.com). You can use an iMac, MacBook (Pro or Air), or Mac Mini for your development. The Apple Store online lets you easily select and configure a Mac, as shown in figure 1.2.

Figure 1.2 Apple Store machine options—the online tool lets you compare different Mac setups.

Apple provides a handy comparison tool so you can easily see the differences between the different lineups at www.apple.com/mac/compare. You can also save some money by buying a refurbished Mac from Apple at www.apple.com/shop/browse/home/specialdeals/mac. Refurbished Macs come with the same one-year warranty as new Macs. If you're in school full time, you can also save money by purchasing from the Apple Education store. Go to the main apple store page (http://store.apple.com), scroll all the way to the bottom of the page, and locate the link For Education.

Make sure you're running the latest operating system (macOS) on the Mac. If you have an older Mac that doesn't have the latest operating system, you can upgrade it by going to the App Store. Depending on how old your operating system is, there may be a fee to upgrade it, but many updates are free.

> ### Sierra OS X 10.12 or newer required for book's exercises
> For consistency with the exercises in this book, you'll want to have at least Sierra (OS X 10.12 or newer) installed. These exercises were all written using macOS Sierra.

If you don't know what version of OS X you have installed now, it's easy to find out. Click the Apple (🍎) in the top-left corner of your screen, and select About This Mac. You can see in figure 1.3 that my MacBook is running macOS Sierra version 10.12.

Figure 1.3   Find the version of your operation system by clicking the Apple icon and then About This Mac.

1.3.2   *Xcode: the iPhone and iPad development environment*

Now that you have your Mac, you need to install Xcode. This IDE is the primary tool you'll use to create your apps. Think of an IDE as a translator between English and the iPhone or iPad. The IDE acts somewhat like Google Translate (http://translate .google.com):

1 You type words into the box for the language you know.
2 You select a language you don't know and click Translate.
3 It gives you the translation.

If you misspell the English words, Google Translate doesn't know what to do with that and shows you an error. If you put in a poorly formed sentence, the translator may give you an error or a response that you weren't expecting.

The IDE acts on the same principles. When you type in well-formed "sentences," the IDE translates it into machine language that the iPhone or iPad can understand. When you misspell words or don't form "sentences" correctly, you'll get errors, or the device will behave in ways you didn't expect. Many programming languages have their own IDEs. Apple uses Xcode for all development, including for iPhones and iPads.

Appendix A has installation instructions for Xcode and details on registering for an Apple Developer account. Once you finish this chapter, you should go to appendix A and complete the steps before starting chapter 2.

Next, we look at some helpful resources to make learning to program for iPhones and iPads easier.

1.3.3   *Helpful resources*

This book will provide you with all the steps necessary to create several apps, and it will teach the underlying concepts of doing so. In some cases, you may want to learn more about a specific topic or you may want to go deeper into a subject. Here are some great resources to help you do that:

- *This book's website*—Here you can download the examples, ask questions about the exercises in the Author Online Forum, and chat with other readers. The website is at www.manning.com/books/anyone-can-create-an-app. I'll try to be as responsive as possible and answer your Forum questions, and you can tell me what you think of this book.
- *Apple*—A good place to start exploring, but it may seem overwhelming at first. There are some "getting started" resources you can review in the Apple Developer Member Center (https://developer.apple.com). You'll need to become a member of the Developer Program first (see appendix A for more info). You do *not* need to read these documents to use this book. I am providing the location for you if you want to learn more about a topic. The first place to start in Apple Developer Member Center is the Develop link at the top of the screen; then select Guides.
- *Stack Overflow*—This site (www.stackoverflow.com) is another great place to get answers about specific questions. You can search on your exact need, and you're almost guaranteed that the question has been asked before and someone else has answered it. Be as specific as possible when searching this or you'll get a lot of information back.

Remember that learning to write apps for iPhones and iPads can be a daunting task if you try to take it on all at once. This book gives you the information when you need it and suggests further resources if you want to learn more about a topic. Think of the old adage: *How do you eat an elephant? One bite at a time.* You can't try to eat the whole elephant in one bite. You need to take it step by step and plan your attack. That's why I want you to learn the important topics "just in time." (So we're clear, I don't condone or recommend eating elephants.) It's time to turn to appendix A to install the tools you'll need to begin developing in Chapter 2.

Concepts to remember

- Hopefully you got excited about creating apps for iPhones and iPads, and you realized that you *can* learn this with the help of this book.
- You learned about *pseudocode*, which means "fake code." You will create your own pseudocode as a type of road map to help you develop your apps.
- You learned about *syntax*, which is the way coding "sentences" are formed. The computer requires you to use the correct syntax so it can understand what you are telling it to do.

(continued)

- You learned about Xcode, the IDE you will you use to create your code. The IDE will compile (translate) your code into a language that iPhones and iPads can understand.
- You know what type of machine it will take to be an iPhone or iPad developer (a Mac).
- You learned what you need to remember, what you can reference later, and what you can look up online.
- You learned where to go for additional help.

1.4 Summary

Congratulations—you just finished the first chapter in a technical book! Remember to take this learning journey step by step. This book will give you what you need to know, when you need to know it. By the end of the book, you'll be comfortable with coding terms. You'll know some coding lingo, and you'll have created multiple apps for iPhones and iPads. Let's get to it and create your first app in the next chapter (but first, go to appendix A).

Building your first app

2

This chapter covers

- Launching Xcode for the first time
- Creating your first application
- Running your first application

You've done all the setup (if you haven't done it yet, please go to appendix A to set up the tools you'll need to complete this chapter). Now you're probably eager to start creating your first app. We're going to start off as almost every programmer ever has: with a Hello World application—a rite of passage for coding. A Hello World application is the first app almost every programmer writes when learning a new programming language, because it's a simple app that accomplishes two goals:

- It gets the programmer using the new tools.
- It proves that the programming tools are set up correctly.

Those are the goals of the application, but what does it actually do? Hello World will launch and display the words "Hello World!" That's it. It may not seem like much, but it's important to take small steps while learning to program.

I'm going to write my own version of pseudocode here so you know what you want to accomplish. As I explained in chapter 1, *pseudocode* is your road map—logical steps required to make the app do what you want it to do. This pseudocode will be a bit more detailed than future chapters, because it's your first app. In my version of the pseudocode, the steps needed to build the Hello World app are as follows:

1 Launch Xcode.
2 Create a new project.
3 Set up your project options.
4 Run the blank app.
5 Add the Hello World text.
6 Run the app.
7 Pat yourself on the back.

It's going to take seven small steps to create your first app. Get ready—we're starting!

2.1 Launching Xcode for the first time

I'm going to quickly walk through Xcode, the integrated development environment (IDE) introduced in chapter 1. I'll show you only what you need to know to create your first app in this chapter. Chapter 4 goes into detail about Xcode if you must jump ahead.

2.1.1 Step 1: Launch Xcode

Step 1 in the pseudocode was to launch Xcode, so find the Xcode icon in Launchpad on your Mac. If you're not familiar with Launchpad, it is the easiest way to find applications installed on your Mac. It looks like a rocket launching (fancy that…Launchpad, a rocket…launching), as shown in figure 2.1. Once Launchpad is on your screen, look for the Xcode icon and click it.

> **Helpful shortcut alert**
> You can also find Xcode by holding down the Command key (⌘) and the spacebar key to launch Spotlight Search. Type *xcode* into the Search bar. Spotlight will help you find anything on your Mac.

Figure 2.1 Use Launchpad (left) to launch Xcode (right).

2.1.2 Step 2: Create a new project

The next step in the pseudocode is to create a new project. Once you've launched Xcode, you should see an initial window that says Welcome to Xcode, as shown in figure 2.2.

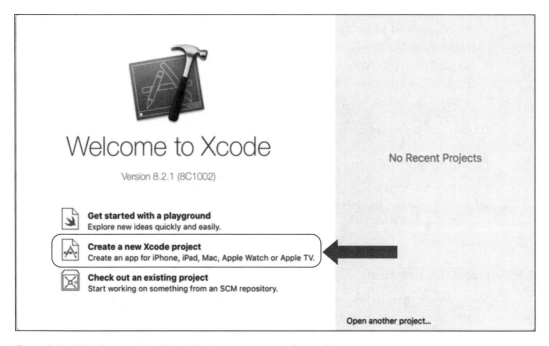

Figure 2.2 Click Create a New Xcode Project to start your first project.

When this appears, click to select the second option, Create a New Xcode Project. The Choose a Template dialog box appears, as shown in figure 2.3.

We'll walk through each option a little later. For now, click Application in the left window pane, if it isn't already selected. On the right, you now have multiple options. Click Single View Application, and then click Next. The Choose Options dialog box will open.

2.1.3 Step 3: Set up your project options

The Choose Options dialog box is used to set up the basic information for your new app, as shown in figure 2.4. You'll see these options for each new app you create, so let's go over them so you know what they do.

Product Name is where you enter the name of your new application. In this case, we're calling it HelloWorld. This product name will be used by Xcode to fill in several areas of the application (I show you those areas in later chapters).

The next box is Organization Name. This field assumes that you are developing for a company or organization. I do have my own company, so I entered *WiseAbility* in this

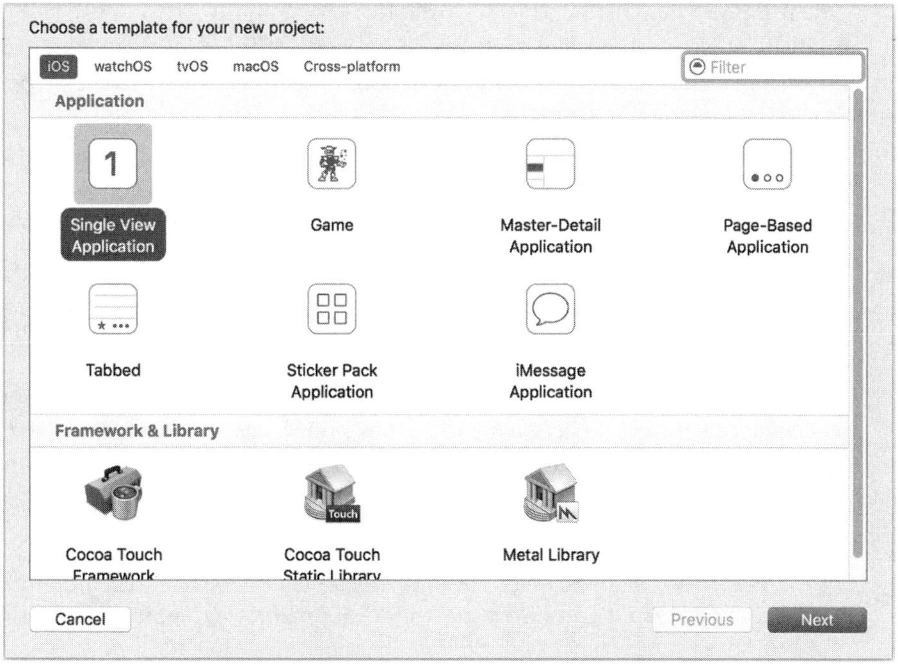

Figure 2.3   Click Single View Application in the iOS Application section.

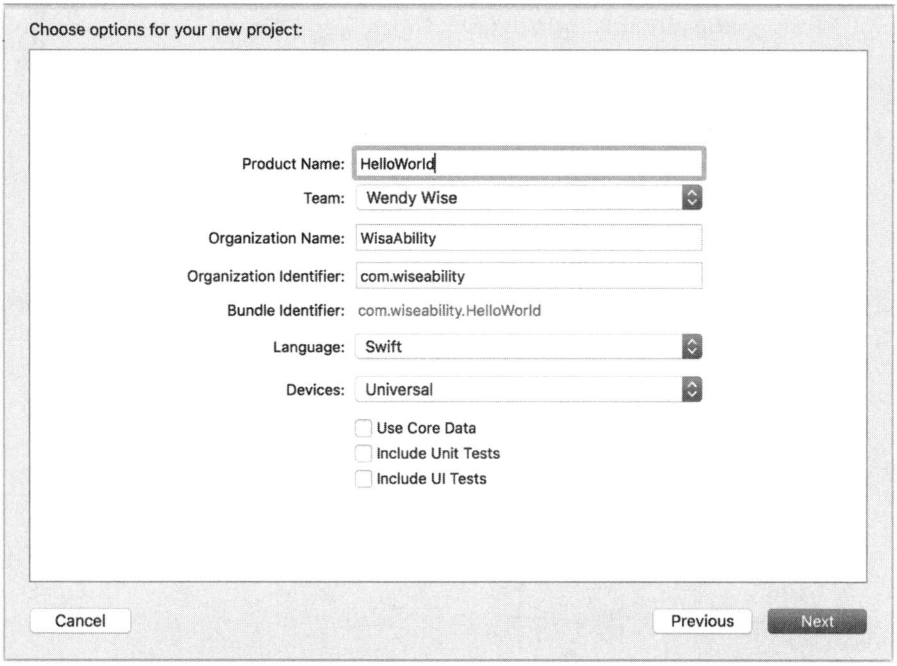

Figure 2.4   Configuring your project options—add HelloWorld to the Product Name, add an Organization Name, and click Next.

field. You don't actually need to be affiliated with a company to develop for iPhones and iPads, so if you don't have a company or aren't affiliated with one, put something here as a placeholder. You can enter a fictional dream company name if you want, or your own name, or leave it blank.

The Organizational Identifier field is used to create unique names for your projects in the event that you want to publish your app to the App Store. It's common practice to use your website domain in reverse for this field. My website is www.wiseability.com, so I use *com.wiseability* for the organizational identifier. You must fill in this field, and if you don't have a website right now, you can use *com.yourlastname* (filling in your last name). You can't have any spaces in this field, so if your last name has spaces, use dashes (-) to replace the spaces.

Once you fill in the Organization Identifier, the Bundle Identifier should show *[your-organization-identifier].HelloWorld*, as mine does: *com.wiseability.HelloWorld*. It isn't important to know the details of these settings right now—we still have a lot of the elephant left to eat that I mentioned in chapter 1.

> **NOTE**   If you name your project Hello World, the Bundle Identifier will show *Hello-World*—what gives? Well, Xcode doesn't allow spaces in the Bundle Identifier field, so if you enter spaces in the product name, it replaces them with dashes (-).

Finally, make sure the Language selection is Swift, and Devices is set to iPhone. Leave the Use Core Data selection blank, and make sure the Include Unit Tests and Include UI Tests options are unchecked. Click Next.

You can now choose where to save your project files on your hard drive. I recommend creating a folder called dev and putting all your work there, so it's easy to keep track of.

Click Create. Xcode will now create a new project for you and open it. This is pretty easy so far, right?

2.1.4   *Step 4: Run the blank app*

I know it doesn't feel like you've actually built an application yet, but Xcode has taken care of the infrastructure and framework for you. How cool is that?

Your next step is to run the blank app. At top left of the current screen is the Run button. It looks like a familiar, triangular play button, as shown in figure 2.5.

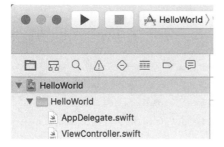

Figure 2.5   Xcode's Run button looks like the play button on most electronics.

This is the universal coding sign for Run. Click it once. The iOS Simulator should pop up with a blank screen, as shown in figure 2.6.

iPhone 7 Plus – iOS 10.2 (14C89)	
Carrier 🔗	6:15 PM

Figure 2.6   If you see a blank simulated iPhone screen, you've set up your project correctly.

The iOS Simulator is an application that Apple built to help developers (like you) test their applications before installing them on an actual iPhone or iPad. Chapter 3 talks a lot more about the iOS Simulator. For now, you're going to launch it so you can see it in action. If you see the blank screen, you're golden.

2.1.5   Step 5: Add the Hello World text

Step 5 of the pseudocode was to add the Hello World text, so let's get to it. Back in Xcode, on the left side of the screen, you should see several filenames, including Main.storyboard.

Click the Main.storyboard file. You should see a screen like figure 2.7.

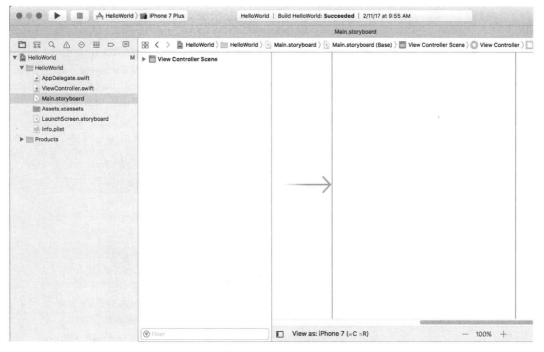

Figure 2.7   Select the Main.storyboard file on the left side of Xcode.

At bottom right on your Xcode screen, if it isn't already selected, select the third button—the one that looks like a circle with a tiny square in it—as shown in figure 2.8. This is the Object Library, which is like a toolbox with all the things that you'll need to build your app. The toolbox is full of items like nuts, bolts, screws, wires, and more. Chapter 4 talks a lot more about the Object Library, but for now, you're going to select a *label* as the item you need for this app.

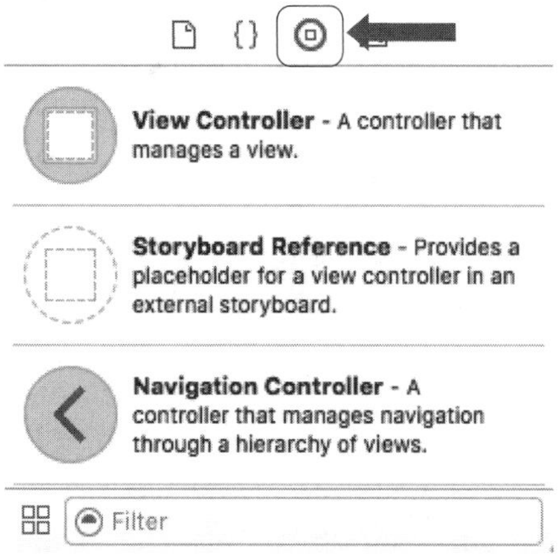

Figure 2.8   Showing the Object Library

At the bottom of the Object Library window, click in the search area, and type *label*. The list should be filtered down to the word *Label* and an icon.

Click and drag the Label icon (the bigger word Label on the left) to the other screen, called the *storyboard* screen, as shown in figure 2.9. Position it near the top-left corner in the storyboard screen, and then drop it by releasing the mouse button.

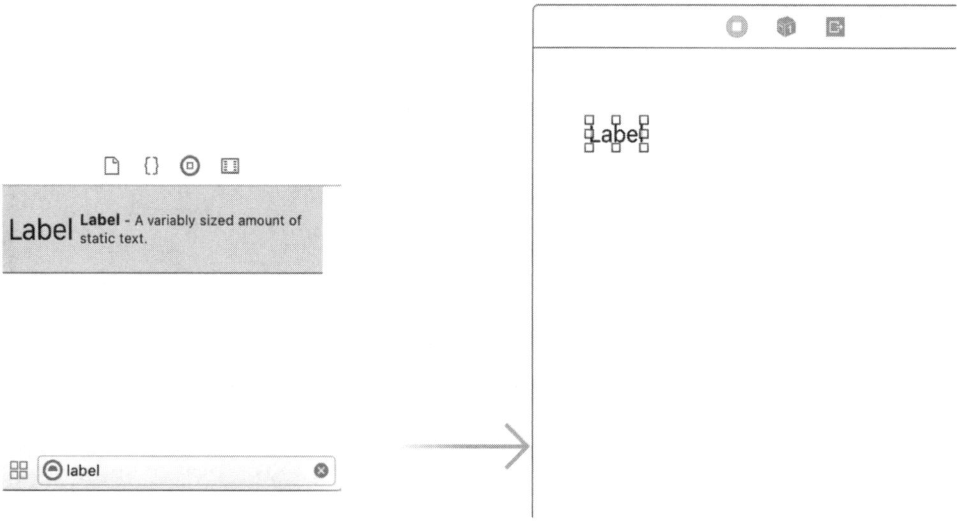

Figure 2.9   Dragging a label onto the storyboard

Once your label is on your storyboard, double-click it so you can edit the text. Type *Hello World!* and then click somewhere else on the storyboard to stop editing the label.

2.1.6   *Step 6: Run the app*

We're finally at step 6 of the pseudocode list: Run the app. You already ran the app once earlier in step 4, but now you'll run it again to see the actual Hello World text.

Click the Run button again. If everything is set up correctly, you should see the iOS Simulator window pop up with the words "Hello World!" displayed, as shown in figure 2.10. The size of the storyboard and the size of the Simulator are different, but you'll fix that in Chapter 7.

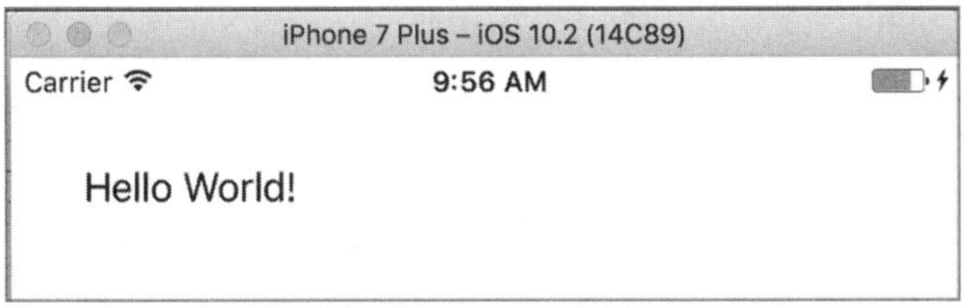

iPhone 7 Plus – iOS 10.2 (14C89)

Carrier   9:56 AM

Hello World!

Figure 2.10   Your first app running—congratulations!

> **Troubleshooting**
>
> If you don't see your label or your app doesn't look like figure 2.10, go back to your storyboard in Xcode, move your label closer to the top left of the storyboard screen, and run the app again.

Congratulations! You wrote your first iOS application. Exciting, right? You're already a success! Revel in it.

> **Terminology alert**
>
> You are now a *newbie*, or *noob*, to iOS programming. That means you are a new, inexperienced developer. Don't let anyone tell you it's a negative term—you're learning. Wear your newbie badge with pride.

2.1.7   *Step 7: Pat yourself on the back (and review)*

Step 7 in the pseudocode steps was to pat yourself on the back. Go for it!

This example was pretty easy, and it's true that we glossed over a lot of stuff. The next chapter will explain the details of what you did and why you did it. Remember, it's important for you to understand the underlying concepts of development, but the details can drown you if you don't wade in slowly. At this point, I want you to focus on remembering some of the basics: how to create an app, where the Object Library is, and how to build and run (with the play button) your code.

> **Concepts to remember**
> - How to launch Xcode
> - How to start a new project—you're going to do this a lot
> - How to run an application—you're going to do this a lot, too
> - How to drag and drop objects to your storyboard
>
> If you don't remember how to do all of these things, walk through this chapter again. You'll do these things many, many times in the upcoming chapters, so you'll have lots of practice. It's good to get the basics down early.

I hope you feel like you accomplished something, because you did. You wrote your first iOS application. It may not have done much, but still—you did it. You may also feel like there's a *lot* you don't know, and that Xcode looks scary with all those buttons, tabs, and icons. Don't worry. I'm going to cover the details of it so it won't look so daunting. We'll do it in small chunks, though, and we'll do it on a *just-in-time* basis so you don't feel like you're drowning.

2.2   *Summary*

I told you in chapter 1 that I'd distinguish key programming concepts in each chapter. This chapter was mostly a how-to—remember, I also told you that you'd learn what you need when you need it. This chapter taught you the actions to take, and the next chapter will tell you why you took them. I hope you're excited about your progress and curious about what you've done so far.

Your first app, explained

This chapter covers

- Xcode templates
- Understanding single-view applications
- Using labels
- The iOS Simulator

In chapter 2, you launched Xcode, created a new project, set your project options, added a label to the app, and ran it in the Simulator for the first time. This chapter will now explain the steps that you took so you'll understand not only what you did, but why you did it.

3.1 Xcode templates, explained

Starting from the top: when you launched Xcode and clicked File > New > Project, a menu item opened a window of templates. What is a *template*, anyway? Apple has created the basic structure or guts of several popular types of mobile applications within the Xcode application. Think of it as though you're preparing a difficult task—like repairing a bicycle. You get out all the parts that you know you're going to need, and in some cases, you assemble some parts before you even touch the bicycle. In the same way, Apple has already made some of the project infrastructure for you, knowing you'll need certain things to complete the project.

The templates are powerful and can help you complete your application in a shorter amount of time, but it's important to understand how they work before you begin relying on them too much. You started your Hello World app in chapter 2 by selecting the Single View Application template (shown in figure 3.1) during the creation of your new project. You may be wondering what that is. I'll explain next.

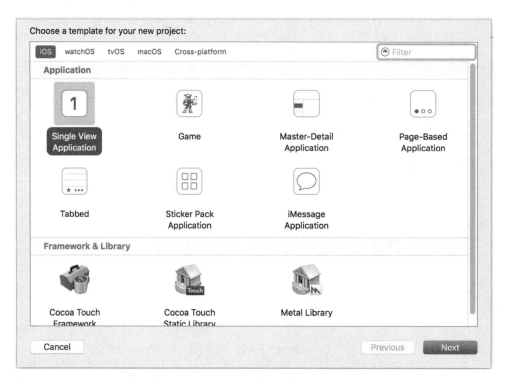

Figure 3.1   Template options for new projects. The Single View Application template is like a blank page in a book, waiting for you to make it into your masterpiece.

3.2   *Understanding the single-view application*

The single-view application is just that: one view that Apple has built for you, which you need to add something to. When you think about a *view*, think of a blank page in a book. There are no words or pictures on the page yet—it's empty. And it has no other parts to it. You can't flip the page to see what's next, because there isn't a next page.

If you think back to the Simulator running Hello World (shown in figure 3.2), you'll notice that there are no buttons or controls to take you to another place or anything. Apple gives you the binding that encloses the book (the application itself) and a blank page for you to do something with (the single view). It's your job to decide what to do with the blank page.

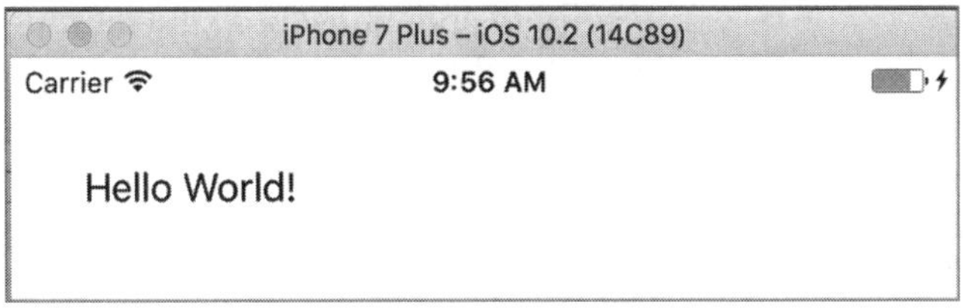

iPhone 7 Plus – iOS 10.2 (14C89)

Carrier 🛜   9:56 AM   🔋⚡

Hello World!

Figure 3.2   **The Hello World app from chapter 2 is a single page with no navigation or buttons.**

In chapter 2, you added a label to the page when you created Hello World. But what is a label? I'm so glad you asked.

3.3   *A label, defined*

A *label* is kind of like a label in the real world—something static that the user can't interact with. If you label something in your house (for example, light switches), you can't do anything with the label. You can look at it, and you can interact with what it labels, but not with the label itself. If you label your master bedroom light switch, you can turn the switch on and off, but the label itself doesn't change. Figure 3.3 takes the empty space (in this case, your app) and adds a label to it. Voilà!

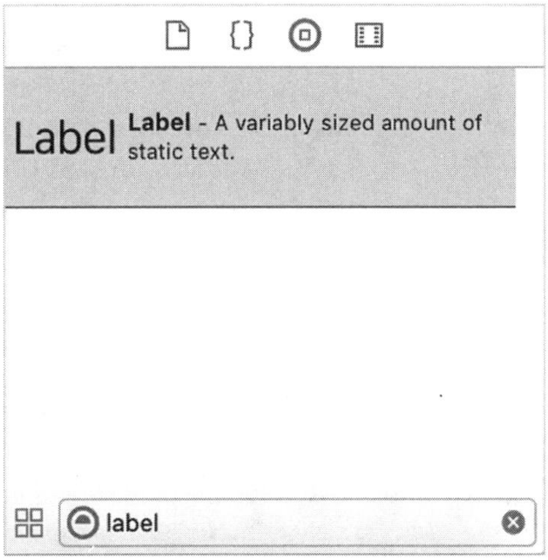

The Apple developer website has its own definition of *label* in its documentation. I talk more about documentation in later chapters, but if you're interested now, you can check out http://mng.bz/xd94, which defines a label as follows:

Label - A variably sized amount of static text.

label

Figure 3.3   **Our good friend, the label**

> *The UILabel class implements a read-only text view. You can use this class to draw one or multiple lines of static text, such as those you might use to identify other parts of your user interface. The base UILabel class provides support for both simple and complex styling of the label text. You can also control over aspects of appearance, such as whether the label uses a shadow or draws with a highlight. If needed, you can customize the appearance of your text further by subclassing.*

This is a lot to try to take in, so let's break it down into simpler terms. Here are a few key points to note about Apple's definition:

- *Apple calls the label a UILabel.* The *UI* prefix stands for *user interface*, which means you can use the label on the part of the application that the user will see. You might see the UI prefix when you're creating apps and adding things that the user sees, such as a label. UI labels are classes.

- *Classes are like the general idea of something in the real world.* Consider a pen. When you think of a pen, you have a pretty good idea of what it is, how it works, and how to use it. It has some kind of ink, it may or may not have a lid or a cap, and it may or may not have a spring-loaded button to enable writing—but it is still a pen. A pen is like a class in programming. It's the definition of a set of expected behaviors (making marks on something) and basic structure (it should be cylindrical and have some way to hold the ink). Again, the pen "definition" here is like a class. Hold that concept in mind as we move on to the definition of objects.

- *Objects are instances of the class.* Imagine you have a pen in front of you that you can touch and hold. That's an object. It is a type of pen (the overall class), but is also an instance of a pen (the object). If you grab a second pen, it may or may not look anything like your first pen, but it is still a pen. You now have two instances of the class *pen*, or two objects of type *pen*. You can think of objects in programming in the same way. Objects of the same type (such as pens in the real world, or labels in the programming world) will behave the same way (making marks on something, displaying text) and will look similar (pens can be a variety of colors and shapes, but you still know they're pens, and labels can be a variety of sizes and colors and they're still labels).

Key concept

It's very important that you understand the concepts of objects and classes. Objects and classes will be used throughout this book and throughout your programming career. It's important that you become clear about these concepts, but don't worry if they're still a little confusing right now. You'll get a lot of experience using them throughout this book, and you'll gain a clearer understanding of them with each chapter.

- *A label is read-only.* Read-only means that the user of the application can't edit the label by clicking on it and typing over it. Don't be confused here. *You* as the programmer can change it, but the user cannot. *Read-only* is a common technical term.

- *A label is used to draw static lines of text.* Static here means that it doesn't move. You can't interact with it, and it is fixed. This is also a common technical term.

- *The definition talks about a base class and subclassing.* These are more advanced topics covered later in the book. Remember that you're learning just in time. You don't need to know everything right now.

Terminology alert: class reference

The Apple definition given earlier is known as the *class reference*. You'll hear the term *class reference* (or *reference docs*) everywhere in the programming world. It refers to the documentation that tells you all about the underlying class of something (something like our definition of pen). You can find the class references in Xcode and on the web. I show how to access them in chapter 4.

That was a lot of theoretical detail in this section. Let's move on to something you *can* interact with: the Simulator. I mentioned it in chapter 2, and now we're going to look at it in more depth.

3.4 The Simulator, defined

Imagine you're a pilot learning to fly a plane. You could read all about the instruments and the physics behind flight and watch flying videos. But if you didn't have a flight simulator to practice on, eventually you'd have to go get in a real plane to see if you learned everything you needed. You would need to practice taking off and landing a plane. There would be little room for error, given that crashes are both dangerous and expensive. To bypass this costly and dangerous method of learning, someone created a flight simulator to simulate different planes and different conditions.

Apple did the same thing. It created the iPhone and iPad Simulator to test apps before installing them on devices. The Simulator lets you see how the app will look and behave when it runs on a device.

What happened when you launched your app by clicking the Run button in chapter 2? Well, Xcode compiled the code and launched the Simulator. I went over this briefly in chapter 2, but let's go into a bit more detail here.

I said Xcode *compiled* the code. A *compiler*, illustrated in figure 3.4, is a translator.

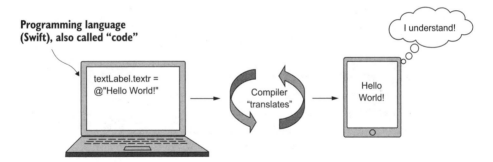

Figure 3.4 The Hello World app is compiled to run on the Simulator.

The compiler takes your written code and translates it into a language the iPhone can understand. (Computers only understand ones and zeros, called *binary code*, and compilers compile your code all the way down to machine-readable ones and zeros.) You don't need to know much about how compilers or their underpinnings work right now. Just know they are powerful and will help you a lot as you test your code.

Back in chapter 2, once the program was compiled, Xcode launched the iPhone Simulator for you, which simulated an iPhone and ran the app. The Simulator lets you test your application quickly and easily without having to put it on an iPhone every time you want to test it. Testing on the Simulator should always be your first step in testing your app. Make sure your app does what you planned for it to do! You'll get a lot of experience with the Simulator in no time, but I want to start by showing you a few neat features.

3.4.1 *Running Hello World in the Simulator*

Run your Hello World app again by clicking the Run button in Xcode (the triangular play button). The Simulator should automatically open in front of the Xcode window so it's your active application—if it doesn't, click the Simulator icon on your toolbar (see figure 3.5).

Within the Simulator application, click Hardware to open the submenu items. You should see some options that are pretty intuitive (shown in figure 3.6), but I'll walk you through them anyway:

Figure 3.5   The Simulator icon

- *Device*—This lets you change what kind of hardware you're simulating your application on. You can choose to see what your app looks like on newer and older iPads and iPhones. To add more types of devices, click Manage Devices. I talk more about adding different kinds of devices later in the book.
- *Rotate Left* and *Rotate Right*—You can change the orientation of the hardware so it's in landscape (long horizontally) or portrait mode (tall vertically). Click the Rotate Left and Rotate Right buttons in the menu to see what I mean.
- *Shake Gesture*—You can also "shake" the iPhone with the Simulator to imitate a user shaking the phone. Apps can implement the shake gesture to erase content or to undo the last entry, for example.

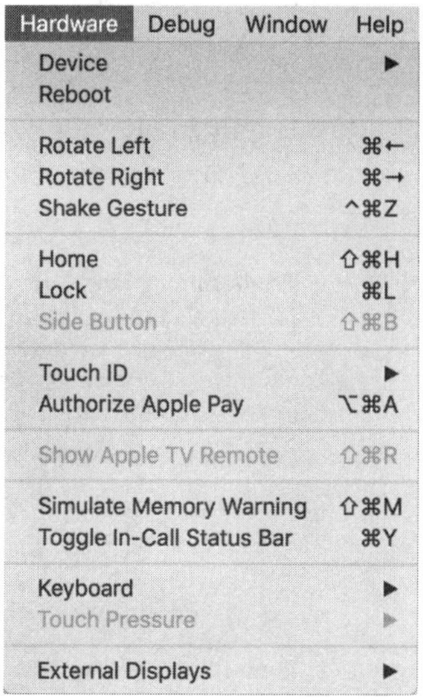

Figure 3.6   The Simulator's Hardware menu options let you simulate different actions and hardware.

There are a lot of features in the Simulator application, and it's powerful. You may find these key combinations helpful as well:

- Press the Command button (⌘) and 1, 2, 3, 4, or 5 to scale the size of the simulated screen up or down.
- Press the Command Button (⌘) and the left or right arrow to change the orientation (portrait or landscape).

You can't hurt anything by playing around with the features, so feel free to explore. You'll use the Simulator in every chapter where you're building apps, so it's important that you're comfortable with the tool.

How are you feeling? You wrote your first iOS application in chapter 2, and you learned all about it in this chapter. The app may not do much, but you made it—pat yourself on the back!

Concepts to remember

- The difference between classes and objects
- The process for running an app (the code is compiled and then run)
- Xcode templates that help get you started quickly

If you don't remember these concepts, you may want to walk through this chapter again. You'll create apps and add classes many, many times in the upcoming chapters, so you'll get lots of practice, but it's good to get the basics down.

3.5   *Summary*

You've learned a lot already, so let's recap to make sure it sticks. *The Hello World application* is your rite of passage into programming. Almost every programming language you learn from here on will start with a Hello World application. The *single-view application* is an Apple template that makes development a little easier, like a blank page in a book. You used a *label*—a read-only piece of text that you can use in your application. The user interface (UI) is the part of the application he user interacts with. A *class* is the underlying definition of something (like the idea of a pen). An *object* is an instance of a class (like a real pen you use). The *Simulator* is a powerful tool to test your application and see what it will look like on a device. The *compiler* is an application that translates your application into machine-readable code.

You're doing great—you've accomplished a lot already. In the next chapter, we'll walk through Xcode so you get more familiar with its tools and functions.

Learning more about your development tools: Xcode

This chapter covers

- Introducing Xcode
- Getting to know the panels and the Standard Editor
- A guide to Xcode's icons

Xcode can look pretty daunting when you first open it. As a beginning programmer, you don't need to know about all the super powerful features, but you do need to get familiar with the basics.

You've already built a simple app using Xcode, and now we'll go a little deeper into Xcode and its features. You'll get to know the different panels and buttons and see how some of them work in this chapter. It isn't terribly important that you remember the name of each panel and button, but if you do, it will definitely make working through this book easier. Apple updates Xcode frequently, so your panels may look slightly different than mine. Don't worry if they don't look exactly the same—some buttons may move around a bit, but the functions should be the same.

4.1 Xcode panels explained

Xcode groups features and buttons into areas called *panels* so programmers can interact with them more easily. (If you've ever used Microsoft Word, you're already familiar with panels. Microsoft Word uses panels to group features like font settings in a panel, and paragraph settings in another panel.)

This section walks you through the various Xcode panels. Remember to focus on picking up programming *concepts* rather than remembering the names of panels.

This chapter is important because you need to feel comfortable working with Xcode. After all, you'll use it for the rest of your iPhone and iPad programming career. Let's get started with the main parts of the Xcode IDE, shown in figure 4.1.

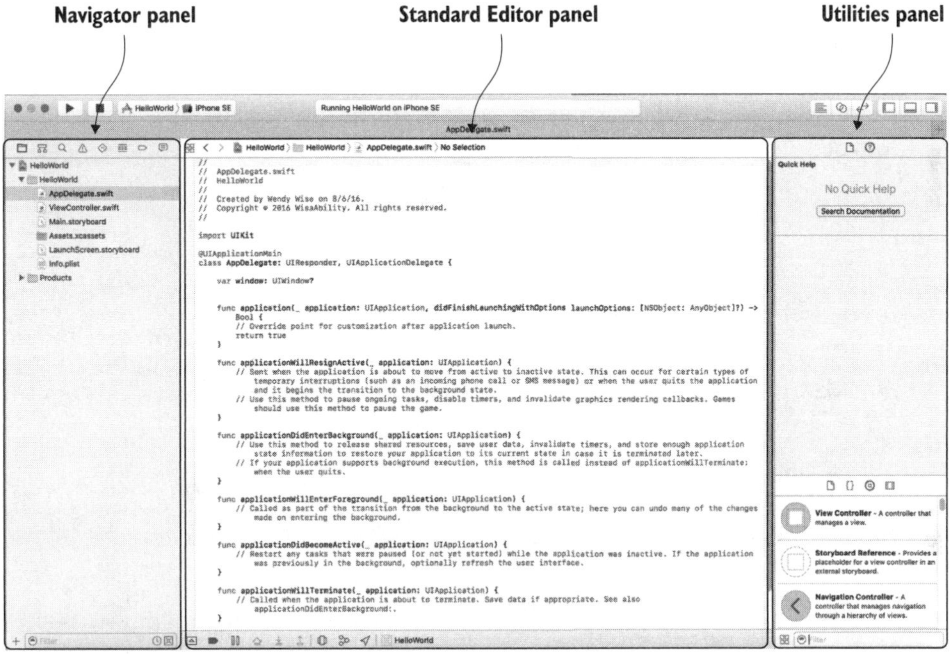

Figure 4.1 Xcode divides the workspace into three panels: Navigator, Standard Editor, and Utility.

Xcode is divided into the three main vertical sections or panels shown in figure 4.1:

- *Navigator (left)*—You use this panel to find your project files (like Windows Explorer on a Windows machine or the Finder window on a Mac). The Apple documentation calls this the Project Navigator or just Navigator.
- *Standard Editor (middle)*—This is where you'll actually write your code. You can think of this space as similar to Microsoft Word—you use it to compose. The Apple documentation calls this the Editor.

- *Utilities (right)*—This panel provides utilities and settings that you need for your app. You can think of the Utilities panel as the ribbon along the top of the Microsoft Word screen—the area that you use to change the font, add bullets, and so forth.

Let's talk a bit more about each panel now.

4.1.1 Standard Editor

The central section is called the Standard Editor, shown in figure 4.2. You'll spend the majority of your time here. This section changes depending on which file you select in the Navigator. Try it now. Click the file AppDelegate.swift, and your Standard Editor should change to show that file. Xcode uses this file as the beginning of every app, so it's kind enough to create it for you (such auto-generation is very helpful to programmers).

```swift
//
//  AppDelegate.swift
//  HelloWorld
//
//  Created by Wendy Wise on 6/17/16.
//  Copyright © 2016 WisaAbility. All rights reserved.
//

import UIKit

@UIApplicationMain
class AppDelegate: UIResponder, UIApplicationDelegate {

    var window: UIWindow?


    func application(application: UIApplication, didFinishLaunchingWithOptions launchOptions: [NSObject: AnyObject]?) -> Bool {
        // Override point for customization after application launch.
        return true
    }

    func applicationWillResignActive(application: UIApplication) {
        // Sent when the application is about to move from active to inactive state. This can occur for certain types of
            temporary interruptions (such as an incoming phone call or SMS message) or when the user quits the application and
            it begins the transition to the background state.
        // Use this method to pause ongoing tasks, disable timers, and throttle down OpenGL ES frame rates. Games should use
            this method to pause the game.
    }

    func applicationDidEnterBackground(application: UIApplication) {
        // Use this method to release shared resources, save user data, invalidate timers, and store enough application state
            information to restore your application to its current state in case it is terminated later.
        // If your application supports background execution, this method is called instead of applicationWillTerminate: when
            the user quits.
    }

    func applicationWillEnterForeground(application: UIApplication) {
        // Called as part of the transition from the background to the inactive state; here you can undo many of the changes
            made on entering the background.
    }

    func applicationDidBecomeActive(application: UIApplication) {
        // Restart any tasks that were paused (or not yet started) while the application was inactive. If the application was
            previously in the background, optionally refresh the user interface.
    }

    func applicationWillTerminate(application: UIApplication) {
        // Called when the application is about to terminate. Save data if appropriate. See also
            applicationDidEnterBackground:.
    }


}
```

Figure 4.2   The Standard Editor is the center panel in Xcode.

I know this AppDelegate file may look complex—there's a lot of code here. You won't need to know much about this yet, but look at the top of the file. The first five or six lines are pretty interesting:

- The first line tells you the name of the file (AppDelegate.swift).
- The second line tells you the name of the application (Hello World). You can then see your name as the creator and the date you created it. Pretty cool!
- The next line shows that Xcode added copyright information to your file.

You're looking more and more like a programmer now. These lines may seem familiar to you—you entered them in the Choose Options dialog box in chapter 2 when you created the Hello World project.

Apple wanted to make coding as easy as possible, so there are a few neat features that show up as you start typing code into the Standard Editor, which I'll demonstrate when you start writing lines of code in chapter 5. Here's a sneak peek for those eager to hear about them:

- *Auto-complete*—This feature tries to figure out what you're going to type and auto-completes it for you.
- *Error notifications*—This feature pops up automatically when you have a syntax error. Back in chapter 1, you found out that *syntax* is the structure of the code, or how you form "sentences" that the computer will understand.

4.1.2   Utilities panel

The right side of the IDE shows the Utilities panel (see figure 4.3). The Utilities panel is the one you'll use the most after

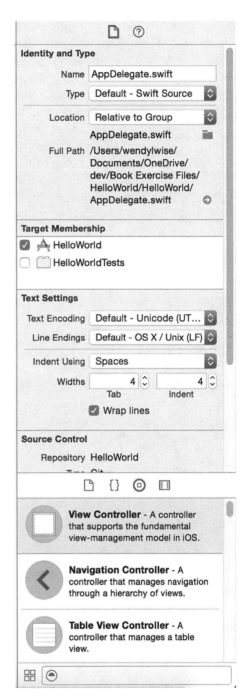

Figure 4.3   Utilities panel—you'll "utilize" this a lot.

the Standard Editor. As you saw in chapter 2, this is where you can find the items you want to add to your application, such as labels and buttons. As we move through the next several chapters, you'll begin to see just how useful the Utilities panel is when you develop your apps.

4.1.3   *Main.storyboard*

Click the Quick Help button at the top of the Utilities panel, the circle with the question mark in the center (see figure 4.3). Note that the panel underneath changes when you click the button.

In the Navigator panel (the left panel), if it isn't already selected, select Main.storyboard, and the center panel should show your storyboard with the label on it. Click the label on your storyboard once, and the Utilities panel (the right panel) will display the help section for that label. It should look like figure 4.4.

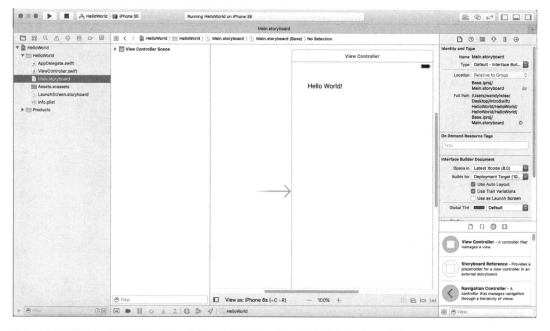

Figure 4.4   Clicking the label on the storyboard displays the Quick Help in the Utilities panel.

Quick Help has a *lot* of information available to you. The label description on the Utilities panel should look familiar to you from chapter 3, where we reviewed Apple's description of the label.

Now that you've had a quick overview of them, let's learn to use these panels. Remember, I'm trying to show you just the bits that you need to understand now rather than go in-depth on a lot of functions and buttons that you won't need until part 3 of this book.

4.1.4 *Navigator panel*

The Navigator panel on the left side of Xcode has three parts, shown in figure 4.5:

- The *navigation bar* is the bar at the top of the panel with the buttons on it.
- The *content area* is the middle part of the panel with the largest amount of space.
- The *filter bar* is the little bar at the bottom of the panel.

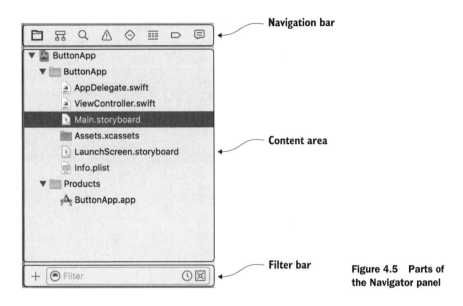

Navigation bar

Content area

Filter bar

Figure 4.5   Parts of the Navigator panel

Make sure the first button in the navigation bar is selected—the one that looks like a file folder. This is the default view: the library view, which shows all the files that are currently part of your project. Xcode created all these files when you selected the Single View Application template. I won't walk through each of these files right now, but I do talk more about each of them in chapter 15.

Several folders and files should appear in the content area now. At the bottom of the screen, in the filter bar, start typing the word *AppDelegate*: you'll notice that the files in the content area are filtered down to a few files that contain that word. This is helpful when you're working with a lot of files.

We're going to skip over a few of the buttons on the navigation bar because you don't need to know or understand them yet. Select the fourth button from the left, the one that looks like a triangle with an exclamation point in it. This is the issue navigator. Every developer has created "issues" in their code—these might be bugs, defects, or other issues. This panel will show you whether there are problems in your code, and it should even give you the name of the file with problem and the problem description. Click the issue, and Xcode will open the file and highlight the problem. I'll go into more detail on this panel and the rest of its buttons, and how to detect, understand, and fix issues, as we create more apps later in the book.

Now that you've seen some of the neat Xcode features, let's move on to neat Xcode buttons.

4.2   Xcode icons explained

You should still have your storyboard displayed. If not, click the file Main.Storyboard in the Navigator panel. Now look at the top right of Xcode, over the Utilities panel. See all those icons up there, which I've enlarged in figure 4.6? They're handy because they help show and hide different parts of the Xcode screens so you can see only what you need to, depending on what you're doing. Let's start with the three buttons on the far right (shown in figure 4.7):

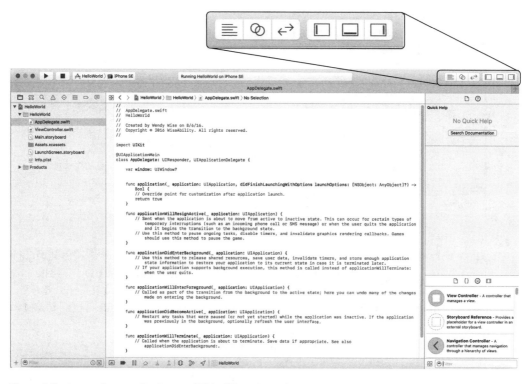

Figure 4.6   Icons allow you to show and hide different panels.

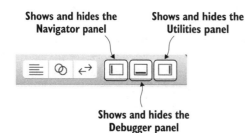

Shows and hides the
Navigator panel

Shows and hides the
Utilities panel

Shows and hides the
Debugger panel

Figure 4.7   Each button serves a purpose in showing and hiding different panels in Xcode.

- *Navigator panel*—The button on the left shows and hides the Navigation panel.
- *Debugger panel*—The middle button shows and hides the Debugger panel. You'll use this panel a lot—it shows when you have errors in your code or if there are warnings. We walk through it in detail in chapter 7.
- *Utilities panel*—The far-right button hides and shows the Utilities panel. Click it on and off to see what I mean.

Now let's look at the three icons on the far left, shown in figure 4.8:

Shows and hides the Standard Editor

Shows and hides the Version Editor

Shows and hides the Assistant Editor

Figure 4.8   You'll use the Standard Editor and Assistant Editor for each app you create.

- *Standard Editor button*—This button looks like a lot of lines in a box. Click it, and you'll see that the Editor shifts back to showing only one file. You can click through all these settings to show and hide panels (I call this "changing the real estate"). When you're doing a lot of typing in the code, you want as much "real estate" as you can get so you can see what you're doing. Make sense?
- *Assistant Editor button*—This button looks like two overlapping circles. If you click it, you'll see that the Editor panel divides into two sections, with two files open. You'll use this Assistant Editor panel quite a bit as you build more apps, but you don't need to know a lot about it right now.
- *Version Editor button*—The button on the right that looks like two arrows pointing in opposite directions is the Version Editor button, which tracks the changes you've made in the project. You don't need to worry about it right now. Click it to see what it does, though, so it doesn't seem intimidating.

If you forget the names of a button, hover your mouse pointer over it, and Xcode will show you a tooltip with the name of the button.

4.3   Feel free to explore

Xcode can look scary because it's packed with functionality and features you aren't familiar with yet. Take time now to click buttons to see what they do, what they show, and what they hide. There isn't much you can do to mess things up, and you need to be comfortable with your IDE and know how to get back to where you need to if you accidentally click something you didn't mean to.

Once you're done clicking through everything, make sure you can get back to the panels and the views that were there when you started. If you're having trouble, begin from the top (literally):

- In the Editor's options at top right in Xcode, make sure the left and right panels are viewable and the bottom panel isn't. You can toggle these on and off by clicking the appropriate buttons again.
- Make sure the Standard Editor is selected (the box with the lines in it). If your Navigator panel and your Utilities panel don't look right, make sure the folder icon in the Navigator panel is selected.
- Once your project files are visible again, click the Main.storyboard file.
- On the Utilities panel, go ahead and select the File Inspector (the first icon that looks like a page with the corner flipped down). This should return you to the view that looks familiar to you.

Concepts to remember

- Xcode is a powerful tool that you'll use for developing your apps. You'll continue to learn about Xcode features in future chapters, so you don't need to understand everything it can do quite yet.
- You do need to remember how to show and hide the different Xcode panels so you have access to the tools you need when you need them. The three buttons at top right in Xcode show and hide the panels, and the next three buttons change how the Editor panel looks.

You learned a lot in this chapter, so I hope you feel proud of yourself. Many people are afraid to click icons and experiment with software tools because they think they'll break something or they don't know what it does. I like to click something, see what it does, and, if it does something I don't understand, try to learn what that is. The other option is to never click anything and never learn about it—but that way, you'll you miss out on features that could be helpful to you. Don't worry; I'll explain each button that you need as you begin to code more apps.

4.4 *Summary*

In this chapter, you learned more about your IDE, you clicked a lot of icons and buttons in Xcode, and you discovered how to get back to where you started. You'll get a lot of experience working with Xcode as you go through the projects in this book. This chapter is just an overview of the Xcode panel terminology and basic features; I'll reference these panels and features in later chapters. You can always refer to this chapter if needed. You're going to build another app in the next chapter, so get ready.

Capturing users' actions: adding buttons

5

This chapter covers

- Creating an app with a button
- Buttons and how to use them
- Changing labels

You're going to create another app in this chapter. This one will have a button the user can tap. *Buttons* are used throughout iPhone and iPad apps to allow the user to do some kind of action, such as make a phone call. Each number on the phone number screen is a button, for example, and the call and hang-up buttons are buttons too.

In this chapter you'll add a label and a button to the app and write some code. The code you write will make the button change what the label displays. You're also going to change how the label looks by implementing cosmetic changes.

Looking at the code

You can download all the projects from this book at www.manning.com/books/anyone-can-create-an-app or https://github.com/wlwise/AnyoneCanCreateAnApp, and you can refer to them anytime.

5.1   *Adding a label and a button*

As usual, we're going to start with pseudocode steps so that we follow a logical road map for completing this project. Here are the steps:

1 Start a new project using the Single View Application template.
2 Add a button and label to the storyboard, and run the app to test it.
3 Connect the button and the label to the code (wire them up), and run the app to test it.
4 Add code to change the text on the label when the button is clicked, and run the app to test it.
5 Change how the label looks, and run the app to test it.

You'll notice that steps 2, 3, 4, and 5 all end with running the app and testing it. I always find it helpful to run the app often to make sure it works the way I expect it to. As you begin adding more and more code to your apps, it's easier to find problems with the code if you test it more frequently. Let's get started.

5.1.1   *Step 1: Start a new project using the Single View Application template*

I want you to get used to starting new projects, so go ahead and create a new one:

1 Click File > New > Project.
2 Remember to select Single View Application, and name it ButtonApp.
3 Make sure the language selection is still Swift. Click OK.
4 Save the project to the dev folder on your computer that you created in chapter 2.

5.1.2   *Step 2: Add a button and label to the storyboard, and run the app to test it*

As before, the project is loaded, and the files are listed down the left side of Xcode. Click Main.storyboard so the storyboard shows up in your Standard Editor panel.

STEP 2A: ADDING THE BUTTON

In the bottom-right palette on the Utilities panel, make sure you have the Object Library showing by clicking the circle with a square inside of it (as you did in chapter 2). Then, at the bottom of the panel, search for *button* instead of *label*. You'll notice that you have three options to choose from for the buttons. In this case, you want to add the top one—the one that says Button. Grab it, and drop it on your storyboard (see figure 5.1). Double-click the new button that you dropped on your storyboard, and change the text to *My Button*.

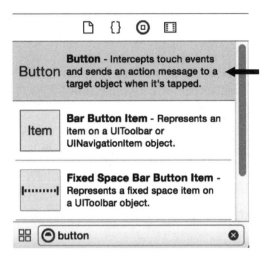

Figure 5.1 Drag a button from the Object Library onto your storyboard.

STEP 2B: ADDING THE LABEL TO THE STORYBOARD

Go back to the Object Library, and search for *label* to add a label to your storyboard. Double-click that label, and change the text to *Button Demo*. (You also did this in chapter 2.)

Now run the app to make sure it looks okay (click the right arrow at top left in the Xcode window). Your Simulator should look similar to figure 5.2.

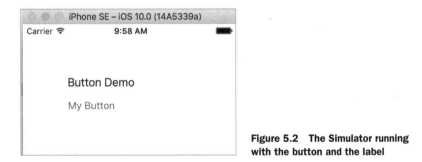

Figure 5.2 The Simulator running with the button and the label

Click the My Button button: it dims when you click it, to show that you're interacting with it. Great! It works, although it doesn't do anything yet. Get ready. You're going to add some code now that will change the title of the button when it is clicked. I'll walk you through it. Stop your Simulator by clicking the square in Xcode (this looks like a stop button on most electronics).

5.1.3   Step 3: Connect the button and the label to the code (wire them up), and run the app to test it

In the next chapter, I'll explain *why* you need to do this step, but for now you need to follow along and make the connections. Okay, let's change the real estate so you can see both the storyboard (with your label and button) and the code.

STEP 3A: CONNECTING THE BUTTON TO THE CODE

You're going to use the Assistant Editor for this, so click the Assistant Editor button (the one that looks like two interlocking circles at top right). You should see the storyboard on the left side and ViewController.swift on the right side, as shown in figure 5.3.

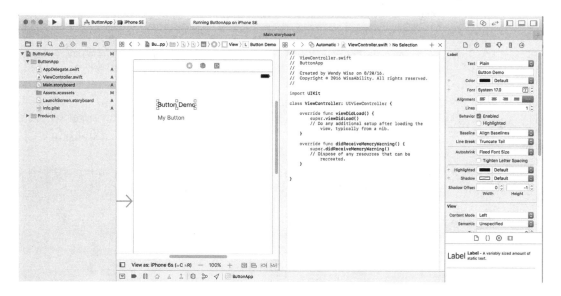

Figure 5.3   The Assistant Editor shows the storyboard on the left and ViewController.swift on the right.

I know the ViewController may look daunting, but we'll walk through it in chapter 13, I promise. For now, think of it as Vanna White from *Wheel of Fortune*. The premise of the show is that three contestants guess letters to a puzzle, and eventually enough letters are guessed so that someone can guess what the puzzle spells. A contestant on the show yells out a letter to the puzzle, and if the letter is in the puzzle, Vanna walks over and turns the letter around so everyone can see it. If the letter is not in the puzzle, she doesn't move. The ViewController is like Vanna: the user presses a button (yells out a letter), and if the button is wired up to your code (if the letter is in the puzzle), the ViewController (Vanna) performs that code (turns the letter around). If the button isn't wired up (the letter is not in the puzzle), nothing happens (Vanna stays still). You can see episodes of the game show here: www.youtube.com/watch?v=rZmWwPN3H2Y.

Again, I'm going to show you how to "wire up the button" first and then I'll explain what you did afterward. I talk more about wiring up buttons in Chapter 6, but for now think about it as if you're connecting Vanna to the puzzle board. Vanna needs to know which puzzle to use:

1 Hold down the Control button on the keyboard, and click My Button on your storyboard.

2 With the mouse button and Control still held down, drag the mouse pointer onto the right side of the screen in the ViewController.

3 Hover the mouse under the words class ViewController: UIViewController {. You should see a blue link that links over to the ViewController and a box that says "Insert Outlet, Action, or Outlet Collection."

4 When you see that, let go of both the mouse and the Control button (with your mouse pointer right under the class ViewController: UIViewController { line. You now see a pop-up that looks like figure 5.4.

Figure 5.4   The pop-up box should appear when you release the mouse button and Control button. Change the Connection option to Action.

5 Change the Connection type (at the top of the pop-up) from Outlet to Action, type *buttonClick* in the Name field, change Type from Any to UIButton, and click Connect (see figure 5.5). You should see on the right panel (the ViewController.swift side) that Xcode added a new line for you. It should state the following:

```
@IBAction func buttonClick(sender: AnyObject) {
```

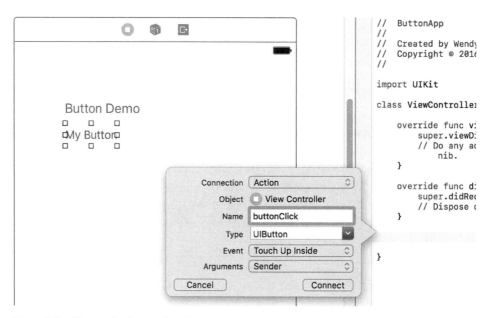

Figure 5.5   Change the Connection, Name, and Type values.

6   If the line says @IBOutlet instead, you need to delete the button and repeat the steps again, but select Action instead of Outlet in the dialog window that pops up. Your code should now look like figure 5.6.

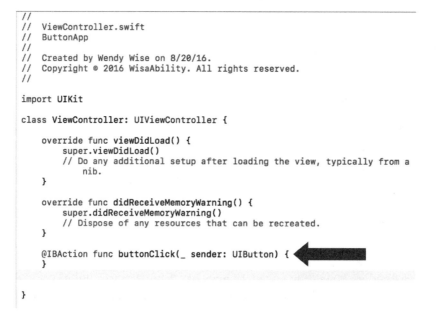

```
//
//  ViewController.swift
//  ButtonApp
//
//  Created by Wendy Wise on 8/20/16.
//  Copyright © 2016 WisaAbility. All rights reserved.
//

import UIKit

class ViewController: UIViewController {

    override func viewDidLoad() {
        super.viewDidLoad()
        // Do any additional setup after loading the view, typically from a
            nib.
    }

    override func didReceiveMemoryWarning() {
        super.didReceiveMemoryWarning()
        // Dispose of any resources that can be recreated.
    }

    @IBAction func buttonClick(_ sender: UIButton) {
    }

}
```

Figure 5.6   Button demo code after you click Connect. The @IBAction line is new. Make sure it looks like this.

STEP 3B: CONNECTING THE LABEL TO THE CODE

Now you're going to connect the label in almost the same way that you connected the button:

1 Control-click your label on the storyboard. With the Control key still held down, drag your mouse pointer over to the ViewController.

2 Let go of the Control key when your mouse is positioned under the class ViewController: UIViewController { line and above the @IBAction line that you added.

3 This time, when the dialog pops up, leave the connection as Outlet (at the top of the box, as shown in figure 5.7).

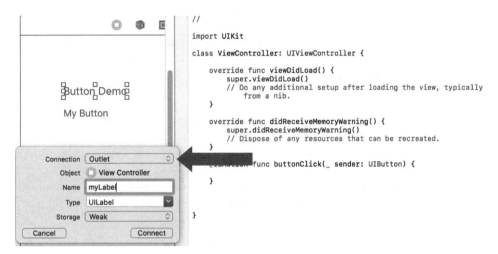

Figure 5.7 Connect the label to the code with the Outlet connection, and change the name to myLabel.

4 Change the name to *myLabel* and leave all the other options set as they are.

5 Click the Connect button.

Your code should look similar to figure 5.8.

Now run the app again to make sure it still works. The app should do exactly what it did before you wired up the label, because you haven't added any code yet. You run it here to make sure that it still works.

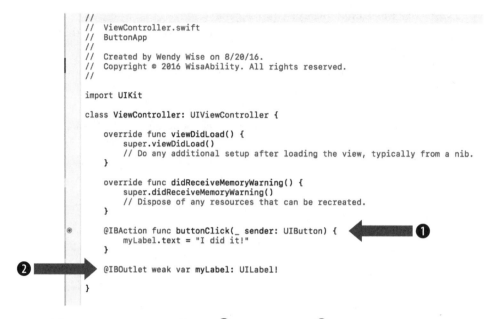

```
//
//  ViewController.swift
//  ButtonApp
//
//  Created by Wendy Wise on 8/20/16.
//  Copyright © 2016 WisaAbility. All rights reserved.
//

import UIKit

class ViewController: UIViewController {

    override func viewDidLoad() {
        super.viewDidLoad()
        // Do any additional setup after loading the view, typically from a nib.
    }

    override func didReceiveMemoryWarning() {
        super.didReceiveMemoryWarning()
        // Dispose of any resources that can be recreated.
    }

    @IBAction func buttonClick(_ sender: UIButton) {
        myLabel.text = "I did it!"
    }

    @IBOutlet weak var myLabel: UILabel!

}
```

Figure 5.8   There should be two additions: ❶ @IBAction and ❷ @IBOutlet.

5.1.4   *Step 4: Add code to change the text on the Label when the button is clicked, and run the app to test it*

Next you'll go back to the code and add the following line right under the @IBAction func buttonClick(sender: UIButton) { line:

```
myLabel.text = "I did it!"
```

Make sure you add this line after the button-click line, but before the next } line. Your code should look like figure 5.9.

That code may look daunting, but I'll explain more about what you're doing and why in chapter 6. Now run the code again, and click the button. If everything worked, your button should now change the label to "I did it!" when you click it, as shown in figure 5.10. Great job!

If it didn't work, look back at your ViewController file and see if there are any red exclamation points with a big red highlight. If so, you have an error in your code. Check to make sure your code looks like my code in figure 5.9, and try again. If you accidentally created the button as an outlet or the label as an action, it won't work. Unfortunately, you can't delete the code in the ViewController because the storyboard still thinks there's a link to the code. To fix this (only if you accidentally created them backwards), you'll need to delete the linkage (the wires) between the

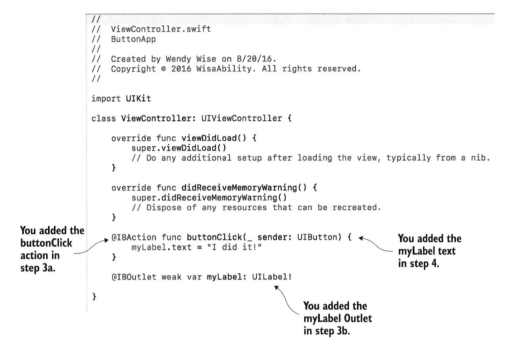

```
//
//  ViewController.swift
//  ButtonApp
//
//  Created by Wendy Wise on 8/20/16.
//  Copyright © 2016 WisaAbility. All rights reserved.
//

import UIKit

class ViewController: UIViewController {

    override func viewDidLoad() {
        super.viewDidLoad()
        // Do any additional setup after loading the view, typically from a nib.
    }

    override func didReceiveMemoryWarning() {
        super.didReceiveMemoryWarning()
        // Dispose of any resources that can be recreated.
    }

    @IBAction func buttonClick(_ sender: UIButton) {
        myLabel.text = "I did it!"
    }

    @IBOutlet weak var myLabel: UILabel!

}
```

You added the buttonClick action in step 3a.

You added the myLabel text in step 4.

You added the myLabel Outlet in step 3b.

Figure 5.9   The final code for the My Button app, with `@IBOutlet`, `@IBAction`, and the line of code to change the text of the label

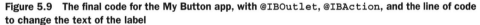

Figure 5.10   The working `buttonDemo` app after you clicked My Button should change the label text to "I did it!"

storyboard and the ViewController. Figure 5.11 assumes you accidentally created your button as an outlet instead of an action, but you can fix any incorrect "wiring" this way.

This is exciting—you made an app with a button that changed the text of a label! Now you'll change how the label looks, and then I'll explain what you did in chapter 6.

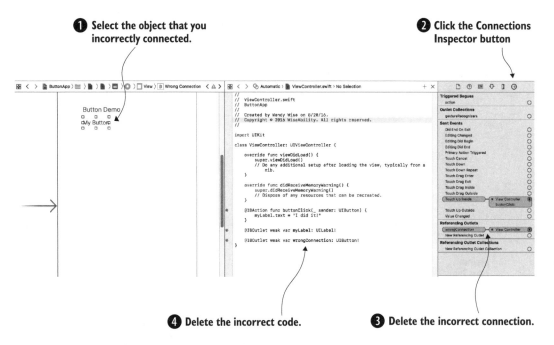

❶ Select the object that you incorrectly connected.

❷ Click the Connections Inspector button

❹ Delete the incorrect code.

❸ Delete the incorrect connection.

Figure 5.11   If you accidentally connected the objects to the code incorrectly, you need to delete the connection (wire) and the code following these steps.

5.2   Changing how the label appears

In this section, you're going to change some attributes of the label. We use the term *attribute* to describe information about something (such as a label). A label has *properties*, or descriptors of that label. Think back to the pen we talked about in chapter 3. Remember, the underlying definition of a pen was a *class*, and the pen in your hand was the *object*. Thinking about that class (the pen definition), what things can be changed on a pen without changing the fact that it's a pen?

You could change the type of pen to ballpoint, felt tip, or fountain. You could change the color of the ink to red, blue, or purple, so the ink color can change and yet it is still a pen. We could say that the color of the ink is a *property* of the pen. In other words, all pens *must* conform to the property of having an ink color. What if you tried to make the ink into lead? Well, that breaks the definition of a pen and makes it a pencil. *Lead* does not conform to the property of the pen. The color of the ink is a pen property, and the available colors that you can make the ink are *attributes* of that individual pen.

Think about the label you added to the My Button app. What was the font? What was the color? How big was the label? Those are all *properties* of the label. One property of the label is color. Color is a property of label, and *red* may be attributed to that property. You can do the same thing with the font. The font of the label is a *property*, and Comic Sans may be the attribute. Again, you can do the same thing with the type of pen. The type is a property of pen, and an attribute could be *ballpoint*. These are key terms in the coding world.

5.2.1   *Step 5: Change how the label looks, and run the app to test it*

Now you'll change some properties of the label you added in the last section:

1 Click once on the label in your storyboard. With the label still highlighted, look at the right side of the Xcode screen.
2 If it isn't selected already, click the icon that looks like a fat arrowhead pointing down—this is your Attributes Inspector panel. It should look like figure 5.12.

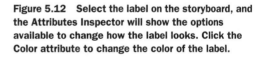

Figure 5.12   Select the label on the storyboard, and the Attributes Inspector will show the options available to change how the label looks. Click the Color attribute to change the color of the label.

These are the options for changing the properties of the label. You can change these settings now. Click the little up arrows next to Font System 17.0. Notice that the size of the font on your label increases as you click the up and down buttons. As you do this, you're changing the *attribute* for the font property:

■ If you make the font too large, some of the letters on the label disappear and are replaced with ellipses (. . .). You can fix this easily by grabbing the corner of the label and dragging it out until your label is completely visible again. Grab the squares on the right side of the label and drag to the right. Voilà! You can see the entire label again.

- Set the Font to System Font 20. Make sure your label is fully visible.

Now you'll change the color property of the label too, because you can:

1 Click the Colors selector right above the Font selector. A color wheel window will open, like the one in figure 5.13.

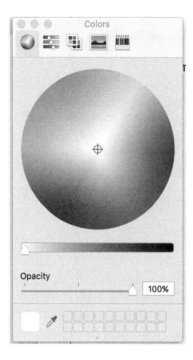

Figure 5.13   The color wheel opens after you click on the text label so you can change the color. Click any color in the wheel.

2 Pick a color you like by clicking inside the circle of colors. When you click the circle, the small box in the lower-left corner changes color to show you what you selected. You can continue to click different colors until you find the one you like.

3 Once you have it, close the panel. The label on your storyboard should now be the color you selected, and the Utilities panel should also show the color. I selected red for the attribute in figure 5.14.

Run the app again, and check that your label looks good in the Simulator. Take a little time and click through the label attributes on the Utilities panel to see what happens to the label. There are a lot of things you can do to make the label look different. If something changes and you can't figure out how to change it back, delete the label by selecting it on your storyboard and pressing the Delete key. Then add another label by following step 2 again.

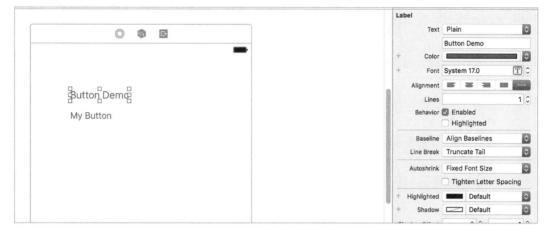

Figure 5.14 Change the label Color property to red by choosing red on the color wheel.

Concepts to remember
- Outlets let you access something on the user interface (the UI) by providing a reference to it (like Vanna being able to touch the letters on the game board and turn them around).
- Actions tell the code what should happen when a user interacts with a control object (like your button) on the UI.
- The most important thing to take away from this chapter is a high-level understanding of outlets, actions, and attributes. Chapter 6 talks more about outlets and actions, so stay tuned. You'll use these concepts for almost every app you build from here on.

5.3 Summary

This chapter covered a lot. You created an app with a label and a button, and you made the words on the button change when you clicked it.

You learned about outlets, but I didn't explain them in depth. Chapter 6 covers them, but for now, think of them as ways for the code to "talk to" the UI elements. The example we used was how our game-show host Vanna knew which puzzle to turn the letters around for.

You learned about actions, which are the way the user interface directs the flow of your code or tells the code to do something differently. In the code example, the "action" was for the user to tap the button and the code to then do something. In our real-world example, it was when the game show contestant yelled out a letter for Vanna. Chapter 6 covers this concept as well. You also learned about changing the attributes of a label, such as the font and the color.

The next chapter further explains the concepts from this chapter. This chapter taught you the basics of wiring up your user controls (buttons and labels) to your code. You'll use these actions throughout the rest of this book, so make sure you understand how to do it.

The button app, explained *6*

This chapter covers

- Explaining the button app you created in chapter 5
- Accessing Apple's documentation
- Learning to comment (appropriately!)

In chapter 5, you created the My Button App with a button and a label, and you added code to change the title of the button when the user taps it. This chapter will explain what you did and why you did it. Additionally, we're going to walk through the Apple documentation so you know where to go when you want more information on topics. We'll also learn to add comments to the code so you'll remember what you did and why you did it when you look back at your code at a later date.

6.1 The button, explained

To refresh your memory, here are the steps you took in chapter 5:

1 Starting a new project using the Single View Application template
2 Adding a button and label to the storyboard, and running the app to test it
3 Connecting the button and the label to the code (wiring them up using an outlet and an action), and running the app to test it

4 Adding code to change the text on the label, and running the app to test it

5 Changing how the label looks by changing the attributes, and running the app to test it

6.1.1 *Creating outlets (or "How do I contact Butch?")*

You should be pretty familiar with steps 1 and 2 now, because you did the same thing in chapters 2 and 5. Step 3 was something totally new, so let's talk more about wiring the button and label. To do that, let's step out of the coding world for a moment and into the real world. Imagine you meet a guy (let's call him Butch) and you want to get to know him better. What is one of the first things you do? You exchange your *deets* (slang for details) such as your *digits* (slang for phone number) or your email address. His phone number and email address are ways in which you can get a hold of him. You have no way of contacting him without that reference. In other words, the email/phone are your *outlets* to Butch (who, by the way, is an *object* because he has all the characteristics of being a guy, but he isn't the only one out there).

In the same way (see figure 6.1), the code has no way to reach the label that you added unless you give the code the details of the label. You created an outlet to the label (the object) and said that the label's name was myLabel. That way, anytime you want to do something with that label, you tell the code to call him using his name: myLabel.

Outlets are used often in iOS coding, and they're useful at times when you want to "call" something on the storyboard (like a button or a label) to exchange details. Once you have the outlet to the object, you can change the properties or attributes of the object (such as color, size, and so on).

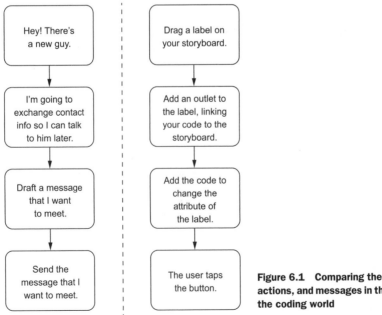

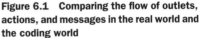

Figure 6.1 Comparing the flow of outlets, actions, and messages in the real world and the coding world

6.1.2 Creating actions

Next, in step 4, you added your first real Swift code to the application, by adding an action for the button. You Control-clicked the button, dragged it to the code, and changed the drop-down on the dialog from Outlet to Action. You may be able to guess at this point what you did, but I'll explain it anyway. In the previous example, you have Butch's phone number (the outlet), and now you want to call him (an action).

The action tells the code that it should do something ("act") when the button is tapped. Then you told the code to change the label's title attribute to "I did it" when the button was tapped. You were able to change the title of the label because you had already told the code how to reach him by using the outlet. Here's the first part of the code you added:

```
myLabel.text = "I did it!"
```

You're telling `myLabel` to set the text "text" to "I did it!".

You're now learning your first bit of *syntax* (how you form coding "sentences") for the Swift language. In this case, `myLabel` is the object (like the pen in your hand mentioned in chapter 3), and you want to send it a message to change an attribute (in this case, text). You're telling the code the following:

```
"object"."message that I want you to do something"
```

If you were going to call Butch and tell him to meet you at 8 p.m., it would look (theoretically) like this:

```
"Butch.setMeetingTime("8pm"...")
```

That seems pretty straightforward, doesn't it?

6.1.3 Is Xcode clairvoyant?

In chapter 4, I told you about some of the neat features of Xcode. I mentioned code completion, which works like a Google search in that it tries to predict what you want to type.

You may have noticed code completion while you were typing in the line of code that sets the label text to "I did it!". If not, go back and try it again, but this time type a little slower to give Xcode a chance to predict what you're typing. Once you start typing *my*, Xcode suggests that you want *myButton* or *myLabel* (shown in figure 6.2). Because you're trying to type *myLabel*, you can press the Tab key to agree with Xcode that you were indeed trying to reference `myLabel`.

```
    @IBAction func buttonClick(sender: AnyObject) {
        myLabel
 V  UILabel! myLabel
 S    mymsg mymsg
      super.viewDidLoad()
```

Figure 6.2 Xcode tries to auto-complete when you begin typing.

Now type a period (.) and you'll see that Xcode pops up a list of messages that you might want to send to the label. The first one that pops up for me is *text*:

- If you press the Tab key again here, you're confirming to Xcode that you want to *set* the message.
- Press Tab again to confirm that you want to set the title.

If you want to set something else in the list, you can either start typing the first letter of the message or use the up and down arrow keys to select different messages. Press Tab again to accept the "text" message. Xcode automatically tells you that you need to type in a title and it needs to be of type `String`, as shown in figure 6.3.

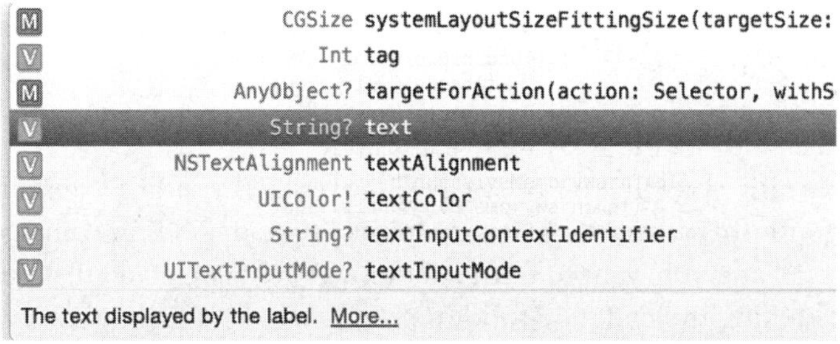

```
 M            CGSize systemLayoutSizeFittingSize(targetSize:
 V               Int tag
 M         AnyObject? targetForAction(action: Selector, withS
 V           String? text
 V   NSTextAlignment textAlignment
 V         UIColor! textColor
 V           String? textInputContextIdentifier
 V   UITextInputMode? textInputMode
```

The text displayed by the label. More...

Figure 6.3   Xcode's first suggestion for changing label attributes is *text*.

Chapter 8 tells you a lot more about *types*, which are different kinds of storage mechanisms, such as strings. For now, you should know that a string needs to have double quotation marks around it—that's how Xcode knows it's a string ("I did it!!!" is a string). Type in your new text, enclosed in double quotation marks (the Shift-apostrophe key), and press Tab again.

6.1.4   *User interfaces and the front end of apps*

Think back to our discussion of labels in chapter 3, where we talked about the term *UI*, meaning *user interface*. The UI is the part of the app that the user can see or interact with, so anything that starts with *UI* pertains to the *front end* of the app. *Front end* is a coding term for the user interface, whereas *back end* is the term used for all the code behind the scenes that the user can't see.

A button is a type of UI *control* (an object the user can interact with that "controls" the flow of an application). When you tapped the button (the UI control object), it went into the code based on the action you defined (the action `buttonClick`). Chapter 9 covers application flow, so don't worry too much about it here.

This may seem like a lot to take in right now, but we'll continue to review these concepts and build on them throughout the book. Remember, the button is an object that's part of the user interface (UI) that can help control the flow of the application—therefore it's a UI control object.

When you ran the myButton app in the Simulator, you may have clicked the button several times to see what happened. You probably noticed that it only changed the label once ("I did it!!!"). It actually set the label text to "I did it!!!" every time you clicked the button, but you didn't see the change because you never told the button to change the title back to its original state (with the title "Button Demo"). I show you how to do that in part 2 of this book, so stay tuned.

6.2 *Documentation*

Let's take a break from the heavier concepts and talk about how to learn what attributes an object has. Think back to your label—you changed the look of it. You made the font larger and changed the color. There are a lot of things you can do to a label, and we've only scratched the surface.

Apple does a great job of documenting such things, so now you're going to learn how to access and read the Apple documentation. The documentation is key to your learning about the different classes, so I want you to get used to accessing Apple documentation. Go back to Xcode and select your label on the storyboard. Now, in the Utilities panel on the far right, select the circle with the question mark in the middle. This opens the Quick Help panel, shown in figure 6.4 (it may look different, depending on your version of Xcode).

You should recognize the description of the label—I showed it to you in chapter 3 when you first added the label. Let's walk through the UILabel Quick Help panel items now:

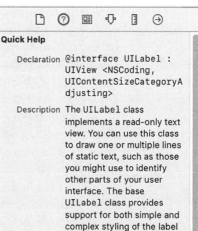

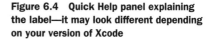

Figure 6.4 Quick Help panel explaining the label—it may look different depending on your version of Xcode

- *Availability*—The Availability line in the panel tells you that this label class has been around since iOS 2.0. That means that the label has been part of iPhone and iPad programming since the second version came out—I'm not sure I can even remember that far back. The supported version of the code (availability) is important to know when coding so you don't use a feature in the code that's only available to the latest release. Some users don't upgrade their iOS version on their iPhones and iPads quickly (for instance, from iOS 9 to iOS 10), so if you release an app that has features only available in iOS 9 and later, iOS 8 users won't be able to use the app.

- *Declared In*—The Declared In line tells you where the underlying class is. If you were looking at the documentation for your pen, for example, this would be the file that describes your theoretical pen and all its properties. These classes are pretty dense and are way too complex for our needs. We would like a document that gives us all we need to know about the class without having to read the code.

- *References*—Enter the Reference line, stage right! This is the documentation that describes everything about what a label is and how you can manipulate it. Go ahead and click the UILabel Class Reference link now. If nothing happens, it means you need to download the documentation. Go to Xcode > Preferences, and a new window will open. Click the Components button, and you should see a screen like figure 6.5.

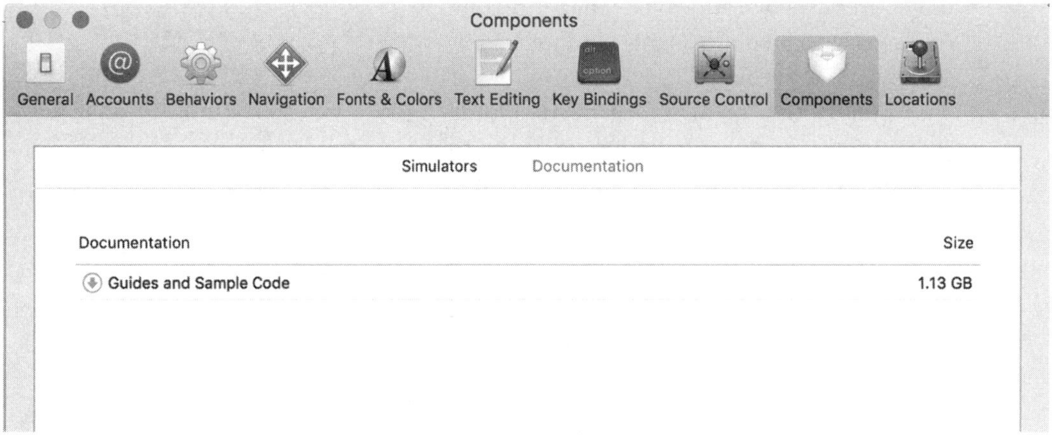

Figure 6.5   Click Xcode > Preferences > Components to download Guides and Sample Code.

Make sure you've downloaded the latest documentation, and then click the Reference link again. This document will be a good reference for you in the future as you begin to interact and customize your apps more and more.

- *Guides*—Apple guides are useful tools for understanding key concepts that Apple wants you to know. They're probably too deep or convoluted to understand at this point in the book, looks just look through them to be familiar with them right now.

- *Sample Code*—The next line provides files of sample code so you can see how to implement certain features. Apple combines a lot of different concepts into the sample code, though, so you won't find a sample that *only* illustrates how to implement a label. Instead, it covers a lot of advanced topics, and these advanced topics happen to implement a label.

- The Quick Help panel is going to be a great ally in your programming career, but don't be too overwhelmed at this point if you don't understand it all. I'll tell you what you need to get started throughout this book, and the rest will come with time and practice.

Now that you've added your first bit of code to an actual app, it's time to talk about commenting your code.

6.3 Commenting: you can never be too wordy, can you?

Remember back in chapter 1 when you created pseudocode for painting a wall? Those steps don't have to be thrown away once your app is created. Sometimes you need to remember what you did, why you did it, and how the app works. Enter comments—stage left!

6.3.1 Comments are your friends

Comments are a way that of documenting your code so that when you or someone else looks through the code, they can easily understand what you did, why you did it, and even how you did it. Adding comments to your code is a good habit to get into now, early in your coding career. Imagine a few weeks into the future when you're creating the LioN app and learning and applying new concepts. What will happen if you take a break for a few days, weeks, or months and then return to your code? Do you think you'll remember where you left off? Or why you wrote a line of code the way you did? It is highly unlikely, which is why comments come in handy. Some developers feel that comments aren't necessary—that code should be written in such a way that comments aren't needed. I think commenting your code is beneficial for you and for anyone who picks up the code after you.

6.3.2 How to comment your code

In Xcode, open the ViewController.swift file by clicking it once in the Navigator panel (the left panel). If you look at the top of the file, you'll see several lines that start with //; some lines have other words behind the // and some don't (as shown in figure 6.6).

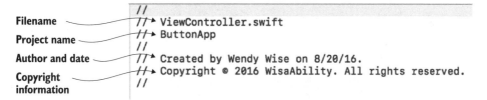

Figure 6.6 Swift creates some comments for you at the top of each file. You can add additional comments throughout your code by starting a line with //.

That section with `//` at the beginning of the line contains comments that Xcode *automagically* (a slang coding term for something done behind the scenes without the programmer having to do anything) adds to all your files.

Syntax: example

You've learned the importance of adding comments to your code and how to add them—by starting the line with `//`. This is important to remember, because you'll need use comments throughout your career!

As I've said, you can add your own comments to code by add the `//` at the beginning of the line you want to comment. Now add a comment right above the line that you added in the ViewController.swift file (the set title line). You might add a comment such as `//this sets the title of the button when it is tapped, but only for the normal state.`

  As with pseudocode, it's important that the comments make sense to you. If you're planning on sharing your code with anyone in the future, or if you plan to have several people work on your code, it's also important that they understand it. But for now, make sure it would make sense to you if you were to come back in a week or two to revisit the code.

Concepts to remember

- Outlets are ways for the code to talk to UI elements. The example we used was contacting your friend Butch—you needed an outlet (his phone number).
- Actions are the way the UI directs the flow of your code, or tells the code to do something differently. In the code example, the action was for the user to tap the button and the code to then do something. In the real-world example, it was the action of calling your friend Butch.
- You learned about messages. In the code, you sent a message to your button to change the title of the button to "I did it!". In the real world, you told Butch to meet you at 8 p.m.
- You looked at the Apple documentation to learn more about labels.
- The most important thing for you to take away from this chapter is a high-level understanding of outlets, actions, and messages. You'll use these concepts for almost every app you build from here on.

6.4   Summary

Wow—this chapter covered a lot! We walked through how you created the app with a label and a button in chapter 5. Remember the difference between outlets and actions: outlets let you access something on the user interface (the UI) by providing a reference to it (like a phone number or email for your friend Butch). Actions tell the code what should happen when a user interacts with a control object (like your button) in the UI. Objects can send messages, like your code sending the message "change your text" to the label.

You learned some syntax: how to comment your code with the // characters. You can (and should) document your code by using // at the beginning of the lines. The comments should be meaningful to you, especially if you revisit your code after some time away. Xcode helps with the syntax for Swift with code completion, and you can accept its guesses by pressing the Tab key. You can access the Apple documentation in Xcode by selecting the object that you want to know more about and clicking the circle with a question mark in it on the Utilities panel (right pane).

In the next chapter, you're going to capture users' input by allowing them to type into the app. The key concepts you learned in this chapter will be used again in the next.

Capturing user input: adding text boxes

This chapter covers

- Creating a new app that shows what's typed into a field
- Capturing user ideas with text boxes
- Connecting objects with actions and outlets again
- Chunking code for a function

You're going to create another app in this chapter, but this time you'll provide a box the user can type in. After typing text, the user will tap a button, and whatever the user typed in the box will appear down below. Such boxes, called *text boxes* (or UITextFields for single lines of text and UITextViews for multiple lines of text), are used throughout iPhone and iPad programming. You've probably seen them numerous times but may not have known that they were called text boxes. Figure 7.1 shows an example.

When you create a new event in the Calendar app on your iPhone, the fields where you type the event's title and location are text boxes. Text boxes are important components to learn, so let's get started.

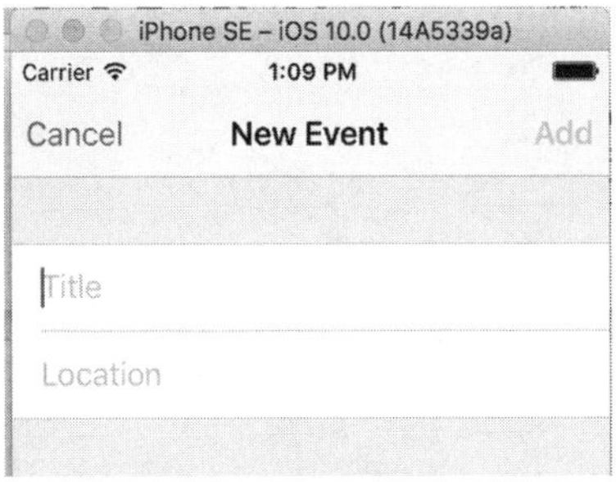

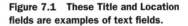

Figure 7.1 These Title and Location fields are examples of text fields.

7.1 Adding text fields

As you know, the best way to start any new project is with pseudocode, so let's write down the steps you need to create this app:

1. Create a new single-view application.
2. Add a button and a label to the view.
3. Add a text box to the view.
4. Connect the button, label, and text box to the code (wire them up), and test the app.
5. Add code to change the label, and test the app.
6. Comment the code.

Let's get started.

7.1.1 Step 1: Create a new single-view application

You should be pretty comfortable by now with creating a new project. In Xcode, start by clicking File > New > Project and selecting the Single View Application template. Name this app TextBoxApp. Save your new project to the same folder you created in chapter 2—mine is named dev.

7.1.2 Step 2: Add a button and a label to the view

When your new project loads in Xcode, you'll see the same set of files loaded down the left side of the Navigator panel (left panel) that were loaded in the new projects you created in chapters 2 and 5. Click the Main.Storyboard file to load the storyboard in the Standard Editor panel (center panel).

You'll first add a label to the storyboard, as you did in chapters 2 and 5. At the bottom left of the Utilities panel (right panel), make sure you have the Object Library showing by clicking the circle with a square inside of it, and then at the bottom of the panel search on *label*. Grab the label and drop it on your storyboard near the middle of the screen. Double-click the label, and change the text to *My Label*.

Go back to the Utilities panel again and search on *button*. You'll have three options to choose from. In this case, you want to add the top one—the one that says Button. Grab it, and drop it on your storyboard above your label. Double-click it, and change the text to *Change My Label.* These actions should be familiar to you from chapter 5—if not, you can review section 5.1.

7.1.3   Step 3: Add a text field to the view

This part is new, but it isn't that different from adding a button or a label. Go back to the Object Library in the bottom-right corner, and search on *text*. You should see two results returned: a text field and a text view. Make sure to select the text field and drop it on your storyboard above your button, as shown in figure 7.2.

Figure 7.2   **Your storyboard should now have a text box, a button, and a label.**

7.1.4   Step 4: Connect the button, label, and text box to the code (wire them up), and test the app

You connected a label and a button in chapter 5, so you should be familiar with this step. The first thing you want to do is change your real estate (how much of each panel is showing) to make it easier to connect the components to the code.

You're going to use the Assistant Editor again. Click the Assistant Editor button (the one that looks like two interlocking circles at top right). You should see the storyboard on the left side and ViewController.swift on the right side. (You saw the View-Controller in chapter 5—we compared it to Vanna White, the game show assistant.) You're going to wire up the button, the label, and the text box using the outlet and actions, and then I'll explain what you did afterward:

1   Holding down the Control button on the keyboard, click the Change My Label button on your storyboard.
2   With the mouse button still pressed down and the Control button still pressed, drag your mouse pointer onto the right side of the screen into the ViewController.
3   Hover your mouse pointer under the following words:

```
class ViewController: UIViewController {
```

You should see a blue link that links over to the ViewController and a black box that says Insert Outlet, Action, or Outlet Collection. When you see that, let go of both the mouse and the control button (with your cursor right under the following line:

```
class ViewController: UIViewController {
```

You should now see a pop-up that looks like figure 7.3.

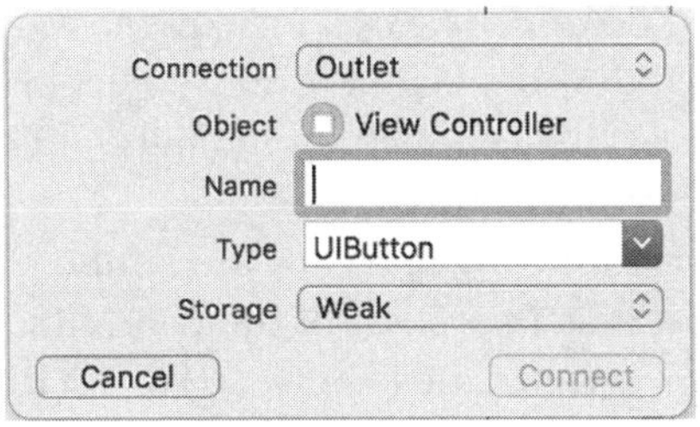

Figure 7.3 **Use the Control button to make a connection between your button and the ViewController file, and this dialog will open when you release the mouse button.**

STEP 4A: WIRE UP THE BUTTON

When the pop-up loads, change the Connection type to Action instead of Outlet, and name the action changeLabelButtonClicked. If you completed that successfully, your code should now have this line in it:

```
@IBAction func changeLabelButtonClicked(_ sender: UIButton) {
    }
```

Now you want to connect the label to the code.

STEP 4B: WIRE UP THE LABEL

First, Control-drag the label into the file, but leave the connection as an outlet and name it myLabel. If you did this correctly, you should see this line of code in your file:

```
@IBOutlet weak var myLabel: UILabel!
```

Finally, you want to connect the text box to the code.

STEP 4C: WIRE UP THE TEXT BOX

Control-drag from the text box to the file, and again leave the connection as outlet. Name it myTxtField. If you did this correctly, you should see the following code:

```
@IBOutlet weak var myTxtField: UITextField!
```

STEP 4D: RUN THE APP TO TEST IT

Run the app again in the Simulator (by clicking the Run button). Nothing should happen if you type in the text box or press the button yet—you want to make sure the app still works after your changes.

Once the Simulator has loaded the app, click the text field—note that the Simulator automatically pops up the iPhone keyboard. How cool is that? You didn't have to do anything to have the keyboard pop up, and you can even type into the text field! This is another way Apple helps by doing some of the work behind the scenes.

I'll tell you a lot more about how to change these behaviors when you start building the LioN app in part 3 of this book.

7.1.5   *Step 5: Add code to change the label, and test the app*

Now you're going to write another line of code. Back in step 4A, you connected the button to the code and specified that the connection should be action instead of outlet. You named it `changeLabelButtonClicked`, which should tell you by reading it that the user tapped (clicked) your Change My Label button.

This part of the code will run every time the user taps the button. This button can *control* the flow of the application because that piece of the code runs every time the button is tapped. This is why a button is called a UI control. (We discussed *UI* in chapter 3; it stands for *user interface.*)

YOU MADE A FUNCTION WITHOUT KNOWING IT

Back in step 4A, when you named the action `changeLabelButtonClicked`, you actually created your first function. *Functions* are self-contained chunks of code that perform a specific task (like sending a message, for instance). If you look at the line of code that was added when you connected the button in step 4A, you see `@IBAction`, which tells you there's an action to be performed:

```
@IBAction func changeLabelButtonClicked(_ sender: UIButton) {
    }
```

You may be wondering where the `@IB` part comes from. You don't really need to know much about it, but it's a carryover from much older versions of Xcode. Right after the `@IBAction` word, you see the word `func`, which stands for *function*. This keyword is telling Xcode that this is a function, or a contained chunk of code. The next piece is `changeLabelButtonClicked`, which you already know as the function name. The part in parentheses around it—`(_ sender: AnyObjectUIButton)`—is called a *parameter*. I'll tell you more about those in part 3 when you're building LioN.

SOME MORE SYNTAX

I said that a function was a "chunk" of code, but how does Xcode know where the chunk starts and where it ends? `{}` to the rescue! These brackets have many names, including curly brackets, brackets, open and close brackets, squiggle brackets, and more. For this book, I'll refer to them as *curly* brackets.

> ### Syntax: example
> The curly brackets `{` and `}` are used extensively in Swift. They're used to start and end functions.

Xcode recognizes the chunk of code as anything inside the curly brackets. You want to tell Xcode to do something when the button is tapped, and in this case, you want myLabel to change to whatever the user typed in the text field:

```
@IBAction func changeLabelButtonClicked(_ sender: UIButton) {
  }
```

Add the following line to your new function between the open curly bracket and the close curly bracket:

```
myLabel.text = mytxtField.text
```

This is saying, "Change the text of myLabel to whatever the text is in myTxtField." Pretty cool, huh? Now your entire file should look like figure 7.4.

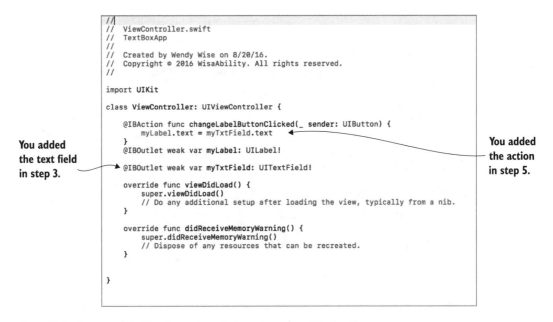

You added the text field in step 3.

You added the action in step 5.

Figure 7.4 The complete ViewController—make sure your code looks like mine.

RUN THE APP, AND TYPE IN THE TEXT FIELD

Now run the app again in the Simulator, type in the text field, and click the Change My Label button. Can you believe it? The label below changed its text to what you typed in the text field! Not only that, it will keep changing the label text every time you update the text field and click the button. Why? Because it's calling the function changeLabelButtonClicked every time the button is clicked. How cool is that? You only wrote one line of code to do that! Amazing, isn't it?

If you get an error when you run the app, make sure you have all the connections connected correctly, that your code looks like mine, and that you have a button, a label, and a text field on your storyboard. If you made connections in error (for instance, you created an action instead of an outlet or vice versa), you'll need to delete the connections for your code to work. (Refer back to figure 5.11 in chapter 5 for how to delete extra connections.)

7.1.6   Step 6: Comment the code

We talked about the importance of commenting your code back in chapter 6, so let's do that here. Remember that the comments are meant for you or a fellow coder to figure out what you did and why you did it when looking at your code at some point in the future. You need to add comments that make sense and that are relevant to you. To add comments, you need to start a line with //; Xcode will ignore whatever else is on that line.

Concepts to remember

- You create outlets and actions for the user interface and code so they're connected.
- Functions are chunks of code that perform a specific task. You'll use these in every app you write.
- You should now be familiar with the basic steps to create an app, add some UI elements like buttons and labels to the storyboard, and connect them to the ViewController. You'll use these basic steps not only throughout the rest of this book, but throughout the rest of your programming career. If you still aren't completely comfortable doing these steps yet, that's okay. You have many more chapters in this book to complete, and you'll be comfortable by the end of the book. You can always rework a previous chapter if you feel you need more practice.

7.2   Summary

I hope you have a sense of accomplishment, because you've written an entire app. As a reminder, you created a new app; added a text field, a button, and a label to the app; and wired those items to the code. You wrote a line of code that told the label to set its text to whatever was in the text field area. You learned about functions (chunks of code), which have an opening curly bracket ({) and a close curly bracket (}) that Xcode uses to know where the function code starts and ends. Xcode can do work for you behind the scenes—you didn't have to write any code to have the keyboard appear when you clicked in the text field.

Playing on the playground

8

This chapter covers

- Swift Playgrounds
- Frameworks
- Types of things

This chapter introduces you to Swift Playgrounds, an Apple app that allows developers to write code and see the results immediately—without having to run the app. We'll also begin discussing the different ways you can manipulate and store things in your code. This chapter will be interactive. You'll create something while also learning.

8.1 Swift Playgrounds: learning to interact with others

Swift Playgrounds is a helpful interactive tool that provides quick feedback on the code you've written. Recall that in part 1, when you created apps, you ran them several times before you were finished writing them, to make sure they still worked. That's because Xcode needed to compile them into a format that the iPhone could work with, and it checked for errors in your code during that process. Chapter 1 explained this process:

- Writing code
- Compiling it
- Running it

Playgrounds provide you with much faster feedback because it doesn't require you to run the code. It takes no time at all to compile and give you almost immediate feedback, so it's a great place to *play* around (see what Apple did there?) and learn. Let's get started with Swift Playgrounds.

Open Xcode and this time, instead of clicking Create a New Xcode Project, click Get Started With a Playground—the first option, as shown in figure 8.1.

Figure 8.1   Start by creating a new playground.

In the next screen that opens, leave the default as MyPlayground, and leave the platform as iOS. Now save it as you did in part 1 of the book when you created new projects. I saved mine in my dev folder again. Once you save the file, the new playground will open, looking like figure 8.2.

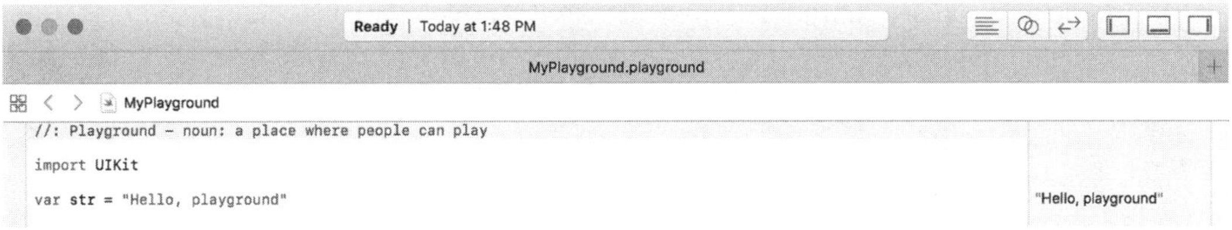

```
● ● ●                    Ready | Today at 1:48 PM                    ≡ ⊘ ↩ □ ▭ ▢

                         MyPlayground.playground                                +

⊞ < >  ▣ MyPlayground
//: Playground – noun: a place where people can play

import UIKit

var str = "Hello, playground"                              "Hello, playground"
```

Figure 8.2 A new playground opens once you click Save.

The first thing you'll notice at the top is that this looks remarkably similar to files you worked with in earlier projects. The top line is obviously a comment, because it starts with //, and it's green, which denotes a comment.

The next line, import UIKit, is also at the top of some files in your projects, but I haven't explained it before, so let's look at it. UIKit is a framework, but what is a framework?

8.2   Frameworks

Imagine trying to build a house and thinking of all the tools that might be required. You may need lots of different kinds of carpentry tools, plumbing tools, electrical tools, roofing tools, tiling tools, painting tools, flooring tools, and so on. Now imagine calling up a supply store and telling them to please deliver all the tools you'll need to build a house. Not only would you have an enormous stack of tools dumped in front of your empty lot, but you probably would spend a lot of time looking for the tool you need when you need it. This isn't efficient and it surely isn't optimized for building a house. The same concepts apply to writing an app.

So many features and so much functionality are built into iPhones and iPads that it would be inefficient if Apple tried to make them all available to the programmer up front. Each app that you wrote would have a huge stack of tools sitting behind it, and you might never even need those tools. Apple's enormous stack of tools might include photo tools, map tools, HealthKit tools, address book tools, sound tools, video tools, game tools, and more.

Now imagine Xcode had to sort through all those tools every time you wanted to compile and run your program. It would take an enormous amount of time, and it wouldn't be efficient or optimized for building an app. Apple packaged together the needed resources for these different types of tools into one package, called a *framework*. This framework is like ordering only the plumbing tools for your house when you need them. You can order the tools (import the framework in Xcode) and have them sitting there ready for you when you need them. Xcode doesn't use the tools until you ask for one—like going out in the front yard and getting a wrench from the pile of plumbing tools instead of bringing them all in at once. A framework is a single grouping of resources and compiled code that Xcode can easily access in your project.

Apple tools such as photos and map are Apple frameworks. You don't need to remember the following list—it's only meant to give you an idea of what they are:

- Photos framework
- MapKit framework
- HealthKit framework
- AddressBook framework
- AVKit framework
- GameKit framework
- And many, many more

Anytime you want to add a feature in your app that has to deal with photos, for instance, you'll need to import the Photos framework. This brings us back to the `import UIKit` statement at the top of your playground file. UI stands for user interface, the part of the application the user can interact with. So UIKit is exactly what it sounds like: a kit that provides you with the tools necessary to create the user interface (or front end) of an application. When you create an app that allows users to interact with it, you must *import* the UIKit framework into your code.

Now let's move on to the final line in the playground: `var str = "Hello, Playground"`.

8.3   *Types of variables*

Let's break down the statement `var str = "Hello, Playground"` into its different components:

- var stands for *variable*, which is the way Swift can store a value and access it again later. It's also "variable" in that you can change it to another value of the same type later if you want.
- str stands for the *name* of the variable in this case.
- = denotes that the variable name should be set to something.
- `"Hello, Playground"` is the string that should be stored in the variable named str.

In pseudocode, I would say, "I would like to store the words *Hello, Playground*, and I want to call it *str*, or, to say it more concisely, set variable *str* equal to *Hello, Playground*."

Syntax: example

When coding in Swift, the syntax for variables is like this: var (which is a *keyword* in swift, or a word that is "reserved" for Swift—developers can't use those words for anything) name_of_variable (this is the name you enter) = some_value (where you decide the value). Or:

```
var name_of_variable = your_value
```

Go back to Xcode, and look at your playground again. Start a new line, type `str`, and press Enter. (Xcode may try to auto-complete the line to `String`, but leave it as `str`—add a space after `str` if you need to.) Your playground should look like figure 8.3.

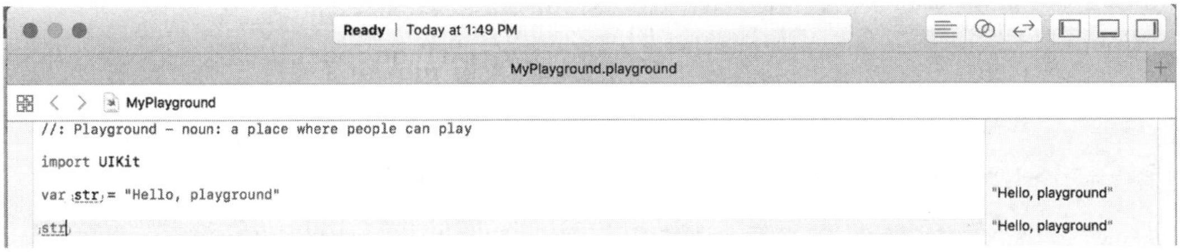

```
//: Playground - noun: a place where people can play

import UIKit

var str = "Hello, playground"                    "Hello, playground"

str                                              "Hello, playground"
```

Figure 8.3   Your playground with another `str`

Notice on the right side of the playground there are now two lines that say "Hello, playground". This is how the playground provides you with instant gratification, by showing results without compiling and running your app:

- The line that starts with `var` shows the output on the right side of the screen in the gray area. Xcode evaluated the variable `str` and said it was equal to "Hello, playground".
- The next line did the same thing because the first line told Xcode to store the value "Hello, playground" in the variable named `str`.
- The next line more or less says, "What is the value of `str`?"

Swift Playgrounds is great in that you can type str and it will show you what's stored in the variable. Xcode doesn't allow you to do that. Now you've learned about variables—or ways to store values in Swift. But what other kinds of variables are there, you ask? I'm so glad you asked!

8.3.1   Not your shoestrings

The first type of variable we'll cover is a string. A *string* can be anything from a single letter to a word or sentence that's enclosed with double quotes (`""`). Xcode and Swift Playgrounds know that "Hello, World" is a string type variable because you surrounded the words with double quotes. Variables can be changed, so you'll change the variable `str` to "This is a string". Go back to your playground, add a new line, and type `str = "This is a string"`. The right side of the playground should now say, "This is a string", as shown in figure 8.4.

Xcode stored the value `"This is a string"` in place of the previous value `"Hello, playground"`. You may be wondering how Xcode knows that the variable `str` should be a string. The Swift language *interprets* the variable type by how you use it. Swift and Xcode recognize the value of the variable `str` as a string because it's surrounded by double quotes.

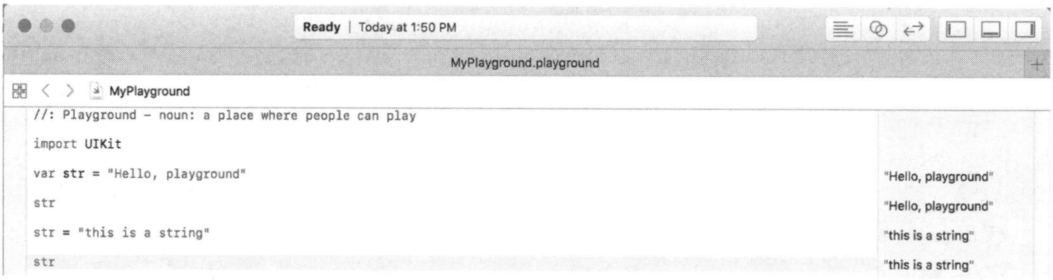

Figure 8.4 Setting the variable `str` to a new value will override the previous value stored in the variable.

You can also explicitly tell Xcode and Swift that this is a string by changing the statement to the following:

```
var myStr: String = "This is a string"
```

In English, that says, "Create a new variable name `myStr` of type string and set it equal to 'This is a String'." You don't often need to explicitly define the variable type, but you should recognize the syntax when you see it. Chapter 9 shows you some examples when we talk about arrays.

Coding conventions: use lowercase for variable names

You may notice that the variable names start with a lowercase letter. This is a common coding convention—the way most people conventionally name variables.

It's much easier to differentiate a variable that you've created (like `str` or `myStr`) from the declaration of a type of variable or class name, which starts with an uppercase letter (`String` or `ViewController`). You *can* use uppercase to start the name of variables, but it makes the code harder to read.

I highly recommend sticking with the coding convention of starting your variable names with lowercase letters. You can learn more about how Apple recommends naming things in the Swift documentation at http://mng.bz/a7Py.

If you enter a new line on your playground and add the statement `var myStr: String = "hello"`, Swift Playgrounds will show you the value of the variable `myStr` on the right side, as shown in figure 8.5.

You'll use strings through the remainder of this book, and you'll be familiar with them by the end. Let's look at other types of variables.

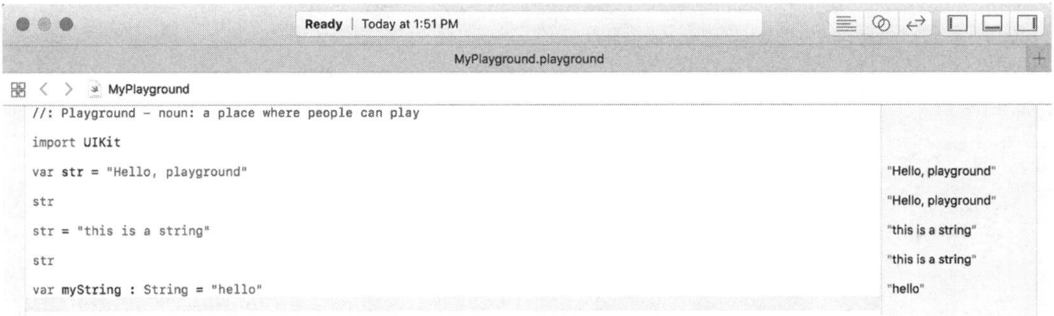

```
//: Playground - noun: a place where people can play

import UIKit

var str = "Hello, playground"                          "Hello, playground"

str                                                     "Hello, playground"

str = "this is a string"                                "this is a string"

str                                                     "this is a string"

var myString : String = "hello"                         "hello"
```

Figure 8.5 Explicitly stating that the variable `myStr` is of type `String` also works, although it isn't necessary.

8.3.2 Going back to math class

Regardless of whether it's been a month or a few decades since you were in a math class, you probably remember that there are different types of numbers: whole numbers, decimals, integers, and so on. If you're like me, you never thought you would need this knowledge outside of math class, but guess what? You now get to use that knowledge again for creating apps, even though you probably thought at the time *I'm never going to use this* (thanks, Mr. Bellamy).

The first type of number we'll discuss is an *integer*. In Swift, we use the variable type `Int` for integers, which are whole numbers (numbers without decimal places). An `Int` can store big numbers like –2,147,483,648 or 2,147,483,648. That's right: an `Int` can be a positive number, negative number, or even zero.

Let's try it in Swift Playgrounds to see an example. Add a new line to your playground, and type the following:

```
"var myCatsAge = 15"
```

Swift Playgrounds shows you that your cat's age is equal to 15 on the right side. Fantastic!

How old will your cat be in five years? Let's check. Add a new line to your playground:

```
"var inFiveYears = myCatsAge + 5"
```

Swift Playgrounds, as shown in figure 8.6, immediately shows you the number 20. Wow—instant gratification!

You should be able to understand this line intuitively: you created a new variable called `inFiveYears` and said that it should be equal to however old your cat is now, `myCatsAge`, plus 5. You can do *math* with integers, like you did in math class. That means you can add (+), multiply (*), divide (/), and subtract (-) integers.

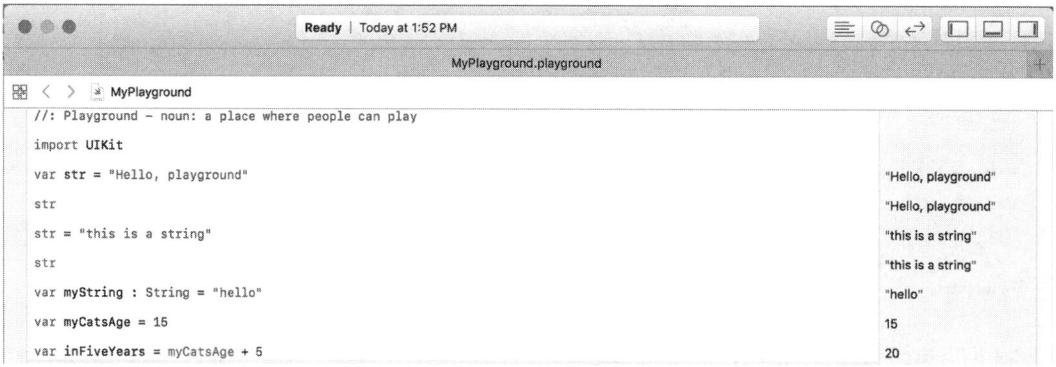

Figure 8.6   Integers can be added together, as shown on the last line.

Write a new line of code to find out how old your cat was 10 years ago. I'll wait here.

Did you do it? You should have added a line something like `var tenYearsAgo = myCatsAge - 10`. Swift Playgrounds should then instantly give you the answer 5.

You'll use the `Int` data type extensively in your programming career and you should be comfortable with it by the end of this book, as we'll use it a lot. Let's head back to math class now and learn about other number types.

8.3.3   *Double, double, toil and trouble*

The next data type we'll discuss is a double. A *double* is a number with decimal points. They're sometimes called *fractional* numbers (whereas a *whole* number can't have decimal points). A double can have up to 15 decimal places (15 numbers to the right of the decimal point) like 3.141592653589793, and it can be positive or negative. Doubles are useful for calculator apps or when trying to find sales tax or a tip percentage.

Let's see how to compute the sales tax for an item in Swift Playgrounds. Try this first, and then check to see if you were right—you can multiply two numbers using the * symbol:

- Create a variable for the price of an item, say 12.47.
- Create a variable for the tax percent, say 1.07.
- Multiply the two together to get the result of 13.3429.

How did that work—did you get it? Check your work by reviewing figure 8.7.

You'll notice in the example that I didn't create a variable to store the final answer in, meaning I can't save the total cost. I could have written it like I did, `cost * tax`, or I could store the value for additional manipulation: `var total = cost * tax`. When coding in Swift for your apps, you'll want to use the second method of storing the value so you can continue to use it in your program. For instance, if I want to print out the total or display it to the user in an app, I would want to store the total in a variable,

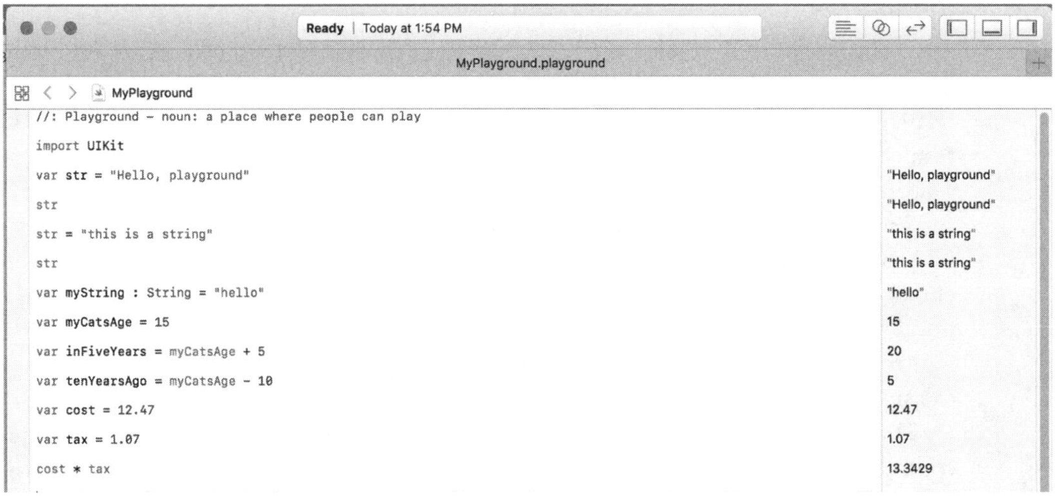
Ready | Today at 1:54 PM
MyPlayground.playground
MyPlayground
//: Playground - noun: a place where people can play
import UIKit
var str = "Hello, playground"
"Hello, playground"
str
"Hello, playground"
str = "this is a string"
"this is a string"
str
"this is a string"
var myString : String = "hello"
"hello"
var myCatsAge = 15
15
var inFiveYears = myCatsAge + 5
20
var tenYearsAgo = myCatsAge - 10
5
var cost = 12.47
12.47
var tax = 1.07
1.07
cost * tax
13.3429

Figure 8.7 Calculating the total cost after tax

so I would need to print or show the variable instead of the calculation. It's also important to note that you can't define the same variable name more than one time in a chunk of code. They must be unique.

There are many more data types that we could cover here, but you won't need to use all of them, and it's better to introduce them to you when you need them rather than have you try to remember them now. I'm trying to give you the information you need just in time rather than overwhelm you with a lot of information that you won't need for a while.

Concepts to remember

- Swift Playgrounds is a great tool to help you learn and try new concepts. You can create new playgrounds and save your work if you want.
- Frameworks are like groups of tools that you'll need for different apps.
- You must import a framework to have access to its tools, like the UIKit for user interfaces.
- Variables are used to store values that you want to access later.
- Variable names should always start with a lowercase letter and can't have any spaces or special characters.
- Data types are different kinds of data, as defined by the types of values that they can take like a string (`String`), a whole number (`Int`), or a decimal number (`Double`). There are many data types, some of which we'll cover later in this book.

8.4   *Summary*

This chapter covered some of the basic data types that you'll use in your programming career, and you'll begin using some of them in the next chapter. You can experiment or play with the different data types in Swift Playgrounds so you can get immediate results. Try adding numbers, dividing, subtracting, and multiplying to get used to working with the number formats.

Swift Playgrounds is a great place to experiment and try things without having to wait for an app to run. *Frameworks* are a grouping of tools or classes that you'll need for different kinds of apps. The primary framework you've been using so far is the UIKit framework, which lets you access the UI features. Remember that *variables* are ways to store information that you want to access later. Variables have data types, or kinds of data they can store and we covered three types in this chapter: String, Int, and Double.

The next chapter will use the information you've learned in this chapter to begin controlling the application flow using different kinds of statements. You'll start learning about what it takes to create your next app: the tip calculator.

The first part of this book introduced you to programming concepts such as classes and objects (chapter 1); technical documentation (chapter 3); object attributes, actions, outlets, and messages (chapter 5); and functions (chapter 7). We'll build on these key concepts in part 2. We'll also begin talking a lot more about the flow of an app and how to create statements to control that flow. The next two parts of the book are even more exciting than the first, so buckle up!

Part 2

The keys to the city: understanding key development concepts

Part 2 teaches you more about programming concepts, including the `while` statement, the `switch` statement, arrays and collections, and navigation. Chapter 9 talks about program flow. In chapter 10, you'll create an app that mimics the game in which one player is asked to guess how many fingers the second player is holding up behind their back. You'll create yet another app in chapter 11, in which you can look up state abbreviations. Chapter 12 explains how to visually lay out application screens using storyboards. In chapter 13, you'll learn about the lifecycle of ViewControllers and create an app to demonstrate that lifecycle. Chapter 14 discusses how to create tab bars; chapter 15 teaches you an important aspect of iOS programming, tables and table views; and chapter 16 wraps up this part of the book by introducing you to design patterns.

Go with the flow, man! Controlling the flow of your app

You learned back in chapter 5 that the *flow* of an application—how an application reacts to different events—can be changed when a user interacts with a control, such as by tapping a button. But there are other ways that the flow can be altered that don't require user intervention like tapping buttons. This chapter introduces some of these ways.

9.1 Control your flow

Controlling the flow of your app is similar to controlling the flow of traffic in the real world. When you're driving to school or work, you either know where you're going or you're following directions of some sort. You may know that you need to turn left at the stop sign, or go through the traffic light and turn right at the second traffic light. If you didn't have directions or if your car only went straight, you wouldn't get to where you needed to be and your ride would be pretty boring. In order to get to where you want to be, you're controlling the direction or flow of your car. Applications are the same: they can be written to flow in a seemingly straight line, but that would be pretty uninteresting, wouldn't it?

One of the ways you get to school or work is by making turns and following traffic laws. While driving, you should obey the traffic laws. If the light is red, you should stop. If it's yellow, you should proceed with caution or stop. These are ways of controlling the traffic and getting where you need to go. You can control the flow of your application similarly:

- If today's date is greater or equal to your birthday, then add 1 to the age.
- If this year is a leap year, then it is possible to have February 29.
- If the user entered a valid entry, then do something.

All of these control the flow because you can react to a situation and do something differently based on what's happening, what day it is, what time it is, and so on. One of the ways you control the flow is by using `if` statements.

9.2   *If you do that again, I'm going to...*

I've already given you several examples of real-world "if" statements, but let's break it down to make it really clear. My mother was clear when I was younger (okay, maybe she still is today) and doing something that she didn't approve of (I rarely did that, by the way). She would always warn me about what I was doing and would tell me the consequences if I did it again. "If you hit your brother one more time, I'm going to take TV away for a week!" (Again, not that this *ever* happened.) There were also the positive "if" statements: "If you cut the grass, I'll give you $5.00." (I was pretty cheap back then.)

Then there were the *compound* "if" statements: "If you cut the grass, I'll give you $5.00, or if you cut the grass and edge the yard, I'll give you $7.50." These statements seem pretty straightforward, but how exactly do you translate that into the coding world? I'm so glad you asked.

I'm going to create a new playground, but you can either continue using the one you used before or create a new one (refer to chapter 8, section 8.1, if you don't remember how). You're going to do the following now, in the usual pseudocode form:

1 Create a variable named x, and set the value to 5.
2 Create a variable named y, and set the value to 10.
3 Create a statement that says, "If x is less than y, then print out the word *yes*."

You should be able to complete the first two steps—you learned about variables in the last chapter. I'll show you how in case you need a refresher:

1 Start your statement by using the keyword var, which stands for *variable*.
2 Type the letter x, which is the name of the variable.
3 Set it = 5.

Simple, right? Do the same thing for y.

Now for the `if` statement, which you haven't seen in code before. The coding *convention* (the coding style that's most widely accepted) for `if` statements is as follows:

```
if (compare statement) {
    Then do something
}
```

The compare statement doesn't need to be enclosed in parentheses, but I did so to make it easier to read. Mine looks as simple as this:

```
if x < y {
```

The greater-than and less-than signs should come back to you from your math classes, but here's an explanation, in case they aren't:

- `<` means the item to the left of the sign is "less than" the item to the right of the sign. So this statement would evaluate as true: `5 < 10`.
- `>` means the item to the left of the sign is "greater than" the item to the right of the sign. So this statement would evaluate as false: `5 > 10`.

Now you can compare the two variables—but I also asked you to do something new: print the word *yes*. Printing out a line is helpful when you're coding, because sometimes the code isn't doing what you think it should be doing. In this case, you want to verify that x is indeed less than y. This is accomplished with the following statement:

```
print()
```

You can read the line as "print line"—because that's what it stands for. If you want to print a string like the word "yes," you put the "yes" between the parentheses like this:

```
print("yes")
```

> **Syntax alert!**
> The print-line statement is going to be one of the best tools in your programming career. There are times when you're developing that you *think* you know what the code is doing, but then you put a `print` statement in there and find out that it isn't doing what you thought. You should definitely remember this statement as you continue to learn the Swift language:
>
> ```
> print()
> ```

If you create your two variables and then evaluate them, your code should look like figure 9.1.

Remember back in chapter 6 where we talked about using the curly brackets to separate chunks of code? You need them in your `if` statements so that Xcode knows

```
//: Playground - noun: a place where people can play

import UIKit

var str = "Hello, playground"

var x = 5
var y = 10

if x<y {
    print("yes")
}
```

Figure 9.1 Comparing the values of x and y, and printing the word "yes" if x is less than y

what chunks belong to which statements. That means your if statements will always have the curly brackets like this:

```
if (statement){
}
```

Note that in this example, I'm only using the parentheses around statement for clarity. You don't need parentheses here. A normal if statement looks like this:

```
if statement {
}
```

> **Syntax alert!**
> if statements always need to be "chunked" up so that Xcode knows what belongs in the if statement and what doesn't. You use the curly brackets { and } to separate the chunks from other chunks.

Now, if you read the preceding code in English, you're saying, "x is equal to 5, y is equal to 10. If x is less then y, then print a line that says *yes*."

I find it helpful to start by thinking about what you want to do and writing pseudocode (as you did earlier), then writing the code, and then verifying by trying to read it in English to make sure the code matches what you intended to do. In this case, the code matches exactly you we wanted it to do. But what if x wasn't less than y? What then?

9.3   *If you do that OR if you... then I'm going to...*

You saw the real-world "if" statement in action earlier. I gave these examples:

- "If you cut the grass, I'll give you $5.00."
- "If you cut the grass, I'll give you $5.00, or if you cut the grass and edge the yard, I'll give you $7.50."

And you've seen the example of a simple if statement: "If x is less than y, print *yes*", so let's move on to the compound if statement, which will give you the ability to use the "or" in the preceding example.

There are cases in programming where you might need to compare three different variables. For example, you already have your variables x and y, but what if you threw a z in the mix? Let's start again by thinking about what you want to do and putting it in pseudocode:

1 Create a variable named a, and set the value to 5.
2 Create a variable named b, and set the value to 10.
3 Create a variable named c, and set the value to 15.
4 Create a statement that says, "If *a* is greater than *b* OR if *b* is less than *c*, then print out the word *yes*."

Notice the last bullet is different than the previous example. First, you want to know if a is greater than b (which it isn't), *or* if b is less than c (which it is). So how do you add an *or* in your code?

The *or* in Swift looks a little weird, I'll admit. You can't type in the word or—you need to use the symbols ||. The key for the || symbols is found on the backslash key \. You press Shift-\. Press this key twice to create the *or* statement: ||.

When I code my compound if statements, I like to separate them by parentheses so they're easier to read. My code in English will look like this: "(if statement one) or (if statement two)."

Try to create this compound if statement in your code now before looking at my code. Figure 9.2 shows my code for this comparison.

```
var a = 5                      5

var b = 10                     10

var c = 15                     15

if a > b || b < c {
       print("yes")            "yes\n"
}
```

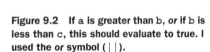

Figure 9.2   If a is greater than b, *or* if b is less than c, this should evaluate to true. I used the *or* symbol (| |).

How did you do? Does your code match my code? I hope so. Notice that I have two if statements and I have the *or* operator in the middle (||).

Now you know how to code a compound if statement using or ||. But what if you want to do the same thing with *and*?

9.4   *If you do that AND you do this, I will…*

Let's revisit the example we've been using: "If you cut the grass, I'll give you $5.00, *or* if you cut the grass *and* edge the yard, I'll give you $7.50." This time, we're looking at the *and* statement: "if (statement 1) AND (statement 2) then …"

Let's see how to create new variables as before and create your pseudocode:

1 Create a variable named d with a value of 5.
2 Create a variable named e with a value of 10.

3 Create a variable named f with a value of 15.

4 Create an if statement to says, "If *d* is less than *e* AND *e* is less than *f*, then print out the word *yes*."

The *and* comparison is && (Shift-7 twice). Take a moment to think about this and then change the code on your playground. Pay attention: this if statement is different than the last one. d is *less* than f in this statement.

Do you see the word *yes* printed on the right? (The \n after the word *yes* is a character in the playground that denotes the next print line will start on a new line.) Figure 9.3 shows how I did it.

```
var d = 5                        5
var e = 10                       10
var f = 15                       15

if (d < e) && (e < f){
    print("yes")                 "yes\n"
}
```

Figure 9.3   I used the *and* operator between my if statements (&&) to print "yes\n".

Notice this looks like the *or* statement earlier, but this time the two comparisons have the *and* (&&) operator between them to denote that both must be true. Good job! You're coming along nicely, Grasshopper. Now you're going to work on the else if statement.

9.5   *If you do this, else if you do this, else if you do this...*

You learned in section 9.3 how to use the *or* || statement, but what if you have several *or* statements that you want to evaluate? In this exercise, you'll do the following in pseudocode:

1 Create a variable named g with a value of 5.

2 Create a variable named h with a value of 10.

3 Create an if statement that says, "If g is less than h, then print a line that shows the value of g is less than the value of h. In other words, I want to see a line that says that 5 is less than 10."

4 Create an else if statement that says, "If g is greater than h, then print a line that shows the value of g is greater than the value of h. In other words, I want to see a line that says that 5 is greater than 10—if that were the case."

There are a few new concepts to discuss here.

9.5.1 *Printing a line with values of variables and strings*

First of all, you need to print a line with actual variable values in them, and you don't know how to do that yet. This is pretty simple, and it's useful to see what's stored in a variable.

If you want to print the value of a variable, you can use

```
print(g)
```

which will print out 5. Remember how to print a string? It looks like this:

```
print("is less than")
```

If you want to print a line that prints the value of the variable and a string, you need do the following:

```
print("\(f) is less than \(h))" \\-> this will print 5 is less than 10\n
```

The quotes are at the beginning and the end of the statement so that Xcode knows the entire line should be printed out as a string, but the backslash and the parentheses around the variable tell Xcode to print the value stored in the variable, not the variable name itself.

> **Where did the \n come from?**
> When you use the print statement with strings, Swift Playgrounds appends \n to the end of each line. This represents *new line* or *carriage return*. Don't worry that it's printing something you didn't want it to or expect.

If you left out the backslash, you would see the following:

```
print("(g) is less than (h)" \\-> this will print (g) is less than (h)
```

> **Syntax alert!**
> Printing the values of variables is incredibly helpful while coding. Sometimes you think a variable is a certain value when it's something different. You can print the values of the variables in one of two ways:
>
> - You can use the statement `print(variable)`, which will print the value of the variable.
> - You can print a string around the variable to make it more human-readable. To do this, you "escape" the variable by adding a backslash in front of it. This is what it would look like: `print("the value of x is \(x)")`.
>
> You'll find these `print` statements useful as you code, so it's important that you learn and remember how to use them. You can always look them up later, but it's faster to memorize it now!

That's one new bit that you didn't know how to do. Let's address the second bit.

ADDING AN ELSE IF STATEMENT

How do you add in an else if? Easy: you add else if. You would have something that looks like this:

```
if (statement 1){
} else if (statement 2) {
}
```

Go back and try to complete the exercise:

- Create an if statement that says, "If g is less than h, then print a line that shows the value of g is less than the value of h. In other words, I want to see a line that says that 5 is less than 10."
- Create an else if statement that says, "If g is greater than h, then print a line that shows the value of g is greater than the value of h. In other words, I want to see a line that says that 5 is greater than 10—if that were the case."

Figure 9.4 shows what my code looks like.

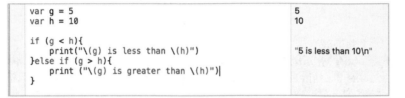

```
var g = 5                                              5
var h = 10                                             10

if (g < h){
    print("\(g) is less than \(h)")                    "5 is less than 10\n"
}else if (g > h){
    print ("\(g) is greater than \(h)")|
}
```

Figure 9.4   Remember to use curly brackets around your if statements and to "escape" your variable names in the print line (use the backslash to print the value rather than the variable name).

How did you do? Did the line print out correctly? When will the second if statement print? In this case, never. The way you coded the variables, g will always be 5, and h will always be 10, and as we know, 5 is always less than 10.

Let's change the values of g and h so you can test the else if statement. Change the value of g to a value larger than h to see what happens. The second line should have printed out. Great job!

Now you know how to use the following:

- if statements
- compound if statements using *and* and *or*
- else ifs

Here's a question for you: what happens in the preceding code if g is equal to h? Let's address that.

9.6   *If you do that, otherwise…*

We need to address the final possible scenario with the `if` statement you created. What happens if g and h are equal? You could add a statement to determine whether they are equal, but in some cases, you want to know that neither of the first two statements was true. I call this the "otherwise" scenario.

Let's start a new comparison with i and j. You'll follow the previous example of printing the lines when i is less than j or i is greater than j, but you'll add a line that says "The value of i is equal to the value of j." In this case, you're going to end your series of `if` statements with the `else` block. This catches every other possible scenario, so if the first `if` statement isn't true, and the second `if` statement isn't true, then do something. It would look like this:

```
If (statement 1){
    Do something
} else if (statement 2) {
    do something else
} else {
    otherwise do this
}
```

Make sense? Try coding the entire statement and make i and j equal to 5. Then code the final `else` statement yourself. Figure 9.5 shows what mine looks like.

```
var i = 5                                            5
var j = 5                                            5

if (i < j) {
    print("\(i) is less than \(j)")
} else if (i > j){
    print("\(i) is greater than \(j)")
} else{
    print("\(i) must be equal to \(j)")              "5 must be equal to 5\n"
}
```

Figure 9.5   I set my variables both equal to 5 and created a final `else` statement to capture all other conditions if i was neither greater nor less than j.

How did you do? I hope you got that! I know we covered a lot with all these `if` statements—but you'll use them a lot in your career.

Concepts to remember

This chapter is full of both syntax and concepts. But the concept you really need to remember in this chapter is controlling the flow of your application through the `if` statement. The `if` statement is logical: "If a variable is this, do something—otherwise do something else."

Syntax alert!
Remember that the `if` statement is this:

```
if (comparison) {
Then do something
}
```

The `if` *or* statement is this:

```
if (comparison1) || (comparison2) {
Then do something
}
```

The `if` *and* statement is this:

```
if (comparison1) && (comparison2) {
Then do something
}
```

9.7   *Summary*

`if` statements are useful tools when you're controlling the flow of your application. You need to be able to handle different situations if one thing happens versus another thing happening. You now have the `if` tool in your tool belt to help direct the flow. You learned several variations of the if statement, including the basic if statement, the compound `if` statement using *or* and *and* (|| and &&), the `if else` statement, and the `else` (or otherwise) statement.

Can you see how this will help change the flow of an application? Imagine you're creating a new contact on your iPhone. You enter all the information, and the app pops up a message that says, "Contact already exists. Merge information?" Now that you know about the `if` statement, behind the scenes the code might be saying, "If the contact already exists, display this message to the user." And when the user clicks Yes or No to merge the two contacts, the code might say, "If the user clicked Yes, then merge—otherwise, don't merge." Make sense?

We'll cover some more helpful statements that help control the flow of the application in the next several chapters, so stay tuned!

While you're doing that...

10

You learned all about the `if` statement and how it can help control the flow of your application in chapter 9. The `if` statement allows you to evaluate variables and then execute different code depending on the outcome of the evaluation. Now you know two ways to control the flow: by the user interacting with your app (by tapping a button, for instance) and by the `if` statement.

There are a lot of other ways to control the flow of your app, though. I'm going to introduce you to a few more now. This chapter will talk about the `while` statement and the `switch` statement, and you'll write another app.

10.1 Using the while statement to control your code

How many times have you been doing something, and someone (usually a parent or a spouse) says, "While you're doing that, will you also do this?" I was hanging a picture in the house the other day—a simple enough task. I got out a hammer, nail, measuring tape, and level (I wanted it to be straight and centered). While I was doing this, my wife came into the room, saw the tools, and said, "While you're doing that, do you mind measuring the height of the bathtub? I want to get a side table." This is a classic example of a *control* statement. I wanted to hang a picture, but the flow of my work was changed by the "while" statement. Of course, I grumbled a bit to register a small complaint, but I did end up measuring the tub.

The `while` statement in Swift works in much the same way as my wife. The flow looks similar:

```
while some condition {
  Do something
}
```

In my real-world example:

```
while you already have the tools out and you're using them {
  Measure the height of the bathtub
}
```

The `while` statement is straightforward and easy to use. I'll show you how now.

10.1.1 *The while statement in action*

Create a new playground in Xcode by clicking File > New > Playground. I saved my playground as Chapter10, but you can name yours whatever you like. In English, our example would read like this: "While *x* is less than *y*, print a line that states that the value of *x* is less than the value of *y*." You learned how to create variables and print lines in chapter 9, and we're going to build on that knowledge here.

Create two new variables (see chapter 9) named x and y. Set the value of x to 5 and the value of y to 10. Let's add a `while` statement now:

```
var x = 5
var y = 10
while x < y {

}
```

These statements are pretty straightforward, but in case you need a refresher, you're creating a variable named x and setting the value equal to 5; then you're creating a variable named y and setting its value equal to 10. Then you see your new `while` statement, which says "While *x* is less than *y*," and you have open and close curly brackets to show the "chunk of code" that should execute when x is less than y.

There isn't any code in there right now, so the playground doesn't do anything yet. You'll add your `print` line now to print out the line of code. You learned how to write the `print` line in section 9.2, so refer back if you need a refresher on the syntax. Add the following line between the two curly brackets:

```
print("\(x) is less than \(y)")
```

This says to print the value of x, then print the words "is less than," and then print the value of y. If you add this in now, you'll notice that Swift Playgrounds begins executing it immediately, and the right side of the playground keeps increasing the number of times the statement is executing with no end in sight. This is called an *infinite loop.* Infinite loops can be bad! Almost every programmer has most likely accidentally created an infinite loop in their lifetime. An infinite loop is a block of code (like your print line statement) that continues to execute with no way out. It's like the fun house mirrors at a carnival, where there's a mirror image of a mirror image of a mirror image, and you see yourself a thousand times over because of the placement of the mirrors. The only way to stop seeing all those images of yourself is to step away from the mirror. In this case, there's no way for the print line of code to stop executing. x will always be less than y because 5 is always less than 10. To fix this, you need to either increment x (add to it) so the statement will not always be true, or you need to decrement y (subtract from it) so the statement will not always be true. Let's increment x, shall we? Add the following line of code under the print line:

```
x = x + 1
```

This line says that x should now equal the value of x plus 1. The first time this statement runs, x will be 6, the second time it runs x will be 7, then 8, and so on. Your print line statement should now run five times and print out the following in your console:

```
5 is less than 10
6 is less than 10
7 is less than 10
8 is less than 10
9 is less than 10
```

That's pretty neat, isn't it? You only needed to write your print line statement once, and it printed out five times.

Now you know how to increment x, so let's see how to change the execution code to decrement y instead. This should be intuitive. You change the line to read as follows:

```
y = y - 1
```

Your print line still writes out five times, but now it shows the following:

```
5 is less than 10
5 is less than 9
5 is less than 8
5 is less than 7
5 is less than 6
```

Again, you only changed one line of code, and the print line executed five times. That's pretty amazing that you could accomplish so much with so little code.

10.1.2 *Wrapping up the while statement discussion*

You learned the while statement, which can be boiled down to the most simplistic statement of "Perform a set of statements while a condition is true." Or, said another way, "Perform a set of statements until a condition is false."

When would you use a while statement in a program? Imagine you're writing a program and you have two variables like x and y from our previous example. This time, though, you have no idea what the values are—you only know they're two numbers. You also know that you need to do something while x is greater than y. In our example, you could probably guess that you needed to print the line 5 times because the difference between 5 and 10 is 5—regardless of whether you add 1 to 5 or subtract 1 from 10. But what if I gave you two different numbers?

Let's assume I gave you 1,024 and 978 and told you to do something while one was greater than the other. You could do the math to see what the difference is between the numbers and then do something that many times, or you could "do while" one is less than the other and let the program figure out the difference. If you update your code with these two numbers, you'll immediately see that the difference is 46. That was so much easier than writing out a print line 46 times, wasn't it? You wouldn't want to use the while statement to do the math mentioned here (1,024 – 978); there are much easier ways to do that.

10.2 *Turn around now switch (remember Will Smith?)—the switch statement*

The next control statement that we're going to talk about is called a switch statement. If you think back to section 9.1, when we talked about the if statement, we evaluated certain conditions by saying something like "If x is less than y, or if y is less than z." What if I wanted to know whether a number was prime or not (prime numbers are those that can't be divided by any number other than 1)? I could write a lot of if statements to say something along the lines of "if x==3, or if x==5, or if x==7" and so on, but that would be a *lot* of if statements. There's a much easier way to accomplish this check, and that is with a switch statement. The switch statement allows you to compare a value to multiple other values. The essence of the switch statement is as follows:

```
switch "the value to consider" {
     case "value 1":
         "do something"
 case "value 2":
         "do something else"
 default:
         "otherwise do this"
}
```

The switch statement evaluates a value and then determines which case it falls into. case is a different way of saying "equals to." You can read the preceding lines and say that if the variable is case 2 or you can say if the variable is equal to 2.

Let's see an example to demonstrate this switch statement. You're going to check to see whether a number is a prime number. Create a variable named a and set the value to 11. 11 is not divisible by any number other than 1, so you know it's a prime number. Now create a switch statement that looks like this:

```
var a = 11

switch a {
case 1, 3, 5,7,11,13:
  print("value is a prime")
case 2,4,6,8,9,10,12:
  print("value is not a prime")
default:
  print("value is not within the range")
}
```

With these few lines of code, you were able to evaluate whether a was prime by comparing it to 14 different numbers. Imagine trying to do these evaluations with an if statement—you would have to write a lot more code than you would if you used a switch statement. The preceding switch statement uses the keywords switch, case, and default. The word switch tells the compiler which statement you're evaluating—in this case, the variable a. The next keyword, case, tells the compiler what to evaluate the variable a against. You can have as many case statements as you want. You aren't limited to two or three. Finally, the default statement says that if none of the cases above evaluate to your variable, then perform that final statement. If your cases don't handle all possible outcomes, you'll get a compile error. The switch statement uses the default keyword, which behaves much like the if else statement. You can see how this works now by changing the value of a to different numbers. Try changing it to 9 or 24 to see how the statement flows.

10.2.1 Assignment

Try this assignment without looking at my code first to see if you can do it. You'll write another switch statement, but this time you're going to use directions. Create a variable named heading and set its value to "east". Now create a switch statement evaluating the heading variable and create a case for each different direction: east, south, north, west, and default. Question: Does it matter what order you put the cases in? No, it doesn't. You can put north first or last and the code will still execute the same. The only case that must go last is the default case—it must be the last case in your switch statement or you'll get an error. For each of your cases, print a line that says "heading north", "heading south", and so on for each of the cases. Ensure that the case matches the print line so if you're evaluating the heading and it is "east", your code should print "heading east". Add a default statement that prints a line and says "Where are you headed again?". Do this now, and I'll wait here.

Okay. How did you do? Here's how I did it:

```
var heading = "east"

switch heading {
  case "north":
    print("heading north")
  case "south":
    print("heading south")
  case "east":
    print("heading east")
  case "west":
    print("heading west")
  default:
    print("where are you headed again?")
}
```

Now change the value of the heading variable to the different cases and make sure it works. Change the heading variable to "north" and make sure it prints the "heading north" line. Change the heading variable to "East" with a capital E; what happens? The strings are case sensitive, so "east" doesn't match "East" and the default line prints. This is important to remember in your programming career: *strings are case-sensitive.* You may spend a long time trying to figure out why your code isn't working the way you expect it to, only to find out that the string you thought you were evaluating was uppercase.

The code that you wrote evaluated the heading variable and then selected which case was appropriate and executed the code in that block—which in this case printed a line. If the value of the heading variable was "north" in the code, then the cases "south", "east", and "west" never would be evaluated. The code skips right over them because it already has a match to the first case. I'll show you a way to continue evaluating the switch statement in chapter 11 after we talk about a few other concepts. The switch statement is powerful, and you can do a lot with it. I've only given you a high-level overview here, but you'll learn more about it in later chapters.

I don't like to go too long without writing an app, and I'm sure you are probably ready now, too. Let's write an app now and put what you've learned into practice.

10.3   *How many fingers am I holding up?*

Do you know the game where you hold your hand behind your back and ask someone to guess how many fingers you're holding up? You're going to write an app to simulate that game now—only your app will be the one holding the numbers behind its back while you guess the number. The WhichNumber app will randomly pick a number between 1 and 5, and you have to guess what the number is. If you're right, the app will tell you that you guessed correctly, and if you're wrong, it will tell you to guess again. Your final app will look like figure 10.1.

The pseudocode for the app looks like this:

1 Add all the components to the story-board.

2 Make the storyboard connections.

3 Create a variable to capture the number guessed: numberGuessed.

4 Change the numberGuessed variable when the stepper is tapped (don't worry—I'll explain stepper in a moment).

5 When the Guess! button is tapped, create a random number and compare it to the numberGuessed variable.

6 Update the view to tell the user whether they were right or wrong.

Figure 10.1   The WhichNumber storyboard will look like this when finished.

10.3.1 Step 1: Add all the components to the storyboard

Start by creating a new project and name it WhichNumber. Then follow these steps:

1 Once the app loads, click the Main.storyboard and drag a label to the top. Double-click it, and change the text to "How many fingers am I holding up?".

2 Drag another label and drop it right under the first one. Double-click it, and change the value to 3.

3 The next component you're going to add is new to you—it's called a *stepper*. It steps the value up or down when the user taps the + or - buttons. The stepper can be seen in dialog boxes where a user can change the number of copies to be printed, for example. Type stepper in the Object Library search bar (at the bottom left of the Xcode window), and you should see the stepper control as the only option. Drag it onto the storyboard below the 3 label.

4 Grab a button from the Object Library, drop it under the stepper, double-click, and change the title to "Guess!".

5 Add another label under the button, and change the text to "are you right?".

6 Make sure your storyboard matches mine (in figure 10.1).

Time to start making connections.

10.3.2 Step 2: Make the storyboard connections

Now you need to begin connecting the components on your storyboard to the code. Do you remember how to do this? (You did it in chapter 3, but I'll remind you here.) Start by changing the Xcode view to the Assistant Editor by clicking the button in the top-right corner that looks like two interlocking rings. This will keep the storyboard open on the left side of your screen but will also open the ViewController on the right side of your screen. If you need more real estate, hide the Navigator panel by clicking the button on the top right of Xcode that looks like a square with a bold vertical line on the left. (This should all be familiar to you, but if not, refer back to chapter 4.)

You made connections between the storyboard and the code back in chapters 5 and 6 when you created the button app. Follow these steps:

1 The first connection you're going to make is between the label that you changed to 3—so Control-click the label and drag it to the ViewController. Leave the connection type as Outlet and name it `"numFingers"`.

2 Do the same with the `stepper` control, but name the outlet `"stepperControl"`.

3 Do the same again with the `"are you right?"` label, but name the outlet `"resultLabel"`. You'll use this label to tell the user whether or not their guess was correct. Make this label wide by dragging the ends of the label so it fits within the window. Using the Attributes Inspector, center the label within the space (click the label in the storyboard, open the Attributes Inspector panel, and click the second button in the Alignment options (fourth from the top).

Next you need to connect the button actions to the code, which you also did in chapter 5. You want the code to do something when the button is clicked and when the stepper is tapped:

1 Control-click the Guess! button, and drag it to the ViewController, but this time change the connection type from Outlet to Action and name the action `guess-ButtonClick`.

2 Do the same for the stepper: Control-click the stepper, drag it to the ViewController, change the connection type to Action, and name the action `stepper-Clicked`. Check your code and make sure you have the following connected:
   - 3 *label outlet connected*—`@IBOutlet weak var numFingers: UILabel!`
   - `"are you right?"` *label outlet connected*—`@IBOutlet weak var resultLabel: UILabel!`
   - stepper *control label outlet connected*—`@IBOutlet weak var stepperControl: UIStepper!`
   - stepper *control action connected*—`@IBAction func stepperClicked(sender: UIStepper) {}`
   - *Guess! button action connected*—`@IBAction func guessButton(sender: UIButton) {}`

If you have all the connections made, run your code to make sure it's still working. If you created connections in error, you'll need to delete them. Refer back to figure 5.11 in chapter 5 if you don't remember how to delete them.

10.3.3 Step 3: Create a variable to capture the number guessed: numberGuessed

You need to create a variable that can store the number that the user guessed. This is different from the label you created on the storyboard—the label is text to show the user what they guessed. You need an Int variable to store a number. Remember that you can store variables as different types, such as an Int for whole numbers (numbers without decimals), a String for words or even sentences, and a Double for numbers with decimals. The numberGuessed variable will start with the number 3, since that's what the label states, but you could start (or initialize) the variable to any number you wanted.

It is important, though, to make sure that the variable you're using in the code is in sync with the label that you're showing the user. You'll add the variable at the top of your class under the ViewController line. Start by adding the keyword var to denote that this is a variable, then add the name of the variable (in this case, numberGuessed, and then set the value equal to 3. The top of your code should look like this:

```
class ViewController: UIViewController {
var numberGuessed = 3
```

10.3.4 Step 4: Change the numberGuess variable when the stepper is tapped

Now you need to increase or decrease the variable numberGuessed when the stepper is clicked. Can you guess where this code needs to go? If you guessed in the stepper-Clicked action, you're right. You'll change numberGuessed based on the value that the stepper tells us. But wait! What's the value of the stepper? You didn't set that anywhere yet, so you need to do that before you can change the value.

Let's go back to your storyboard for a minute and click the stepper control. In the Attributes Inspector panel, notice at the top that you can set the minimum and maximum values for the stepper, as well as the current value and the step value. The values that you need to put in here should be intuitive to you, but let's walk through them.

The minimum value is going to be the smallest number you can guess. In this case, you want to let the user guess that you aren't holding any fingers up, so set the value to 0. The maximum number you can guess is five, unless you're the six-fingered man who commissions swords and then doesn't pay.[1] You set the current value of your numberGuessed variable to 3, and you set the label on the storyboard to 3, so set the current value of the stepper to 3 so you're consistent. You want the user to be able to guess each of the numbers between 1 and 5, so the step should be 1. This means your stepper will increase by 1 each time the + is tapped and decrease by 1 each time – is tapped.

Now that you've set up the stepper, let's go back to the code so you can capture the value that the stepper is incrementing and decrementing. numberGuessed should

---

[1] "Hello, my name is Inigo Montoya. You killed my father—prepare to die," from the classic movie *The Princess Bride*. If you haven't seen it yet, go see it. The book is awesome, too.

equal the value of the stepper, so add the following code in between the two brackets of the `stepperClicked` action:

```
numberGuessed = stepperControl.value
```

This does exactly what you want it to do: It gets the value of the `stepperControl` and sets it to the `numberGuessed`, but there's an error in the code. The error says you "cannot assign a value of type 'Double' to a value of type 'Int'." We talked about data types back in chapter 8, so you probably remember that a `Double` is used to store values with decimal points, whereas `Ints` are used to store whole numbers. You have two options here: you can either change the `numberGuessed` data type to `Double`, or you can create a new `Int` using the value of the `Double`. That's a heavy sentence, right? The details about why you can do this are too deep for this book, but know that you can construct a new `Int` by using the `Double` in the constructor (or how the `Int` is made). Remember that the learning strategy of this book is to give you enough information to get you coding but not to overwhelm you.

Let's talk about the *how* instead. This is the easy part. To get rid of the error, you need to create a new `Int` using the `Double` and assign that value to the `number-Guessed`. To do this, add `Int` in front of `stepperControl.value` and put parentheses around what you're changing. Your code should look like this:

```
numberGuessed = Int(stepperControl.value)
```

Now you want to update the label on your storyboard to match the `numberGuessed` and the stepper. Add the following line right below:

```
numFingers.text = "\(numberGuessed)"
```

This line sets the text of the `numFingers` label to value of `numberGuessed`. You added the quotes around the `numberGuessed` so you could use the value of the variable in your `String`. If you don't put the backslash and the parenthesis around the variable name, it will print the word *numberGuessed*. You must put the backslash and the parentheses around the variable if you want to print the value stored in the variable. Now if you run the code again, pressing the stepper up and down should change the label to the different numbers. Pretty cool, huh?

Next you'll hook up the Guess! button.

10.3.5   *Connecting the Guess! button*

Step 5 of the pseudocode says that you should create a random number and then compare it to what the user guessed when the user tapped the Guess! button. It should be easy for you to figure out where this code goes now because you've coded several actions before. Add your code between the curly brackets of the `@IBAction func guessButton(sender: UIButton) {}` function.

The first thing you need to do is create a random number. This code is most definitely more than you need to understand right now, so copy it down as is:

```
let randomNumber = Int(arc4random_uniform(6))
```

Some of that should look familiar to you. The `let` keyword indicates that you're creating a *constant*, or a value that you can't change once it's set. You named the constant `randomNumber` and then set it equal to a random number that was cast to an `Int`. The `(arc4random_uniform(6))` is a function that returns a random value between 0 and 5. In Swift, counting always starts with 0 when you're programming, so the 6 is inclusive of 0 and 5.

Part of being a good programmer is knowing which tools to use when you need to do something. Just as a plumber knows which tools to use for a specific problem, you'll learn to determine which types of control statements will work best for certain situations. You might be trying to figure out how to create a `switch` statement or a `while` statement to compare the random number to the guessed number. In this case, the simplest way to compare the two numbers is an `if` statement. Some programmers spend a lot of time trying to figure out the most elegant way to solve a problem when sometimes the simplest tools work best. I recommend solving the problems in the easiest possible way. Then, once it's working, you can go back and try to make it more "elegant." In this case, the `if` statement is the easiest way to compare the two numbers.

You need to create an `if` statement that compares the random number to what the user guessed and then tells the user whether they were right or wrong (pseudocode step 6) by updating the `resultLabel`. It would also be nice to show the user what number they guessed and what the number was so they know you aren't cheating.

Here's what my code looks like for the `if` statement:

```
@IBAction func guessButton(sender: UIButton) {
  let randomNumber = Int(arc4random_uniform(6))
  if numberGuessed == randomNumber {
    resultLabel.text = "Congrats! I was holding \(numberGuessed) fingers up!"
  } else {
    resultLabel.text = "You guessed \(numberGuessed), but it was
      \(randomNumber)."
  }
}
```

Run your code in the Simulator and see if it works. You can click the stepper button all the way up to 5 and all the way down to 0 and click the Guess! button, and it should display the results. You can guess as many times as you want, and each time the app will generate a new random number between 0 and 5, compare it to the number you guessed, and tell you the answer. Pretty cool!

```
//
//  ViewController.swift
//  WhichNumber
//
//  Created by Wendy Wise on 8/21/16.
//  Copyright © 2016 WisaAbility. All rights reserved.
//

import UIKit

class ViewController: UIViewController {

    var numberGuessed = 3

    @IBOutlet weak var numFingers: UILabel!
    @IBOutlet weak var stepperControl: UIStepper!
    @IBOutlet weak var resultLabel: UILabel!

    @IBAction func guessButtonClick(_ sender: UIButton) {
        let randomNumber = Int(arc4random_uniform(6))
        if numberGuessed == randomNumber {
            resultLabel.text = "Congrats!  I was holding \(numberGuessed) fingers up!"
        } else {
            resultLabel.text = "You guessed \(numberGuessed), but it was \(randomNumber)."
        }
    }

    @IBAction func stepperClick(_ sender: UIStepper) {
        numberGuessed = Int(stepperControl.value)
        numFingers.text = "\(numberGuessed)"
    }

    override func viewDidLoad() {
        super.viewDidLoad()
        // Do any additional setup after loading the view, typically from a nib.
    }

    override func didReceiveMemoryWarning() {
        super.didReceiveMemoryWarning()
        // Dispose of any resources that can be recreated.
    }

}
```

Figure 10.2   The entire ViewController code for the app. Check your code against mine if your app isn't working.

Figure 10.2 shows the full listing of my code. You can download the entire project from www.manning.com/books/anyone-can-create-an-app or from GitHub (https://github.com/wlwise/AnyoneCanCreateAnApp).

Syntax: example

You learned some great syntax in this chapter:

- *The* while *statement—*while *comparison* { *do something*}
- *The* switch *statement—*switch *variable* { case: *case to compare*}

Concepts to remember

- The `while` statement tells your application to perform a set of statements until a condition becomes false.
- The `switch` statement can help you reduce the comparisons you need to do if you were using an `if` statement.
- Infinite loops are generally not a good thing and can use all the memory in a device until the app is shut down.

10.4 Summary

In this chapter, you learned about the `while` statement, the infinite loop—which is generally not a good thing—and `switch` statements. You also built an app that put your `if` statement knowledge to good use. You're going to learn about how to store multiple values with arrays in the next chapter, so stay tuned.

Collections

11

Almost every app you'll ever write will need some way to store data. You already learned about storing data in variables in chapter 8, but sometimes you need to store several pieces of data together in a grouping of some sort. This is where the idea of *collections* comes in—a collection of values that can be stored together. Imagine if you went to the grocery store and had to buy one egg at a time instead of a nice dozen packaged together. It would be a bit annoying, for sure. This chapter covers two different collection types (egg cartons) to store your data.

11.1 Quantum arrays: not really, but that sounds scary, right?

The first kind of collection that we'll discuss is called the *array*. Let's go back to the egg carton example—but this time, the eggs are numbered 0 through 11 (remember, in the programming world, counting starts with 0). The eggs were put in the carton in order, starting with egg 0 and ending with egg 11. The only way to get the eggs out of the carton is also in order. If you want to start cooking and you need an egg, you must start with the first egg—or to write it in a programming way, you want egg[0]. When you want the second egg, you get egg[1], and so on.

Let's assume for a moment that the seventh egg (egg[6]) in the carton appears to be slightly larger than the rest. You have a recipe that is precise and you want to use that slightly larger egg. I said you can only get the eggs out in order, so does that mean you have to pull eggs 0 through 6 out to get egg 7? No! If you know the exact number of the item you want, you can get that one out by itself. It's only when you don't know the exact number of the one item that you want that you have to go in order to pull them out. In this case, you want egg[6] from the carton.

What if you wanted to store some cheese in your egg carton? That wouldn't make sense because the storage type is for eggs, not cheese. The same applies to arrays. You can only store one kind of data type in an array. (You learned about data types in chapter 8, in case you need a review.) The egg carton is specific and can only store one type of object, and in this case we said it was eggs.

You'll create an array now so you can see how easy they are. Create a new playground and save it (I saved mine as Chapter11). Now make a list (array) of tools that you might need to paint a wall. Your shopping list array will hold the names of items that you need to buy, and the names will be stored with the data type String. The first part of the array statement should be familiar to you by now. You're going to create a variable named shoppingList. Add the following to your playground:

```
var shoppingList = ["paint", "painter tape", "roller", "drop cloth"]
```

The preceding statement creates an array named shoppingList and adds four items to the list. Notice that there's nowhere on that line that says the word *array*, but you can tell this is an array because it has the square brackets [and] around the strings. When you see these brackets, you know it's a collection. You can see that all the types added are of type String. You can tell pretty clearly that there are four items in the list, but what if you didn't know exactly how many were in there? You could easily check by getting the count of the array as follows: shoppingList.count, which will return a number as an Int. Check it on your playground by printing out the count:

```
print(shoppingList.count)
```

You'll see that Xcode returned the number 4—which is great! How easy is this? Now you know that "roller" is stored in the third position (or *index*) of 2 (remember, you start counting from 0). If you wanted to get that item and print it out, you would do the following:

```
print(shoppingList[2])
```

The preceding statement says the following: "Print the item stored in index 2 in the shoppingList array." You should see "painter tape" printed on the right side of the playground. Now you have a shopping list of four items, but that's hardly worth going to the hardware store for, so add a few more items to the list. Add a pan:

```
shoppingList.append("pan")
```

You can check the count to make sure you now have five items in your array:

```
print(shoppingList.count)
```

The append statement adds an item to the end of the list, and the count of the array is increased by 1.

Back to the egg example: I said you couldn't store cheese in the egg carton because they're not the same type of object. The same applies to arrays. Try to add an Int (in this case, the 5 is an Int) to the array so you can see what kind of error is produced in the playground:

```
shoppingList.append(5)
```

You can see the big red exclamation point that shows up on the left-hand margin. If you click it, you'll see an error message that says, "Cannot invoke append with an argument type (Int)." This is telling you that you can't append an object of type Int to an array of Strings. Makes sense, right?

I talked to my wife, and she said she had already bought a pan, so I need to remove that item from my list:

```
shoppingList.removeLast()
```

Great! Now I'm back to having four items on my list. What if I wanted to print out each item on my list? I could use a print() statement for each item, or I could use what's called the for statement.

Syntax alert!

Arrays are used to stored several of the same kind of objects in a collection. They are created:

```
var arrayName = [item1, item 2, item3]
```

You can add an item to an array:

```
arrayName.append(item4)
```

You can remove the last item from an array:

```
arrayName.removeLast()
```

11.2 *The for statement and loop*

The `for` statement is used when you want to *iterate* through an array—move through the values in the array one item at a time. The syntax is straightforward: `for item in` *array* `{ }`, where *array* is the name of your array and `item` is the variable name that you want to use for the items. An example would make this clearer. Add the following to your playground:

```
for item in shoppingList {
  print(item)
}
```

This `for` statement is iterating through your shopping list starting with index 0 (the first item in the array). It assigns the value of the item stored to the variable named `item` and then prints out the item. It prints this out for each item in your array. This is much easier than writing four `print()` statements. You can name the variable anything you want. Try changing the word `item` to `x`, for example:

```
for x in shoppingList {
  print(x)
}
```

You'll notice that nothing changed—you got the exact same results. You can use any variable name in the `for` statement.

Syntax alert!

The `for` statement is used for iterating through an array. The `for` statement looks like this:

```
for variableName in arrayName {
  do something
}
```

11.3 *Dictionaries*

The next kind of collection type we'll discuss is the dictionary. Dictionaries are exactly what they sound like. You have a key and you want the corresponding value—or you have a word and you want to know the definition. Where the array uses indexes (`[0]`, `[1]`, and so on) for the objects, dictionaries use keys. The syntax looks like this:

```
var nameOfDictionary = [key : value, key : value ]
```

Again, let's look at an example to make this clearer. Assume you want to know state abbreviations and the state names. You'll create a dictionary so you can store them for easy lookup later:

```
var states = ["GA": "Georgia", "WA": "Washington"]
```

This stores two key/value pairs in the dictionary named states. As with the array, you might want to know how many values are stored in the dictionary. The syntax should look similar:

```
print(states.count)
```

And if you want to add a key/value pair to the dictionary, do the following:

```
states["OR"] = "Orogon"
```

Now if you print out the count, you'll see a total of three states:

```
print(states.count)
```

I meant to have the value of "OR" be "Oregon", so update that:

```
states["OR"] = "Oregon"
```

The value for key "OR" has now been updated to "Oregon". Now make sure it was updated by printing out the value of key "OR":

```
print(states["OR"])
```

You may notice that Swift Playgrounds is showing a yellow triangle warning. This is because you're printing the value of the key OR, and Swift Playgrounds doesn't know what kind of variable this is. It will still work, but that yellow triangle is annoying. Click it to see what Xcode tells you: "Expression implicitly coerced from 'String?' to Any." That sounds deep, doesn't it?

You're asking Swift Playgrounds to evaluate and print out the value of the key OR without knowing what might be stored in there. Swift Playgrounds isn't sure how to handle that, so it gives you three suggestions. The first is to provide a default value. You can provide a default value to print out in case nothing is stored in the OR key. To do so, change your code to

```
print(states["OR"] ?? "no state")
```

The ?? operator is a shorthand way of saying, "If there isn't a value stored for the OR key, use "no state" instead.

The second option available to you is to *force unwrap* the value. Use the Force, Luke! Okay—not that Force; but you can't fault a girl for trying. You can force unwrap a variable by using the ! symbol, which tells Xcode that you're absolutely sure an appropriate value is stored in the variable and that it isn't nil. You can do this by adding the following:

```
print(states["OR"]!)
```

You should use this only when you're positive the variable has a value and isn't `nil`; otherwise, your app will crash and burn when you run it (okay, it will throw an exception and stop working, but "crash and burn" sounds more exciting).

The third option is to cast the value to "As Any"—to tell Swift Playgrounds to treat the variable as the nonspecific type `Any`. This lets Xcode and Swift Playgrounds know that the variable type could be any of the supported types. This approach is called *casting* or *typecasting*, and you'll learn more about it in chapter 19. The code looks like this:

```
print(states["OR"] as Any)
```

You don't use the `print` statement often when creating real iPhone or iPad apps—it's used mostly for debugging and testing, to check the values stored in variables. You do need to know and remember how to handle variables when Xcode may not know what type a variable is or whether it's `nil`.

Let's get back to some other states in the example. Next, check to see whether you added Indiana into the dictionary:

```
print(states["IN"])
```

You'll see that Swift Playgrounds printed the word `nil`, which means there's no key or value (key/value pair) for the key `"IN"`. If you want to remove a value from the dictionary, you could set its key to `nil`, which would delete the key/value pair from the dictionary. Remove the misspelled `"Oregon"` from the dictionary:

```
states["OR"] = nil
```

If you print out the count of the dictionary again, you'll see that you're back to two key/value pairs in the dictionary. If you try to print the name of `"OR"` again, you'll see that `nil` is returned:

```
print(states["OR"])
```

You were able to print all the values in the `shoppingList` array earlier by using the `for` statement, and you can do the same type of thing with the dictionary. You'll do that now with the following syntax:

```
for (dictionaryKey, dictionaryValue) in dictionaryName {
  do something
}
```

Go back to Swift Playgrounds, and add the following:

```
for (stateAbb, stateName) in states{
  print("\(stateAbb) : \(stateName)")
}
```

You should see the state keys and values printed out:

```
WA : Washington
GA : Georgia
```

> **Syntax alert!**
> You can create a dictionary:
>
> ```
> var dictionaryName = ["keyName" : "keyValue1", "keyName2" : "keyValue2"]
> ```
>
> You can get the number of key/value pairs in the dictionary by getting the count:
>
> ```
> dictionaryName.count
> ```
>
> You can add to the dictionary:
>
> ```
> dictionaryName[newKey] = newValue
> ```
>
> You remove an item from the dictionary by setting the key to `nil`:
>
> ```
> dictionaryName[keyToDelete] = nil
> ```

Remember that you can use any variable names in the `for` statement, but I used `stateAbb` and `stateName` to make what I'm doing easy to remember. I could use x and y, but that doesn't describe the key/values in the dictionary, and if I put the code away and come back in a few months, it would be much more helpful to have descriptive variable names.

This might seem like a lot to take in, so next you'll write an app to see how useful dictionaries and for statements are.

11.4   *Creating a state name lookup app*

You're going to create an app that allows the user to type in a state name and the app will display the abbreviation of the state. If the state name isn't found, the app will display a message that the abbreviation couldn't be found. The pseudocode looks like this:

1 Create an app named StateAbbreviationLookup.
2 Add the UI components to the storyboard: a descriptive label, a text box for the user to type into, a lookup button for the user to tap, and a result label to display the state name.
3 Connect the UI components to the code.
4 Create the dictionary of state abbreviations and names.
5 Create the code to look up the state abbreviation when the user types in the state name.

Let's get started.

11.4.1 Step 1: Create an app named StateAbbreviationLookup

This should be pretty familiar to you by now, but click File > New > Project and select the SingleViewApplication template. Leave the default settings in the New Project dialog when that appears. Name your project StateAbbreviationLookup and save it into your dev folder.

11.4.2 Step 2: Add the UI components to the storyboard

In Xcode, click the Main.storyboard so the Standard Editor shows the storyboard in the center panel. Drag a label from the Object Library to the top of the storyboard, double-click the label, and change the text to "Enter the State Name:". Now drag a text box and put it right under the label. Drag a button to the storyboard, and place it right under the text box. Double-click it, and change the text to *Lookup State Abbreviation.* Grab one more label and put it right under the button. Double-click it, and change the text to *Result.* Make sure your result label is long enough to handle the names of your states. Hover your mouse pointer over the end of the label until the resizing squares appear on all sides, and then drag it out so it's longer, as shown in figure 11.1. Your storyboard should look similar to figure 11.2.

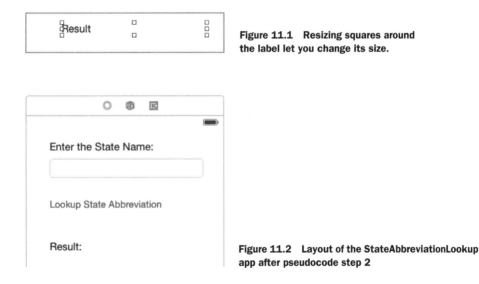

Figure 11.1 Resizing squares around the label let you change its size.

Figure 11.2 Layout of the StateAbbreviationLookup app after pseudocode step 2

11.4.3 Step 3: Connect the UI components to the code

The next step is to wire the components up to the code, as you've done in each of the apps you've created since chapter 3. Start by changing the Xcode layout to the Assistant Editor (the button on the top right of Xcode that looks like two interlocking rings). Control-click the text box, drag it to the ViewController on the right side of the screen, and connect it using an outlet named stateTextField, as shown in figure 11.3.

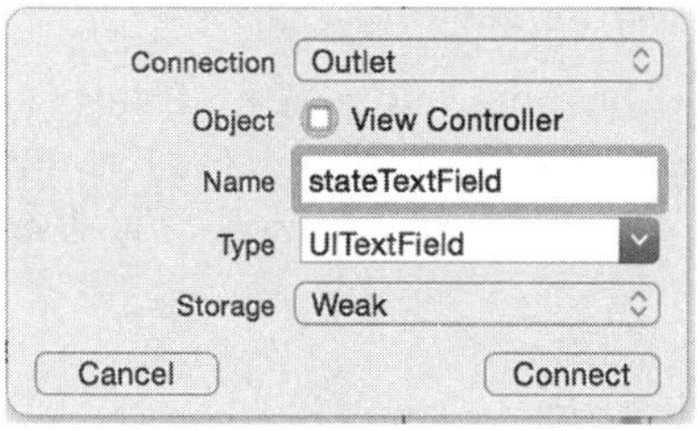

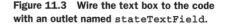

Figure 11.3   Wire the text box to the code with an outlet named `stateTextField`.

Wire up the result label using an outlet also, but name it `resultLabel`. Now wire up the action for the app. You'll need to capture the action from the button, so Control-click the button, drag over to the ViewController, and change the connection type to Action. Name the action `lookupClicked`.

Notice that I try to name my variables and connections to be consistent with what they are or what they do. You can name your variables and connections anything you want, but the closer you name them to what they do, the easier it will be to understand your code.

That's all the connections you need from your storyboard to your ViewController, so switch back to the Standard Editor (the button at the top right of Xcode that looks like left aligned text) and select the ViewController in the Navigator panel so it's showing in the center panel.

11.4.4 *Step 4: Create the dictionary of state abbreviations and names*

The next step from our pseudocode is to create a dictionary with the state abbreviations and names. I'm just going to create a few state dictionary entries, but you can create as many as you'd like from whichever states you want. If you don't know your state abbreviations, you can use mine here or look them up at http://pe.usps.gov/text/pub28/28apb.htm.

Add the following code to your `ViewController` class, under the line `class View-Controller: UIViewController {`:

```
var stateDict = ["Georgia" : "GA", "Washington" : "WA", "North Carolina" :
➡ "NC", "Oregon" : "OR", "Indiana" : "IN"]
```

This creates a dictionary named `stateDict` and adds five key/value pairs for states. Remember, here's the syntax:

```
var dictionaryName = ["key1" : "value1", "key2" : "value2"]
```

Next, you'll create the code that will take the key that the user entered, search your dictionary for the key, and display the value of the state abbreviation if there is one.

11.4.5 *Step 5: Create the code to look up the state abbreviation when the user types in the state name*

The first thing you want to do is to look up the key that the user entered to see if it's in the dictionary. As you'll remember from chapter 7, you know how to get the value from the text box that the user entered the state key into by using `codeText-Field.text`. You'll create a new variable named `dictionaryKey` and set it equal to the value that the user entered into the text field:

```
let dictionaryKey = stateTextField.text
```

Now check the dictionary to see if that value is in there (add this to the `lookup-Click()` function):

```
if let stateAbb = stateDict[dictionaryKey!]{
  resultLabel.text = stateAbb
}
```

This statement looks a bit different from the `if` statements you've seen before. Ignore the `if` at the front of the statement, and it might look more familiar. You're first creating a constant variable name state abbreviation (`let stateAbb =`) and then setting it equal to the value that will hopefully be returned from your dictionary lookup (`stateDict[dictionaryKey!]`). The dictionary lookup should look familiar since you did it in the preceding with the `print(states["OR"])` code.

Now, if you add the `if` statement back into the line, you're saying if the `stateAbb` variable that you just created isn't `nil` when you look up the value from the dictionary (as you did earlier when you tried to print the abbreviation of Oregon after deleting it). In English, we're saying "If the state abbreviation for the key that the user typed in isn't *nil*, then set the result label to the abbreviation." Make sense? Chapter 20 covers this concept in more depth.

What if the user enters a value that isn't in the dictionary? Add an `else` to your `if` statement to respond to that situation:

```
if let stateAbb = stateDict[dictionaryKey!]{
    resultLabel.text = stateAbb
  }else{
    resultLabel.text = "No state abbreviation found"
  }
```

Now this `else` statement should display the message that no state abbreviation was found for the value that the user entered. Try it now to make sure it works. Remember that strings are case-sensitive, so you have to type in the state name in camel case (*camel case* is another coding term meaning you use uppercase for the first letter of words all squished together—thisIsCamelCase). Did that work for you? Great!

Syntax alert!
You may have noticed in the preceding `if let` statement that the `dictionaryKey` has an exclamation point (`!`) at the end of it. That has to do with a concept covered later in the book, but it tells Xcode that there should be something in the variable and to please look at it.

It isn't good practice to make the user type in a capital for the first letter—it's better to just not give them an option, so you need to fix that. Go back to the storyboard and select the text box so it's active. Now on the Attribute inspector on the right side of Xcode (the button that looks like a big down arrow—if you need a refresher on Xcode panels, go back to Chapter 4 for review). If you look about halfway down the Attributes Inspector panel, you'll see a drop-down for Capitalization. Click it to see the options and choose Words, as shown in figure 11.4. Run your app again. You should see now that the user doesn't need to make the first letter uppercase, which is exactly what you need.

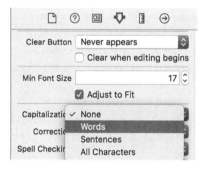

Figure 11.4   Change the attribute for Capitalization to Words.

You know what else is not good practice? Having that result label show up before you've entered any states to look up. The user doesn't need to see that if there aren't any results, so you'll fix that too. Back in Xcode, click the results label so it's that active component and then look over in the Attributes Inspector panel again. You have to scroll down to the near bottom of the panel to see the Hidden Attribute. Once you find it, click it and then look at your storyboard again. The *Result* text now shows in light gray to indicate that it isn't visible. If you run your app again, you'll see that the result label is indeed hidden from view. That's great—except now it doesn't show up after you searched. You'll fix that by going back to the ViewController code and adding the following line in the `lookupClicked` function:

```
resultLabel.isHidden = false
```

Now when you run your code, the result label shows up after you click the lookup button. Great!

There's one more thing that would make this app a little better. What if the user clicks the lookup button without entering any text? You should handle that—and you can.

You're going to surround your previous if statement with another if statement, making it a *nested* if statement. Add another if statement checking for no text ("") and then update the result label to instruct the user to enter a code:

```
if dictionaryKey == ""{
 resultLabel.text = "Please enter a state name"
}else{
 //this is where your other code is...
}
```

Make sure to add the final curly bracket } at the end, right before you unhide the result label.

Here's what my entire lookupClicked function looks like now:

```
@IBAction func lookupClick(_ sender: AnyObject) {
    let dictionaryKey = stateTextField.text
    if dictionaryKey == ""{
      resultLabel.text = "Please enter a state name"
    }else{
      if let stateAbb = stateDict[dictionaryKey!]{
        resultLabel.text = stateAbb
      }else{
        resultLabel.text = "No state abbreviation found"
      }
    }
    resultLabel.isHidden = false
  }
```

That's it! You created an app that will do the following:

- Look up an abbreviation based on the state name
- Handle the situation where the user doesn't enter anything
- Handle the situation where there is no state abbreviation in the dictionary
- Make sure the state name entered starts with a capital letter

Great job!

Concepts to remember

- You can't mix data types in arrays or dictionaries. Once you create the collection, you must be consistent with the datatypes (much as you can't add store cheese in an egg carton).
- The for statement allows you to iterate through arrays and dictionaries so you can execute some code for each item in the collection.

(continued)

- The syntax for arrays and dictionaries is important, but not as important as remembering how the collections are used. You can use them to store data when you have more than one value that you need.

11.5 Summary

This chapter covered some important topics related to collections. I find in my programming that I generally use arrays more than I use dictionaries, but you'll probably need to use both in your programming career. As a reminder, you learned about arrays, which are ordered, accessed using an index [Int], and can be added to using array.append(). You also learned about dictionaries, which are not ordered, are accessed using keys, and can be added to by simply creating another item. We touched a little on the for statement, which has a few variations that you haven't learned yet, but that you'll use in upcoming chapters.

If you want to challenge yourself, try creating another app that works like the state-abbreviation lookup app but that looks up airport codes instead. The only differences should be the values of the labels and dictionaries. I posted the code for both apps, so you can see how I did it at www.manning.com/books/anyone-can-create-an-app or https://github.com/wlwise/AnyoneCanCreateAnApp.

Telling stories
with storyboards

This chapter covers

- Storyboards and how to use them
- More about segues

All the apps you've created so far have been single view applications with only one screen that updates based on a user action. In this chapter, you're going to learn how to create apps with multiple screens that link to each other through user actions.

12.1 Storyboards

Storyboards are a little bit like what they sound like—a way to visualize a story and how the parts of the story are related. If you imagine a graphic novel (that's what the cool kids are calling comic books these days), there are multiple panels that together tell a story. Each panel flows into the next so the reader can follow the story. If you were writing your own graphic novel, you might start out with several blank panels and lay them out so you could begin planning the novel. You might sketch in a few details on each panel to start, and then begin filling in more details as time progresses.

Storyboards in Xcode are similar to creating a graphic novel. You can lay out multiple panels (henceforth known as *scenes*), show how these scenes interact, and then add more detail to each scene. The storyboards give you a conceptual view of your application and how the scenes fit together and flow. Let's create an app so we can walk through storyboards and see some of the coolness in action.

12.2   Creating an example storyboard app

Our example app will just have a button on the first scene that links to the second scene, and then a back button on the second scene that returns the user to the first scene. Here's the pseudocode:

1 Create a new app called StoryboardExample using the Single View Application template, and add a button.
2 Add a second scene to the app, and link the button action to the second scene.
3 Add a navigation bar to the second scene, and add a Cancel button.
4 Link the Cancel button action to the first scene.

Now that we have the pseudocode laid out, let's get started.

12.2.1   Step 1: Create a new app called StoryboardExample

Let's start by creating a new application and saving the project as Storyboard-Example. Select the Single View Application template. Now add a button to the app—click Main.storyboard from the Project Navigator (on the left side of Xcode). Once the storyboard loads in the center pane, use the Object Library to add a button to the storyboard. Change the title of the button to Push Me (sometimes I amaze myself with my creativity).

12.2.2   Step 2: Add a second scene to the app

You haven't added a second scene to any of the apps you've built so far, so this is something new. You'll start by changing your real estate so the Storyboard Editor takes up more of the panel. Hide the Navigation panel (the left panel in Xcode) by clicking on the third button from the right at the top of Xcode. Now scroll the main editor a little so there's some white space next to the storyboard scene with your button. Mosey on over to the Object Library and grab the topmost item in the list—the ViewController—and drop it just to the right of the first scene on your storyboard. It should look like figure 12.1.

Now you need to connect the action of the Push Me button to the second scene. You've connected the actions of buttons to the code in previous chapters, but this time you're going to connect it to the new scene. Control-click the Push Me button and drag your mouse over to the new scene (this is the same action you used to connect the button to the code). When your mouse pointer is over the new scene, release the mouse button, and you'll see something like figure 12.2 pop up.

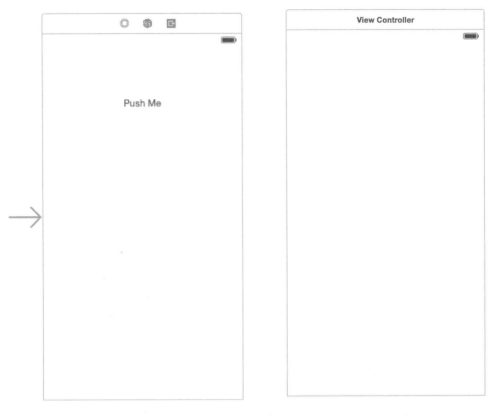

Figure 12.1   Add a ViewController to the storyboard, and drop it to the right of the first scene.

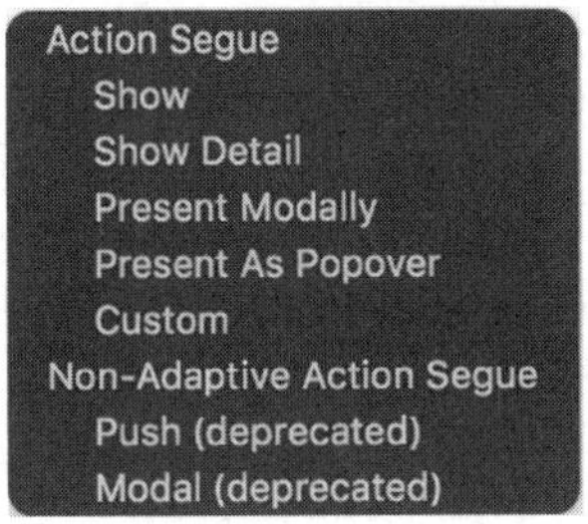

Figure 12.2   Control-click the Push Me button and drag to the new scene, and you'll see this dialog box pop up.

When the black box pops up, there will be several options to select. I explain these options later in chapter 15, but for now select Present Modally. If the connection was successful, you're storyboard should look like figure 12.3.

Notice the arrow pointing from the first scene to the second scene. This is called a *segue*. I'll tell you more about these when I explain the app later in the chapter. For

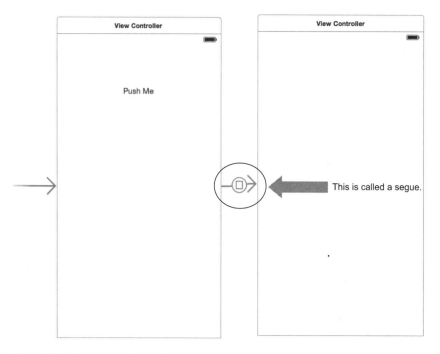

Figure 12.3   Connect the Push Me button to the second scene, and Xcode adds a segue to the storyboard.

now, know that the segue is a way to visually represent that the Push Me button, when clicked, will show the second scene.

Run the app to test the Push Me button and make sure it works as you expect it to. Once you click the Push Me button, it should disappear because the second scene loaded. It may be hard to see this, so you'll add a label to the second scene to make it obvious that it has loaded. Go back to the Object Library, search on *label*, and drag it onto the second scene. Double-click the new label and change it to "You have arrived!" Run the app again, and now when you click the Push Me button, the scene should change to show the "You have arrived!" scene.

This is starting to look like an app with two scenes, but there's a major problem with the app right now. You led the user into a dead end: there's no way to return to the first scene! Users get annoyed when they find dead ends in your app, and they'll let you know about it on your app reviews, so let's fix that now.

12.2.3 Step 3: Add a navigation bar to the second scene

In order to return to the initial scene in your app, you'll add a navigation bar to the top of the app. If you open your Phone app on your iPhone, you'll notice the bar at the top that displays the title of the scene you're on (Favorites, Contacts, Voicemail) as well as buttons to the left and right of the title on some scenes. For instance, on the Favorites scene, you have the Edit button on one side of the title and the add (+) button on the other. This bar, called a navigation bar, serves several purposes. The title clearly tells the user which scene they're on, which is a nice navigational aid so they don't get lost in the app. The navigation bar also provides an area to add buttons such as Back, Cancel, Edit, and Add. You'll add a navigation bar to the second scene now so you can let the user go back to the first scene.

In Xcode, search the Object Library for *navigation*. You'll notice that several items are returned, including Navigation Controller, navigation bar, and navigation item. In this case, you want the navigation bar. Grab the navigation bar and drag it to the top of the second scene so it looks like figure 12.4.

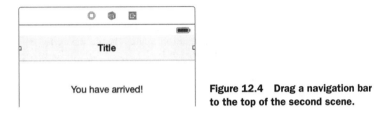

Figure 12.4 Drag a navigation bar to the top of the second scene.

Now double-click the title in the navigation bar and change it to *Second Screen*. Run the app again in the Simulator, and you should see the Second Screen title in the navigation bar when you click the Push Me button. Next, you can add a Cancel (or Done) button the navigation bar so the user can return to the previous scene. In general, you want to use a Cancel button when there's something that the user was doing that they want to cancel out of (for instance, adding a new contact to the address book). You want to use a Done button when the user is finished with an action.

Your first inclination may be to look at the Object Library and add a navigation item to the bar, and that would seem logical—but in this case, it isn't what you need. Search the Object Library again for a button. Grab the object Bar Button Item, and drag it up to the left side of the navigation bar. Once you drop it on the bar, it should say Item on the button, as shown in figure 12.5.

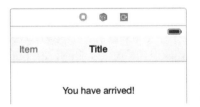

Figure 12.5 Drag a bar button item to the navigation bar, and drop it to the left of the title.

Now you need to change the Item button to a Cancel button. Apple was kind enough to add several standard button titles to the Object Library so you don't have to change the title for a Cancel button. These options can do a lot more than just change the title, but that's all they'll do for you right now in this chapter. You'll learn a lot more about them in the next chapter.

Back in Xcode, click the Item button so it's selected, and then go to Attributes Inspector on the right panel, as shown in figure 12.6. Click the drop-down for Identifier and you'll see all of your button options. In this case, you want to use the Cancel option.

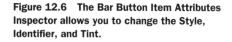

Figure 12.6   The Bar Button Item Attributes Inspector allows you to change the Style, Identifier, and Tint.

Run the app again, and click the Push Me button to get to the second scene. Then click the Cancel button. Nothing happened—because you haven't specified what kind of action should happen when the button is clicked. Let's specify that now.

12.2.4 *Step 4: Link the Cancel button to the first scene*

Next you're going to connect the Cancel button's action to the first scene, much as you did with the Push Me button. Control-click the Cancel button, and drag it back to the first scene. Be careful to select the Cancel button and *not* the entire bar. You'll see the same dialog box pop up that you saw when you connected the Push Me button (figure 12.2). Select Present Modally again. Run the app, and you'll see that the Cancel button now takes the user back to the first scene.

When you look at your storyboard, you'll see that there are now two segues (see figure 12.7)—one that goes from the first scene to the second scene, and one that goes from the second scene back to the first scene. Congratulations! You just added a second scene to your app and allowed the user to navigate to it and back.

12.3   *Segue animation types*

When you ran the application in the preceding section, you may have noticed that the second scene slides up from the bottom when you click on the Push Me button. The same happens when you click the Cancel button. You can easily change how these pages are displayed by changing the Transition property of the segue. Select the first segue that you created (the one going from the first scene to the second scene) and you'll notice that there are several options in the Attributes Inspector, including one called Transition, as shown in figure 12.8.

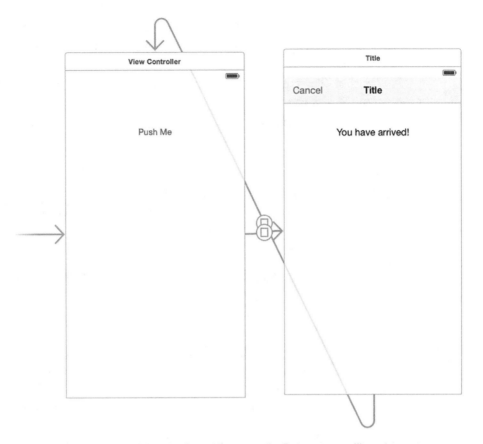

Figure 12.7   Once you connect the Cancel button to the first scene, you'll see two segues.

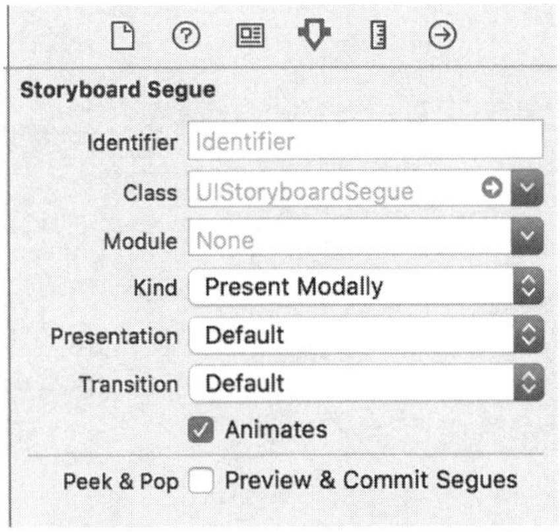

Figure 12.8   Storyboard segues have transition types. Select a different one to see what happens.

There are four basic transition types for scene loading:

- *Cover Vertical*—Loads the new scene by sliding it up from the bottom.
- *Flip Horizontal*—The scene rotates horizontally to load the new scene.
- *Cross Dissolve*—The page fades or dissolves to load the new scene.
- *Partial Curl*—The page flips up from the bottom of the scene.

You can change your segue to any of these to see how they work. It's amazing how changing one attribute of a segue can change the way the scene loads.

Concepts to remember

- *Storyboards* are a great way to see what scenes look like as you add components to them. They also help you visualize the flow of the application, or how one scene leads to another.
- *Segues* are visual representation of the transition between two scenes. You can choose how the transition is animated by changing the transition type.

12.4 Summary

Storyboards and segues are important to programming in Swift, and you should feel comfortable adding components to a scene and creating segues from one scene to the next. You'll need to do this for the rest of your programming career. You'll get plenty of practice throughout the remainder of this book, but make sure you understand the basics from this chapter.

The next chapter talks in a lot of detail about ViewControllers, so grab a cup of coffee if you need one.

ViewControllers in depth

You've created several apps now and in each app you've had a ViewController. What exactly is a ViewController, anyway? The name definitely gives away a lot: it's the code that controls the view that you created. We're going to go more in depth now and look at the details of the ViewController, which means we'll need to talk about some new programming concepts as well. This chapter includes some underlying programming principles, so make sure you understand it before you move on to the next chapter.

13.1 Inheritance

I know you may be excited here because you think you may get money from an inheritance, but in this case, it means something different—sorry. Please keep reading anyway, though. Let's start by going back to Xcode and looking at the ViewController file. You'll need to be familiar with ViewControllers in your programming career, so it's important that you get comfortable with them. You can either look at one of the ViewControllers that you used in a previous app that you wrote or you can create a new app so you can look at it. Either way, in Xcode, click the ViewController.Swift in your Project Navigator tab (the leftmost tab).

You should see something like figure 13.1. The first line of code is the import UIKit line, which is importing the UIKit framework so that you'll have access to classes needed for the ViewController. The UIKit offers much more than classes needed for the ViewController, but you'll learn more about that later.

```
//
//  ViewController.swift
//  TabBarControllerExample
//
//  Created by Wendy Wise on 5/25/15.
//  Copyright (c) 2015 WiseAbility. All rights reserved.
//

import UIKit

class ViewController: UIViewController {

    override func viewDidLoad() {
        super.viewDidLoad()
        // Do any additional setup after loading the view, typically from a nib.
    }

    override func didReceiveMemoryWarning() {
        super.didReceiveMemoryWarning()
        // Dispose of any resources that can be recreated.
    }

}
```

Figure 13.1   The ViewController.swift file controls the view.

As a quick refresher, in chapter 8 we talked about *frameworks*, which are groupings of classes that are packaged together so you can use them when needed (I used the example of a package of plumbing tools when you're building a house). The next line is the class definition:

```
class ViewController: UIViewController {
```

It's telling you that this is a class with the name of ViewController and it is a *subclass* of UIViewController. What is a subclass, you may be wondering?

Remember back in chapter 3 when we talked about the "pen" object? Imagine now that the pen object is a class. PenClass describes what kind of properties the pen can have (it has ink, a clicker, and so on), and the kinds of things it can do—called *functions*—such as writing, or the action of clicking the pen so it can write, or taking the cap off the pen. In this example, the PenClass class is called a *base class* or *superclass*. It's the fundamental class that describes the pen. It has methods and functions that are common to all pens. If you want to create a class about a specific pen that is a felt-tip pen, you would create a *subclass* of that pen, such as the FeltTipPenClass, and Felt-TipPenClass would *inherit* the properties and functions from the PenClass class. Felt-TipPenClass is a subclass of PenClass, and PenClass is a *superclass* of FeltTipPenClass (see figure 13.2). Imagine if you had to define the basic behavior of a pen every time you wanted to use one. It would get old fast and you would probably stop using pens altogether.

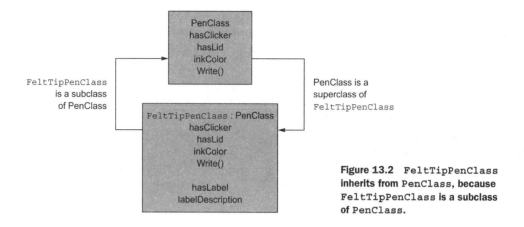

Figure 13.2 **FeltTipPenClass** inherits from **PenClass, because FeltTipPenClass is a subclass of PenClass.**

Notice in figure 13.2 that PenClass has properties: hasClicker, hasLid, and ink-Color. It also has one function called write(). You can tell it's a function because of the () after the name. The properties and the function are defined in the superclass, so when FeltTipPenClass declares itself to be a subclass of PenClass, it automatically has access to those properties and that function. The superclass can choose which functions and properties to make available to subclasses, and we'll talk about how later in the book. The PenClass automatically gives its properties and functions to its subclass. It can also then define new properties and functions as well. In this case, FeltTipPenClass also has a property for hasLabel and labelDescription.

I bring all this up now because ViewController.swift is a *subclass* of UIViewController. That means it has access to the functions and properties that the UIViewController class has. How do you know that the ViewController is a subclass of the UIViewController? Simple—look at the class definition at the top of the file again:

```
class ViewController: UIViewController {
```

This line is saying that the class ViewController is a subclass of UIViewController. The syntax is as follows:

```
(Keyword) class className : SuperClass {
```

I know I got you excited at the beginning of this section when I mentioned the word *inheritance*, but then I never used it again. How rude! The topics covered—a class being based on another class and specifying behaviors that both classes use—describe inheritance. Consider dogs. If you were trying to tell someone who had never seen a dog before what a dog looks like, how would you explain it? You couldn't specify the color because different dogs have different colors and patterns of color. You have to go to the base definition of dog so it could cover all possible types, sizes, colors, and shapes of dogs. This is the overall concept of *Dog*—or the superclass of dog.

Let's talk about breeds of puppies and dogs. There are certain properties that you expect all healthy puppies to inherit from the overall concept of Dog. For instance, they will all have four legs, a tail, two ears, eyes, awesome puppy breath, and little wet noses. These puppies inherited those properties from the Dog superclass, regardless of the breed. A puppy is a subclass of the Dog class, and the dog is a superclass of puppy. The puppy has certain properties that are inherent to the definition of a dog. What about a specific breed of puppy, like an Airedale? Does it look exactly like the Wikipedia picture for "Dog" (or the first Google Image that pops up)? No. It's a different class or breed and has properties set differently than the superclass of Dog. What about the puppy behaviors? Do all puppies act alike? No. You do know the puppy should be able to walk (or at least scamper), bark, poop (preferably outside) and eat. Not all dogs do these things in the exact same way, so let's talk about how subclasses can override their inherent behavior next.

13.2 *The override keyword*

If you look back at `ViewController.swift` in Xcode, you'll see two functions that were added to the class when you created it as part of the Xcode template for the ViewController:

```
override func viewDidLoad() {
    super.viewDidLoad()
    // Do any additional setup after loading the view, typically from a nib.
}

  override func didReceiveMemoryWarning() {
    super.didReceiveMemoryWarning()
    // Dispose of any resources that can be recreated.
}
```

Now you're finally going to learn what these things mean. I said earlier that healthy puppies should have inherited the ability to walk, bark, poop, and eat from their parents, but they all do it a little differently. I have one dog that looks regal when she walks. It's almost as if she's strutting her stuff. I have another dog that looks goofy when he walks, as if walking is an afterthought for him and his mind is elsewhere. They both are Airedales (the breed), they both are puppies (dogs), and they both perform the function of walking, but they both implement it slightly differently. They have inherited the ability to walk from the Dog superclass, which means that to implement their own version of walking they had to override the superclass definition of walking. They still move all four legs in a rhythmic fashion (okay, one doesn't look rhythmic so much, but cut him a little slack). So let's compare the dog examples to `ViewController` now.

`ViewController` is a subclass of `UIViewController`, as mentioned earlier. It has access to the `UIVIewController` functions, including the functions `viewDidLoad()`

and `didReceiveMemoryWarning()`. These two functions are part of the superclass, so Xcode adds the keyword `override` to tell the compiler to use this version of the functions instead of the functions in the `UIViewController`. The `override` keyword tells the compiler that you did intend to overwrite a parent function. If you didn't have this keyword, the compiler wouldn't know whether to call the superclass function or this function, and it would throw an error. The `override` might look something like this:

```
override func walk() {
    super.walk()
    // Do any additional setup after loading the view, typically from a nib.
}
```

This tells the compiler that the `puppyBreed` class should override the superclass `walk` and implement its own version. In my example, I have one dog that sort of flops his legs around when he walks (like a clown with enormous shoes on) and another dog that looks regal when she walks. They both implement their own version of `walk`, but they both definitely walk. So in my `puppyBreed` class, I would show that my dog either walks regally or floppily.

When you look inside the function, you see the keyword `super`, which tells the compiler to call the function found in the parent class, or superclass (parents, don't let that go to your head; it doesn't mean parents are all "super"). But I thought we were overriding the superclass function? In order to explain the `super` keyword, I need to first talk about application lifecycle (or puppy lifecycles in our example).

13.3 *ViewController lifecycles*

When my dogs get up in the morning, they usually stretch, yawn (loudly), let me know they need to go outside to take care of their personal business (poop), and then expect to eat. This is the beginning of their daily routine, which figure 13.3 compares to an application lifecycle.

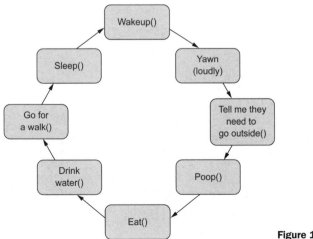

Figure 13.3 My dogs' daily lifecycle

This lifecycle repeats a few times per day as they seem to nap a lot. The interesting thing that you'll note about this lifecycle is that there are no times associated with any of the activities. sleep() could last 20 minutes or 12 hours, but I know that they yawn and then want to go out afterward. walk() could last 15 minutes or an hour, but it happens at least once each day. This isn't all that my dogs do, or we would all probably go a little crazy. I've simplified it a bit to make it easier to understand and create a repeating lifecycle. What does this have to do with programming, you may be wondering? I'm glad you asked.

The ViewController has the same type of lifecycle when it is launched and when it is hidden. For the lifecycle shown in figure 13.4, assume that the application has launched and your ViewController is ready to be shown (the ViewController on your storyboard that has an arrow point into it from the left).

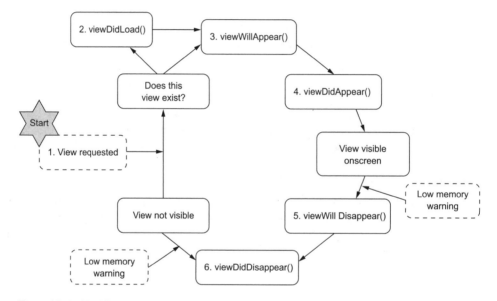

Figure 13.4   The ViewController lifecycle

As you can see from figure 13.4, the steps are as follows:

1 A view is requested.
2 If the view does not already exist, viewDidLoad() is called.
3 Once viewDidLoad() is complete, viewWillAppear() is called.
4 Then viewDidAppear() is called and the view is now visible on the screen.
5 At some point, the view is going to disappear, either through the application loading a different view or if there is a low memory warning (more on low memory warnings later). viewWillDisappear() is called at this point.
6 Finally, viewDidDisappear() is called.

You may be wondering why it's important to know the lifecycle of the ViewController. It's okay if you're not wondering—I'm going to tell you anyway. I'm cool like that. In some cases, you need to do some setup work in your ViewController when it loads—for instance, if you need to initialize a value. You many also be wondering how this maps to the dog lifecycle above. When the app requests a view for the first time, it is created between steps 1 and 2 (view requested and `viewDidLoad`). The view is now stored in memory for as long as the app is running or until we explicitly destroy it. This is slightly different then my dog's daily routine, only in that I assume my dog is always "running." I don't need to create the dog in the morning and destroy it at night (yikes!).

This will be easier if you write an app so you can experiment and see how the different functions are called.

13.4 The Lifecycle app

This app is going to be a simple one, with two screens and two buttons. The first button will be on the first screen, and its only purpose will be to load the second screen. The second button will be on the second screen, and its only purpose will be to go back to the first screen. I know that doesn't sound exciting, but the point of this app is for you to understand the lifecycle of the ViewController. You're going to override the five functions mentioned earlier so you can see when they're called. As usual, let's start out with pseudocode:

1. Create a new project called Lifecycle.
2. Add a second ViewController to the storyboard, add buttons, and wire up the first button.
3. Create an unwind segue (this is a new concept—as if there weren't enough already!).
4. Override the five functions mentioned earlier.
5. Test the app.

Let's get started.

13.4.1 Step 1: Create a new project called Lifecycle

I know you know the drill by now, but go ahead and create a new project called Lifecycle and make sure it's using the Swift language and is for the iPhone only. Save the project to your dev folder as you have in previous chapters.

13.4.2 Step 2: Add a second ViewController

Once the project is loaded, open the main.storyboard file and change your real estate so you can see the storyboard clearly. Go to the Object Library (bottom right panel) and drag a ViewController to the right of the existing ViewController. Back in the Object Library, search on *button*, add a button to the first ViewController, and change the title to "Load second view." Remember, in order to add the button to a specific screen, you need to tap that screen to make it the active screen. Add another button to the second ViewController and change the title to "Go back to first view."

Now you want to wire up the first button so it loads the second view when the user taps it. Do you remember how to do this? Control-click the first button and drag it to the second ViewController. When the second ViewController is highlighted, let go of your mouse button and select the option Show. Run the app to make sure the button works. I'll wait.

13.4.3 *Step 3: Create an unwind segue*

You may be tempted to wire up the second button in the same way that you did the first, but you're going to do something a little different this time. Apple gave us the ability to unwind—or go back to—previous ViewControllers. This type of segue is easy to implement and is helpful when you have a series of ViewControllers loaded and you want to go back to one of the earlier ones. In your ViewController.swift file, add this function anywhere in the code (I usually add all @IBAction and @IBOutlets at the top of my code):

```
@IBAction func unwindHome(_ segue: UIStoryboardSegue) {
}
```

Now go back to your storyboard and click your second ViewController. Notice the three buttons at the top of the ViewController. If you hover your mouse pointer over each, you'll see that the first one is ViewController, the second is First Responder, and the third is Exit. I'll explain the first two buttons later, but for now you want to use the third button, which looks like figure 13.5.

Figure 13.5   The Exit button on the ViewController lets you unwind your segues.

Right-click the Exit button (the third button on the second ViewController), and you should see the function you added to the first ViewController as an option. Don't do anything to it—just verify that the function appears in the black box.

You need to wire the second button to the Exit segue now. This is pretty easy. Control-click the second button and drag it up to the Exit button, and you'll have one option to select to connect it, as shown in figure 13.6.

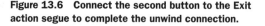

Figure 13.6   Connect the second button to the Exit action segue to complete the unwind connection.

Now you can test the app to make sure both buttons work. The first button should load the second ViewController, and the second button should load the first ViewController.

13.4.4 *Step 4: Override the five functions*

Now you need to go back to ViewController.swift and override some of the functions. For each function that you override, you need to first call the superclass's implementation of the function to make sure that everything that's supposed to happen in the function happens before you add your own implementation. Next, you want to add a line that will print a message to the console. You'll start with viewDidLoad(). Add the following print statement, so your function looks like this:

```
override func viewDidLoad() {
    super.viewDidLoad()
    print("view did load")
    // Do any additional setup after loading the view, typically from a nib.
}
```

The only thing I added for this function was the print statement. Now you need to add the other four functions to the code. Remember that you need to use the keyword override to ensure that the compiler knows you're intentionally overriding an existing function. Add the following four functions—and remember to let the auto-complete function do as much of the work for you as possible so you don't create any typos:

```
override func viewWillAppear(_ animated: Bool) {
  super.viewWillAppear(true)s
  print("view will appear")
}

override func viewDidAppear(_ animated: Bool) {
  super.viewDidAppear(true)
  print("view did appear")
}

override func viewWillDisappear(_ animated: Bool) {
  super.viewWillDisappear(true)
  print("view will disappear")
}

override func viewDidDisappear(_ animated: Bool) {
  super.viewDidDisappear(true)
  print("view did disappear")
}
```

Make sure your code has these functions added and that you don't have any errors.

13.4.5 *Step 5: Test the app*

Now run the app again and watch the console for the different print statements that you created. Click the first button, then the second button, and then the first button again. What do you notice? The viewDidLoad() function is only called once. Why is this? Look back at figure 13.4 to see the lifecycle and pay specific attention to the left side of the diagram. If the view already exists, the viewWillAppear() function is called, but the viewDidLoad() function is not called. This is part of how Apple makes sure the apps are as responsive and fast as possible—the views are stored in memory rather than disposing of them and having to recreate them each time they're needed.

Why is this important, you may ask? Let's add a few more things to your code so you can see why. You'll create a variable called counter at the top of your code and initialize it to 0. When you add a variable at the top of the code and not in a specific function, it is a *class level variable* and it will be available to all the functions in your class.

> ### Key concept: class-level variable
> When you add a variable at the top of the code and not in a specific function, it's a class-level variable, and it will be available to all the functions in your class.

You're going to use this counter to see how many times the functions are called. Add this line to your ViewController.swift class, putting it right under the class definition:

```
var counter = 0
```

Increment the counter by 1 in the viewDidLoad() function, and print the value of the counter:

```
counter = counter + 1
print(counter)
```

Run the app again. No matter how many times you switch between the first and second ViewControllers, the counter is still set to 1. The viewDidLoad() function is only called once, when the view is first loaded. Next you'll add the counter to the viewWillAppear() function and increment it there too:

```
override func viewWillAppear(animated: Bool) {
  super.viewWillAppear(true)
  print("view will appear")
  counter = counter + 1
  print(counter)
}
```

Now run the app again and switch between the two screens. Notice that the counter increments each time you switch between screens. This is important to understand: you should know where to place your code when you need to update values when new ViewControllers are loading and unloading.

Concepts to remember

- Inheritance
- Subclasses
- Superclasses

It's also important that you understand the ViewController lifecycle and know that every object has a lifecycle. It may not have the same functions, but every object in your code will be created and destroyed, and you'll need to keep this in mind as you code.

13.5 Summary

This chapter provides a foundation for key concepts in the programming world. It's important that you understand these items, so stay with this chapter for a while if they aren't clear to you. You should have a basic understanding of inheritance, subclasses, superclasses, and the ViewController lifecycle. You'll definitely use these in the LioN app in part 3 of the book.

14

Put it on my tab:
creating tab bars

This chapter covers

- Using Tab Bar Controllers
- Creating tab bars
- Adding labels to tabs

You use a Tab Bar Controller every time you use the phone app on your iPhone, although you probably didn't know what it was called until now. The *tab bar* is the bar at the bottom of many apps that has several buttons with icons on it. For example, in the Phone app, you have bottom icons for Favorites, Recents, Contacts, Keypad, and Voicemail. Tab Bar Controllers are powerful and allow for attractive and smooth navigation through your app.

14.1 The Tab Bar Controller

The easiest way to learn about Tab Bar Controllers is to create an app so you can see them in action. Let's do that now, starting with pseudocode as usual:

1 Create a new app called TabBarControllerExample, using the Single View Application template.
2 Delete the existing scene.
3 Add a Tab Bar Controller to the storyboard and set it as the main interface.

4 Add labels to the different tabs and change the tab attributes.

5 Add a third tab to the app.

Let's get started.

14.1.1 Step 1: Create a new app

Create a new app in Xcode, and call it TabBarControllerExample. Make sure to use the Single View Application Template. Notice that there's a Tabbed Application template, but you need to understand how the Tab Bar Controller works from a high level first.

14.1.2 Step 2: Delete the existing scene

Change your real estate now so that you can view more of the storyboard. Hide the Navigation panel (the left side panel) using the button in the top right of Xcode, third from the right, or press Command and the 0 key at the same time (⌘-0). Notice in the Storyboard Editor that the ViewController has an arrow pointing into it from the left (as shown in figure 14.1).

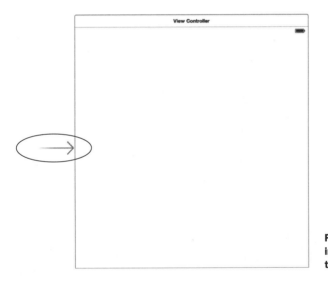
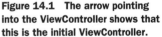

Figure 14.1 The arrow pointing into the ViewController shows that this is the initial ViewController.

This arrow indicates that this ViewController is the initial ViewController, which means this is the first view and controller when the application starts. Every app needs to have an initial ViewController for it to work correctly, or Xcode doesn't know which scene to display first or which controller to use. In this app, however, you don't want this ViewController at all, because you're going to create a new and different one, so you're going to delete it. Click the scene once, and press Delete. The first time I deleted a scene from a storyboard, I felt like I had ruined the app—but I fixed it, and you can too.

If you try to run the app now, Xcode will give you an error message: "Failed to instantiate the default view controller for UIMainStoryboardFile 'Main' - perhaps the designated entry point is not set?" This is a clear error message telling you that you need to have an initial ViewController set, which is designating the entry point for the app. You'll add one now.

14.1.3 *Step 3: Add a Tab Bar Controller to the storyboard*

In the Object Library, you can either scroll down a few rows or search on *tab* to find the Tab Bar Controller. Grab the object, drag it to the middle of your storyboard, and drop it.

You'll immediately notice that this doesn't look like the other apps you've built before. The Tab Bar Controller adds what appear to be three scenes on the storyboard (as shown in figure 14.2).

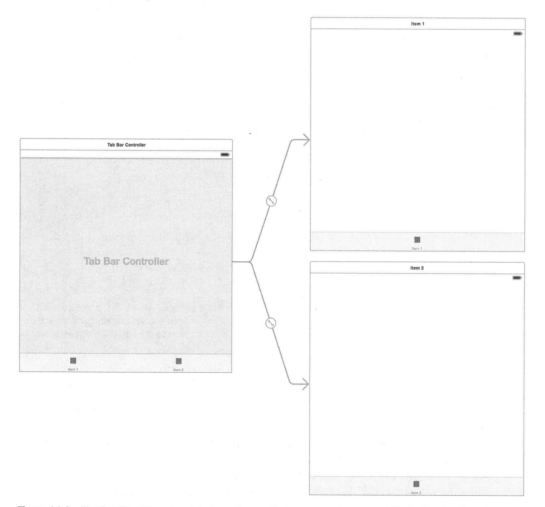

Figure 14.2   The Tab Bar Controller object creates multiple scenes when you add it to the storyboard.

These aren't three scenes, though, because the Tab Bar Controller is known as a *container ViewController*—meaning it contains other views but doesn't display itself. The first object on the storyboard says Tab Bar Controller at the top and is grayed out, letting you know that you can't add visual components to it. Its primary purpose is to control the two views it's connected to, called Item 1 and Item 2.

The easiest way to understand this is to run the app, but before you can do that, you need to set the initial ViewController so Xcode knows which controller to load first. Click the Tab Bar Controller (the first object) in your storyboard so it is the active object. In the Attributes Inspector, click the Is Initial View Controller check box to set it as the initial ViewController, as shown in figure 14.3.

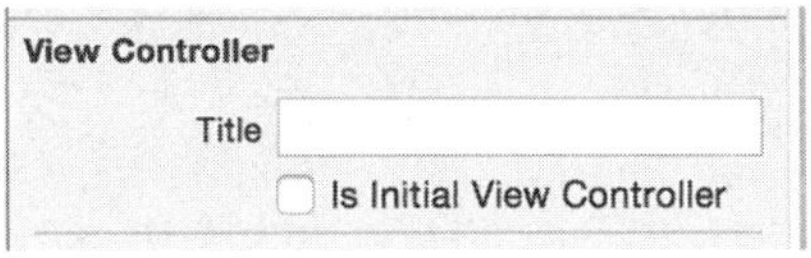

Figure 14.3   Making the Tab Bar Controller the initial controller

Now run the app, and you'll see two tabs at the bottom of the app: Item 1 and Item 2. This is pretty powerful stuff, right? You didn't even have to add a scene or a segue to have two different scenes with a tab bar controlling them. Let's add some UI to the different tabs so you can see them differentiated.

14.1.4 Step 4: Add labels to the different tabs

Drag a label onto the first tab—named Item 1—and change the text to "Tab 1" (or something more creative if you'd like). Drag another label onto the second tab (Item 2) and change the text to "Tab 2" (again, feel free to be creative). When you run the app now, you should see the different labels on the different tabs when you select the tab buttons at the bottom of the screen.

Items 1 and 2 aren't exciting scenes or button names, so let's change those, too. The easiest way to change the tab button labels is to use the Document Outline of the storyboard. The Document Outline can be shown and hidden using the button at the bottom left of the storyboard—see figure 14.4.

Let's take a moment and look at the Document Outline more closely. Near the bottom you'll see Tab Bar Controller Scene in bold text, as shown in figure 14.5.

The Tab Bar Controller scene displays all the items that make up the Tab Bar Controller scene, including the Tab Bar Controller itself, which you added to the storyboard in step 3 earlier. When you added the controller, it automatically added a tab bar, which is the tab bar that you see at the bottom of the scenes in your storyboard. I'm going to skip over the First Responder and Exit items right now, because you don't need to understand what they do yet. I'll tell you more about them in part 3 of this book.

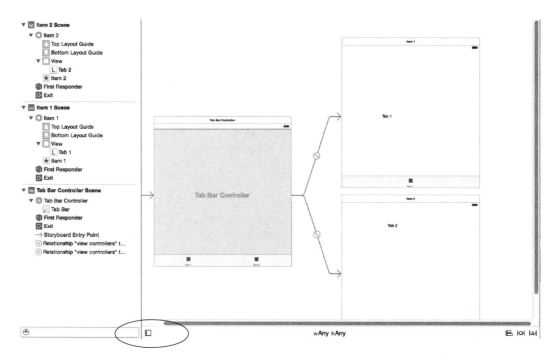

Figure 14.4   **Show and hide the Document Outline by clicking this button.**

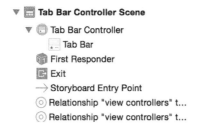

Notice that the Tab Bar Controller scene has something called a Storyboard Entry Point. This is the initial View Controller that you set earlier in step 3. Finally, notice that there are two relationships below the entry point. These are the segues between the Tab Bar Controller and the scenes currently called Items 1 and 2. Now let's look at the Item 1 Scene components in the Document Outline (figure 14.6).

Figure 14.5   **The Tab Bar Controller scene in the Document Outline shows all the components of the scene.**

If you click the Top Layout Guide item in the list, you'll see that a blue line appears in the ViewController on the storyboard. This is a visual representation of the top of the view—meaning you shouldn't try to add any components (such as labels or buttons) above this guide. There is also a Bottom Layout Guide that does the exact same thing except for the bottom of the view. Next, the View is the primary area where you

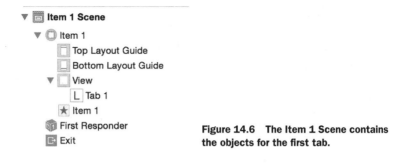

▼ 🖼 **Item 1 Scene**
   ▼ ⭕ Item 1
        ⬜ Top Layout Guide
        ⬜ Bottom Layout Guide
     ▼ ⬜ View
        ⬜L Tab 1
      ⭐ Item 1
   🗊 First Responder
   🖥 Exit

Figure 14.6   The Item 1 Scene contains the objects for the first tab.

can add components to the tab. You can see the label that you added, and you can tell by looking at it that it's a label because its icon appears as an uppercase L with a box around it (as in figure 14.6). Xcode tries to give you visual cues like this in many places, and as you continue to code you'll begin learning them. You don't have to learn them all right now, but do notice them.

Underneath the Tab 1 label, notice the star icon that says Item 1. This is the actual tab bar button for Tab 1. You want to change the text from *Item 1* to *Tab 1* so you can see the difference. Click once on this row so Item 1 is highlighted in the Document Outline. In the Attributes Inspector on the right side of the screen, change the Title field from `Item 1` to `Tab 1`, as shown in figure 14.7.

Tab Bar Item

Badge	
System Item	Custom
Selected Image	
Title Position	Default Position

Bar Item

Title	Tab 1
Image	
Tag	0

☑ Enabled

Figure 14.7   Change the title of the tab bar Item to Tab 1 in the Attributes Inspector.

As soon as you click out of the Attributes Inspector, you'll notice that the button at the bottom of Scene 1 changes to say Tab 1. That was easy! You'll also notice that the Tab Bar Controller on the left also changed the button title to Tab 1. Do the same thing for the second tab, but call it Tab 2. If you run the app again, you'll see that the tab bar buttons at the bottom of the app changed to Tab 1 and Tab 2.

What if you really wanted Tab 2 to be the first button and Tab 1 to be the second button? Easy. On the Tab Bar Controller on the left side of the storyboard, grab the Tab 2 button and drag and drop it to the left of the Tab 1 button. Run your app again, and see that they changed places.

Another fun and exciting thing you can do with the tab bar buttons is change the icon. Right now the icons are rather unattractive squares (I'm not saying all squares are unattractive; I try to be PC), so let's change that. Click Tab 1 Item in the Document Outline again, but this time in the Attributes Inspector, click the drop-down for System Item.

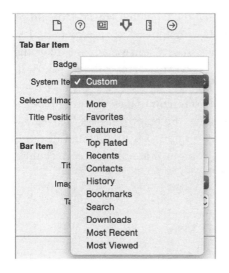

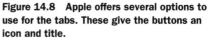

Figure 14.8   Apple offers several options to use for the tabs. These give the buttons an icon and title.

Change the System Item to different options to see how the tab button changes. This method makes it easy to add the most common types of tabs.

Now let's add a third tab to the app so you know how to do it.

14.1.5   *Step 5: Add a third tab to the app*

The Tab Bar Controller has two tabs already created when you add it to the storyboard. What if you want more than two tabs? I'm glad you asked. Let's go back to Xcode, and, in the Object Library, find a ViewController. Make sure you grab a View-Controller and not a view or other kind of controller. Drag it to the storyboard, and drop it below the Tab Bar Controller. Now you're going to add a segue as you did in chapter 12. Control-click from the Tab Bar Controller to the new ViewController, and, when the black pop-up appears, select the Relationship Segue / View Controllers option, as seen in figure 14.9.

Once selected, you'll notice that a third tab bar item has now been added to the controller, named Item by default. Run the app again, and you'll see that you now

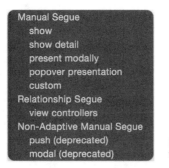

**Figure 14.9   Click the Relationship Segue /
View Controllers option for the segue.**

have three tabs working in your dummy app. Xcode and Apple make it easy to create these kinds of UI, but it's important to know what is going on behind the scenes (pun intended!).

> **Concepts to remember**
> - The Tab Bar Controller is a powerful tool to help you build apps faster, with great-looking navigation.
> - There are a lot more things you can do with Tab Bar Controllers, but that's outside the scope of this book. I encourage you to experiment with them!

14.2 Summary

In this chapter, you learned about the Tab Bar Controller, which is used in many iPhone and iPad apps. It's an important tool that provides navigation for users and is easy for you, the developer, to implement. You can change the color and icons of the tab bars, although I don't have room to cover that in this book. Play around with this app—change the settings, add more components, and experiment.

I encourage you to build a few apps to practice implementing the features you've learned so far. You're getting closer to building the LioN app, which will pull all these concepts together.

15
Table views: more than a coffee table picture book

This chapter covers

- Delegation and protocols
- Data source
- Table views
- Tuples

Table views are powerful tools that allow you to present data to your users in a clean, organized way. You've seen table views on your iPhone and iPad many times, though you probably didn't know they were called table views. Open your Phone app, and navigate to the Favorites screen if it isn't open already. If you aren't horribly lonely, you should have at least one or two people that you call frequently enough that you've added them to your Favorites. If you don't have any favorites added, look at the Contacts screen to see a list of your contacts. Each of your favorites is a row in a table. Each of your contacts is a row in a different table. Who knew?

You're going to learn all about table views in this chapter, but we need to cover some underlying concepts first, so bear with me. Don't worry—this is fun stuff.

15.1 Delegation

Swift uses a concept known as *delegation*, and you've used it in the real world, I'm sure. Let's say you want pizza for dinner. There are many options for pizza, including heating up a frozen pizza, ordering a pizza from a variety of different pizza places, or making a pizza from scratch. Let's start by making a pizza from scratch.

15.1.1 Making pizza from scratch

Think about making pizza in the same way you planned painting a wall way back in chapter 1. You got out all the things you needed and you painted. In this case, you get out your ingredients, get out a pizza pan, and so on. Now make the dough for the crust and spread it out in the pan, add sauce, add cheese, and add pepperoni to the top. Pop it in the oven (or on the grill—mmmmm) for some time until you have a warm, yummy, gooey pile of goodness.

Back in the programming world, let's make that a method: `makePizza()`. You're method might look a little like this:

```
func makePizza()
{
    makeDough()
    addSauce()
    addToppings(cheese, pepperoni)
    cook()
}
```

Great job. Now I'm hungry for pizza, so I'll be back in bit.

15.1.2 Delegating pizza making

Let's say you've been working for a while and still have a lot more to do, so you don't want to stop to go make pizza. You wish someone else would do it for you. Wait—you can delegate making pizza to someone else! Let's say you want to get a carry-out pepperoni pizza from a restaurant. Either you can call the restaurant and tell them you want a pepperoni pizza, or you can go there and tell them in person. Either way, you're not making the pizza yourself. You're delegating to a pizza restaurant.

Each pizza restaurant understands the method `makePizza()`, but they may implement it in different ways. Some make thin crusts, some make thick crusts, and some make double crusts. Some cook in a wood-fired oven, some grill, some cook in an electric or gas oven, and some probably put it under a heat lamp (doesn't sound tasty, and it's probably square). No matter how they implement `makePizza()`, the cool thing is that you aren't required to make the pizza yourself—all you have to do is call their version of `makePizza()`. (They would appreciate it if you also call their version of `payForPizza()`, too.) Once you've delegated pizza-making to someone else, you don't have to worry about the implementation details of how to make pizzas. This is fantastic!

15.2   Protocols

Although each pizza restaurant implements `makePizza()` differently, they all have a method for `makePizza()`, or they wouldn't be a pizza restaurant. This means they must follow the protocol required to be a pizza restaurant. So every pizza restaurant conforms to what we might call the *Pizza Restaurant protocol*, which has a method for `makePizza()`.

If every restaurant implemented `makePizza()` the same way, all pizza would taste the same, look the same, and smell the same, which doesn't seem like a good idea. So Pizza Restaurant has a protocol called `makePizza()`, which told every class, or pizza restaurant, that wanted to be a Pizza Restaurant that it needed to have a method called `makePizza()`so it could conform but could implement it its own way. Pizza Restaurant is moving responsibility for the *details* of `makePizza()` to the individual pizza restaurants. Pizza Restaurant may also have other methods that are considered optional that not all pizza restaurants need to conform to. For instance, Pizza Restaurant may have additional methods like `serveSoda()`, `serveBeer()`, `serveSalad()`, and `servePasta()`. Not all pizza restaurants have these methods, but some do.

A *protocol* is a contract that says any class that wants to conform to the protocol *must* implement the required methods. In this case, a pizza restaurant *must* implement `makePizza()` if it wants to conform to the Pizza Restaurant protocol. This will be easier to understand when you create the app, so stick with me. We need to cover one more concept before you create your first table view.

15.3   Data sources

Data sources are exactly what they sound like—sources for data. If you look back at your iPhone and check out the Phone app again, all of those contacts are stored somewhere on your phone. The table views that display the data conform to the table view data source, which is to say, the table view asks the data source how many rows to display, what should be in the row, how many sections should be displayed, and more. There are two distinct concepts here:

- The data that you want to display to a user is stored in a data source that you create (like an *array*).
- The table view that you create must conform to `UITableViewDataSource`, which means you must implement two required methods each time you implement a table view.

You'll learn a lot more about data sources and `UITableViewDataSource` when you create an app next.

15.4 Creating a table view app

You're going to create an app now to see a demonstration of the concepts covered so far. The app is a simple one that displays the ingredients used to make pizzas and their associated fictional nutritional values. You'll follow these steps:

1   Create a new app called PizzaIngredients.
2   Add a table view to the ViewController and set the properties.
3   Set up a prototype cell.
4   Set the protocols for UITableView.
5   Create a data source for the pizza.
6   Connect the data to a table to display the rows of data.

15.4.1 Step 1: Create a new app

Let's get started by creating the app. I called mine PizzaIngredients. Save it to your dev folder as you have all your other apps. Use the same Single View Application template, and set the Device to iPhone.

15.4.2 Step 2: Add a table view to the ViewController

Once the project loads, open the Storyboard.storyboard file and change your real estate so you can view the storyboard easily. In the Object Library, search on *tableview*, and three objects should be returned: TableViewController, TableView, and TableViewCell. In this instance, you want the middle option: TableView. Drag the object to your ViewController on the storyboard and size it so it takes up the entire ViewController screen. Now run the app to see your table view. You'll notice that you have an entire screen of empty rows and you can scroll up and down—pretty cool, given that you haven't written any code yet, right?

Now you'll connect the table view properties to the ViewController. While still in your storyboard, right-click the table view, and you'll see the connections that are available for you by default, as shown in figure 15.1.

NOTE Make sure you right-clicked the table view and not the table-view cell. The table-view cell's first option at the top of the menu is Triggered Segue. If you see that, you right-clicked the cell, not the table view. Click off of it, and try again.

Figure 15.1 The Table View connections properties are available when you right-click the table view in the storyboard.

As you've learned in previous chapters, these outlets connect the table view to the ViewController. Once connected, the table view will look to the ViewController for the `dataSource` and `delegate` properties. With this dialog open, click the open circle for `dataSource` and drag it to the yellow icon at the top of the ViewController in the storyboard, as shown in figure 15.2.

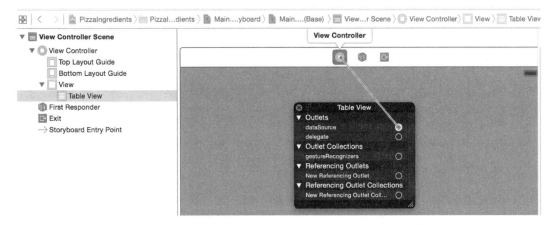

Figure 15.2   Connect the `dataSource` property for the table view to the ViewController in the storyboard.

There's another way you can connect the outlets to the ViewController. On the right side of Xcode, in the Utilities panel, the last button on the top of the panel is the Connections Inspector. Click this button to display the panel (figure 15.3).

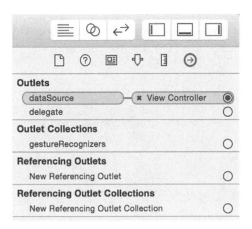

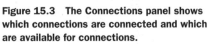

Figure 15.3   The Connections panel shows which connections are connected and which are available for connections.

Click the circle next to `delegate`, and drag it over to the storyboard ViewController icon (the yellow icon at the top of the view) to make the connection. Now your connections are made for the table view. Like your other apps in earlier chapters, you need to first make the connections in the storyboard, and then in the code. You'll connect the code later in this chapter, but first I want to show you the prototype cell.

15.4.3 Step 3: Set up a prototype cell

I mentioned in the introduction to this chapter that the table has rows of data (like the Favorites in your Phone app). Each of the rows has data that's provided by a data source (more on that in a minute). The rows of data are displayed in a *cell* in your table view.

Again, it will be easier to see when you do it, so open up the storyboard again. Select the table view in the storyboard, and make sure the Attributes Inspector panel is open. The top option says that you want Dynamic Prototypes as content, and the second line says Prototype Cells with the option currently set to 0. Change it to 1, and notice that a new row appears on the table view in the storyboard. Cool!

Now, on the storyboard, select the prototype cell so the Attributes Inspector panel shows the cell's attributes. The first attribute you can change is the cell style. Change it to *Basic*, and notice that the word *Title* appears in the cell. This is the primary data that will be displayed in the cell—in the Favorites tab of your Phone app, it would be the name of your contact. Change it to *Right Detail*—again, the prototype cell changes and shows the word *Detail* on the right of the cell. In your Phone app, this would correspond to the contact type (mobile, home, iPhone, work, and so on). Next, select Left Detail, and you'll notice that Title is to the left and the detail comes after. Select Sub-Title, and you'll notice the Title is on top of the detail. This is what the left of the cells looks like in your Voicemail tab. You can play around with the different types of cell attributes that you can change. It's pretty fun. I'll wait—take your time.

Before you leave the prototype cell, set the properties as follows:

- *Style*—`Basic`
- *Identifier*—`myCell`
- *Accessory*—`None`
- *Editing Accessory*—`None`

15.4.4 Step 4: Set the protocols for UITableView

I talked about protocols in section 1.2. *Protocols* allow the defining class to delegate the implementation of the methods to other classes. The classes that will implement the methods must conform to the protocol. You added a `UITableView` to your storyboard, so the `ViewController` class that controls that view must conform to the protocols for `UITableView` in order for the application to work properly. If you tried to run your app now, you'd get a long error message in your console (in the All Output pane, scroll to the top) that looks something like this:

```
'NSInvalidArgumentException', reason: '-[PizzaIngredients.ViewController
tableView:numberOfRowsInSection:]: unrecognized selector sent to instance
0x7fb7aaf94280'
```

Well, doesn't that look foreign? If you look through your `ViewController` code, you'll notice there isn't anything that says `numberOfRowsInSection`, so where is this coming from? You added a table view to the storyboard and didn't implement the required method for the `ViewController` to conform to the protocol. This is telling you that the table view tried to call `numberOfRowsInSection` but couldn't find the method in your code. At this point, you're not conforming to the protocol.

ADD THE PROTOCOLS TO THE VIEWCONTROLLER

Look back at figure 15.2. See the black box where you connected the table view data source and delegate to the ViewController? You need to do the same thing in your code. In the `ViewController` source code, you'll see the definition near the top of the file:

```
class ViewController: UIViewController {
```

You need to change that to show that you'll conform to the protocols for the table view. Add to the class definition so it looks like this:

```
class ViewController: UIViewController, UITableViewDelegate,
UITableViewDataSource {
```

As you can see, you added the `UITableViewDelegate` and the `UITableViewDataSource` to the definition. You told Xcode that you want the class to inherit from `UIView-Controller` and to conform to `UITableViewDelegate` and `UITableViewDataSource`. Fantastic! Except now there's a big red exclamation point in the code that shows something isn't right, as you can see in figure 15.4.

```
import UIKit

class ViewController: UIViewController, UITableViewDelegate, UITableViewDataSource {
                                                             Type 'ViewController' does not conform to protocol 'UITableViewDataSource'
```

Figure 15.4   Xcode says that the `ViewController` class does not conform to the `UITableViewDataSource` protocol. You need to add the methods that are required.

If you click the red exclamation point, Xcode tells you that the class doesn't conform to the `UITableViewDataSource` protocol. What gives? What you did in the class definition is tell it that you *want* it to conform to the protocol, but you haven't implemented the required methods for it to conform yet. If you think back to the pizza restaurant analogy, it's as if the pizza store said it wants to be a Pizza Restaurant but it didn't implement `makePizza()`. You need to implement the methods that will make your ViewController conform to the `UITableViewDataSource` protocol.

There are two ways to find out what methods you must implement to conform. The first is more educational, and the second is more expedient. I'll show you both of them, and you can choose which you find more effective based on your learning style. The first way is to look at the reference documentation, which can be accessed by Option-clicking the word `UITableViewDataSource` that you added to the class definition. When you do this, a new Quick Help window will open (shown in figure 15.5). If you don't see this, make sure you hold the Option key down when you click.

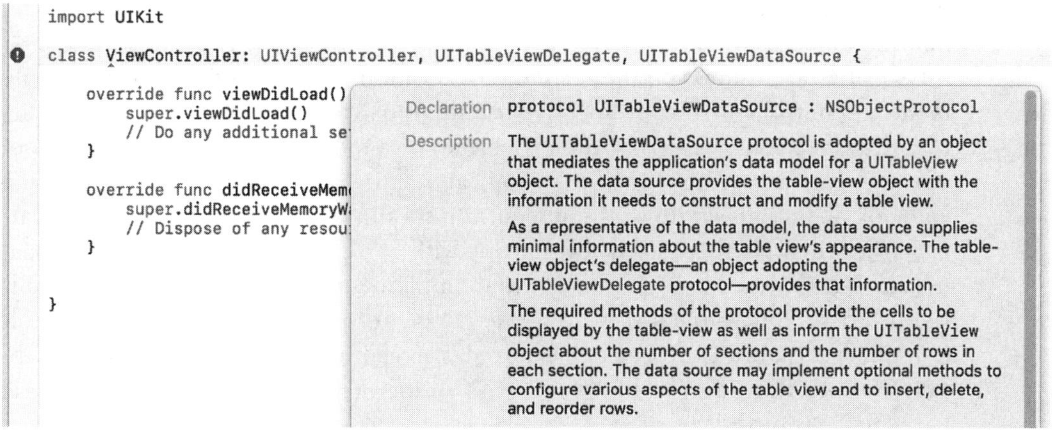

```
import UIKit

class ViewController: UIViewController, UITableViewDelegate, UITableViewDataSource {

    override func viewDidLoad()
        super.viewDidLoad()
        // Do any additional se
    }

    override func didReceiveMem
        super.didReceiveMemoryW
        // Dispose of any resou
    }

}
```

Declaration	protocol UITableViewDataSource : NSObjectProtocol
Description	The UITableViewDataSource protocol is adopted by an object that mediates the application's data model for a UITableView object. The data source provides the table-view object with the information it needs to construct and modify a table view.
	As a representative of the data model, the data source supplies minimal information about the table view's appearance. The table-view object's delegate—an object adopting the UITableViewDelegate protocol—provides that information.
	The required methods of the protocol provide the cells to be displayed by the table-view as well as inform the UITableView object about the number of sections and the number of rows in each section. The data source may implement optional methods to configure various aspects of the table view and to insert, delete, and reorder rows.

Figure 15.5   Option-clicking the `UITableViewDataSource` **protocol opens the Quick Help dialog.**

At the bottom of the Quick Help window, you'll see a link to the Protocol Reference document. Click this to open the reference doc. Reading this doc is a great way to learn about the different methods that you can implement, and it also tells you which methods you *must* implement. If you scroll down a bit through the documentation, you'll see something like figure 15.6 (this may change slightly depending on when Apple updates the documentation and the code, but the definition will remain the same).

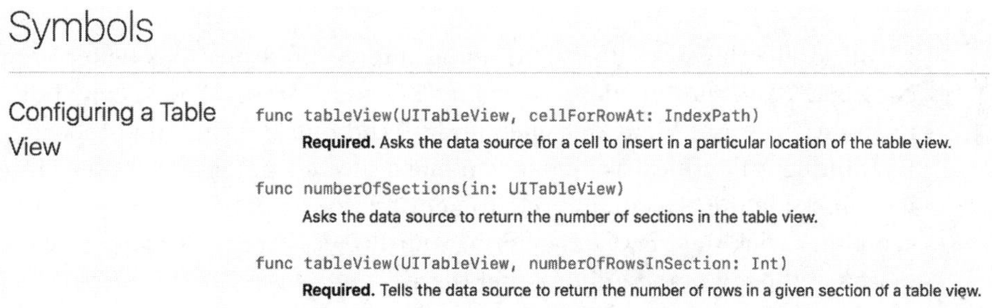

Symbols

Configuring a Table View	func tableView(UITableView, cellForRowAt: IndexPath)
	Required. Asks the data source for a cell to insert in a particular location of the table view.
	func numberOfSections(in: UITableView)
	Asks the data source to return the number of sections in the table view.
	func tableView(UITableView, numberOfRowsInSection: Int)
	Required. Tells the data source to return the number of rows in a given section of a table view.

Figure 15.6   The Apple `UITableViewDataSource` **Protocol Reference document tells you which methods must be implemented in order to conform to the protocol.**

Notice that the `tableView(UITableView, cellForRowAt: IndexPath)` method must be implemented (denoted by the word *Required*). The methods are named in a way that should help you understand what they do, but there's also a simple explanation below the definition. In this case, the method is asking the data source to provide a cell (which contains the data) for the table to display. You changed the attributes of your prototype cell in section 15.4.3, so you understand more about how the cell looks—and this is the method that will provide the cell with the data for the cell (like the contact information in your Phone app).

Now I want to show you the second way to find the methods that you *must* implement to conform to the protocol. Back in your ViewController, Command-click `UITableViewDataSource` this time (instead of Option-click). This time, Xcode opens the actual `UITableView` file so you can see the code behind the class. Cool! If you look about halfway down the screen, you should see two methods that start with `func`, and then the methods below starting with `optional func`. The word `optional` means—you guessed it—you don't have to implement these methods to conform to the protocol, but you can if you choose. This means the other two methods that don't have the word `optional` are required. You can see, as shown in figure 15.7, the two methods that you must implement in order to conform to the `UITableView-DataSource` protocol.

```
public protocol UITableViewDataSource : NSObjectProtocol {


    @available(iOS 2.0, *)
    public func tableView(_ tableView: UITableView, numberOfRowsInSection section: Int) -> Int


    // Row display. Implementers should *always* try to reuse cells by setting each cell's reuseIdentifier and querying
        for available reusable cells with dequeueReusableCellWithIdentifier:
    // Cell gets various attributes set automatically based on table (separators) and data source (accessory views,
        editing controls)

    @available(iOS 2.0, *)
    public func tableView(_ tableView: UITableView, cellForRowAt indexPath: IndexPath) -> UITableViewCell
```

Figure 15.7   You may copy the required function definitions from the source file.

I tend to like this second way of finding the required methods better because I can copy and paste the functions right into my code. Do that now: copy both required functions into your ViewController, under (and outside) the `viewDidLoad()` method. Positioning isn't critical as long as you make sure it's not inside another function and it's still inside the class definition. To get back to the previous file you had open, you can either click the ViewController in your Project Navigator panel or click the back button at the top of the Editor panel (figure 15.8).

⊞ ‹ ›   Ⓜ UIKit ⟩ 🔷 UITableView ⟩ Ⓜ tableView(_:numberOfRowsInSection:)

Figure 15.8   You can use the back button at the top of the Editor panel to navigate back to the previous file you were working on.

Once you've copied the two functions in to your code, you'll need to add the curly brackets to the functions: add a { at the end of the method definition line, press Enter, and add a } to close the function. Xcode is helpful here. Once you enter the opening bracket on the line and press Enter, Xcode should close it for you so you don't need to type the }. Great! Now you have two different errors in your file. Let's fix those next.

IMPLEMENT THE CODE FOR THE REQUIRED METHODS

The first function you added is to return the number of rows in section. You can see that it has `-> Int` at the end of the method, so it is expecting the function to return an `Int`. This is called the *return type* of a function and is part of the function definition. You'll eventually return the number of rows in your data source, but for now return 1. Add the line `return 1` inside the curly brackets for that method. Yeah! One of errors is fixed. Now you need to fix the second one.

The second method you added is asking for the cell that should be displayed at an index path. What is an index path, anyway? Officially speaking, it's a path into a specific node in a tree of nested array collections. Clear as mud, right? The index path is basically the index of the row of data you want, but it's robust enough that if you had an array with one or more arrays inside it, you could get to the data you needed easily. In this case, though, you're only going to have one array of data, so consider it a simple index of an array. (Remember, arrays start at base 0, so if you wanted the first row, you'd ask for `array[0]` to get the first row. In this case, the 0 is the `indexPath`.)

You'll also notice that the function is looking for an actual `UITableViewCell` as the return object. Add the following code to the `cellForRowAtIndexPath` function, and then we'll walk through it:

```
let cell = tableView.dequeueReusableCell(withIdentifier: "myCell", for:
    indexPath)
cell.textLabel?.text = "cell \(indexPath.row)"
 return cell;
```

Let's start by looking at the first line. `let cell` is creating a new object called `cell`—you should remember this from the earlier chapters. The `let` keyword is making the object a *constant* object, or one that can't be changed once it's created (although its properties can be changed). Next, you're calling a function on the `tableView` called `dequeueResuableCellWithIdentifier`. Remember the lifecycle of a ViewController (or a dog) that we talked about back in chapter 13? The lifecycle applies to objects as well, like the cell. Imagine a table with 200 cells in it. You could create a new cell for every row, but that would take up a lot of memory on a phone. We always want to be cognizant of the memory use of our app so we don't use too much and make users unhappy.

Instead of creating 200 cells every time, you're going to create as many as can be displayed on one screen. As the user scrolls down, the cells at the top of the screen are *dequeued* so they can be used again at the bottom of the screen. Remember earlier when you set the identifier attribute of your cell to `myCell` on the storyboard? This is why! You can now tell Xcode to create a new cell with the name (or identifier) of `myCell` for the `indexPath` that was passed into the function, or reuse a dequeued cell if one exists. Pretty slick, huh?

The next line sets the text on the cell to the word *cell* and the `indexPath` row number of the cell that was created. So you're setting the `text` property of the `textLabel` attribute of the cell to `"cell 0"`, `"cell 1"`, based on which row is being displayed. We'll talk more about the ? after the `textLabel` in later chapters: this says that the `textLabel` attribute may not exist, but if it does, assign it value `"cell 0"`, and so on. Finally, you need to return the cell so the `tableView` can display it. Go ahead and run the app now—you should see one row of data. How cool!

15.4.5 Step 5: Create a data source for the pizza

You want to create a list of ingredients that will be displayed in the table and then display more details about the ingredient when the user taps on the row. We talked about collections back in chapter 11, and you learned about arrays and dictionaries. Let's talk about another way to store and pass data around: the tuple. A *tuple* is a grouping of values that can be stored as one value. Think about the name of a person: Arlene Brown is the full name of one person. But what if you wanted to reference her first name only? You could do it like this:

```
var name = ("Arlene", "Brown")
var firstName = name.0
var lastName = name.1
```

Gives the first name Arlene

Gives the last name Brown

You could also name the elements in a tuple so they are easier to reference. Let's show this for a person named Matthew Drooker:

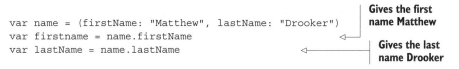

```
var name = (firstName: "Matthew", lastName: "Drooker")
var firstname = name.firstName
var lastName = name.lastName
```

Gives the first name Matthew

Gives the last name Drooker

You could add more to this tuple if you wanted—like this:

```
var name = (firstName: "Matthew", lastName: "Drooker", nationality:
    "Canadian, eh? ")
var firstname = name.firstName
var lastName = name.lastName
var nationality = name.nationality
```

Gives the first name Matthew

Gives the last name Drooker

Gives "Canadian, eh?"

Let's create a tuple for your pizza ingredients. The easiest way to create a variable that can be accessed from all the functions in a class is to make it a *class-level* variable. If you create a variable inside a function, it will only be available to that function. If you create it at the class level, all functions in the class can access it (this is referred to as *scope*). So you'll create a tuple at the class level and call it `ingredient`. Add the following line of code right under your class definition:

```
typealias ingredient = (name:String, desc: String, calories: String, fat:
String)
```

Whoa! That's a new keyword: `typealias`. A *type alias* is a way to give a simpler name to a data type you've created. The ingredient definition, which has four named strings, can now be known as `ingredient` instead (it was an array of four strings). This will be much easier to reference. And because you created this at the class level, you can access it inside all of your other functions. Next you'll create an ingredient.

You're going to create a new ingredient (tuple) called `pepperoni` with the following properties:

- `Name`—"pepperoni"
- `Description`—"yummy goodness"
- `Calories`—"probably none"
- `Fat`—"less than 0 percent"

Obviously, my love for pepperoni isn't based on reality, but go with me anyway.

This is what my code looks like here (I put this code right under the `super.view-DidLoad()` line within the `viewDidLoad()` function):

```
let pepperoni : (ingredient) = ("pepperoni", "yummy goodness", "probably
➡ none", "less than 0 percent")
```

Can you see how handy that `typealias` was? I was able to create a constant variable (pepperoni) of type `ingredient`, with the properties that I defined. I can add a second ingredient, too. Let's call it `cheese`:

- `Name`—"cheese"
- `Description`—"yummy gooeyness"
- `Calories`—"less than 0 calories"
- `Fat`—"less than 0 percent"

This is what my code looks like for adding the `cheese` variable:

```
let cheese: (ingredient) = ("cheese", "yummy gooeyness", "less than 0
➡ calories", "less than 0 percent")
```

Now we have two ingredients. Let's add both ingredients to a new array called `ingredients`. The array is going to be at the class level, too, so you can access it in all of your functions. Remember how to create an array? Add this line to your code:

```
var ingredients:[ingredient] = []
```

Here you're creating an array named `ingredients`, which will have a type of `ingredient` in it. Notice that I used the plural of *ingredients* for my array because it will have many items stored in there. This is a good practice so you can easily identify your arrays.

Let's add both ingredients to the array and print the name of `pepperoni` to make sure it worked correctly. Add this just under the `let cheese:` line in the `viewDidLoad()` function:

```
ingredients.append(pepperoni)
ingredients.append(cheese)
print(ingredients[0].name)
```

Notice that you can print the name of the first ingredient in your array by referencing name—this is because you created a type alias of the `ingredient`, which makes the code much easier to understand. Run the app, and make sure you see `pepperoni` printed in your console. Great! Now all you have to do is make the array your actual data source! This is what my `viewDidLoad()` function looks like right:

```
override func viewDidLoad() {
super.viewDidLoad()
// Do any additional setup after loading the view, typically from a nib.
let pepperoni : ingredient = ("pepperoni", "yummy goodness", "probably
➡ none", "less than 0 percent")

let cheese: ingredient = ("cheese", "yummy gooeyness", "less than 0
➡ calories", "less than 0 percent")

ingredients.append(pepperoni)
ingredients.append(cheese)
print(ingredients[0].name)
}
```

15.4.6 Step 6: Connect the data to a table

We are so close to having this whole thing work that I can taste it (pun intended—pizza on my brain for some reason). So let's recap before we finish wiring this up. You added a table view to the storyboard. Then you connected the table view properties for the data source and delegate to the ViewController in the storyboard. Next, you added the required methods for the data source to the code with dummy data (you hardcoded the number 1 into the number of rows returned and hardcoded the word `cell` with the row index for the cell data). Then you created an array of data for your pizza ingredients. Finally, you need to remove your hardcoding of the data source values and replace them with your array values. Let's finish this thing!

Go back to your ViewController, and replace the 1 in `numberOfRowsInSection` with the count of your ingredients array. My code looks like this:

```
return ingredients.count
```

This will now return the value 2: the count of the array `ingredients`. If you remove the cheese, it will return the value 1. If you add an ingredient called `sauce` to the array ingredients, it will return 3. Pretty brilliant, huh? That's all you have to do to have the `tableView` display the actual number of cells that you have data for. But you also want the cell to display the value of your data, not your hardcoded "cell" label. Let's fix that now.

Remove the portion of code in your cellForRowAtIndexPath function that sets the textLabel?.text to your hardcoded value "cell \(indexPath.row)". Add the following in its place: ingredients[indexPath.row].name. The line should look like this:

```
cell.textLabel?.text = ingredients[indexPath.row].name
```

Run your app again, and make sure your table view is displaying two rows of data—one that says pepperoni and one that says cheese. Wow! Amazing! You made your first table with dynamic data!

Now that you've come this far, why don't you play around with this to get more comfortable with it? How about adding a few more ingredients to the array? Or, instead of displaying the name of the ingredient, displaying the description?

Figure 15.9 shows what my entire code base looks like so you can check yours against it. (Don't forget, you can also go to www.manning.com/books/anyone-can-create-an-app or https://github.com/wlwise/AnyoneCanCreateAnApp and download the full solution.)

```
//
//  ViewController.swift
//  PizzaIngredients
//
//  Created by Wendy Wise on 9/11/16.
//  Copyright © 2016 WisaAbility. All rights reserved.
//

import UIKit

class ViewController: UIViewController, UITableViewDelegate, UITableViewDataSource {
    typealias ingredient = (name: String, desc : String, calories: String, fat : String)
    var ingredients : [ingredient] = []

    func tableView(_ tableView: UITableView, cellForRowAt indexPath: IndexPath) -> UITableViewCell{
        let cell = tableView.dequeueReusableCell(withIdentifier: "myCell", for: indexPath)
        cell.textLabel?.text = ingredients[indexPath.row].name

        return cell;
    }

    func tableView(_ tableView: UITableView, numberOfRowsInSection section: Int) -> Int{
        return ingredients.count
    }
    override func viewDidLoad() {
        super.viewDidLoad()
        let pepperoni : ingredient = ("Pepperoni", "yummy goodness", "probably none", "less than 0 percent")
        let cheese: ingredient = ("cheese", "yummy gooeyness", "less than 0 calories", "less than 0 percent")
        ingredients.append(pepperoni)
        ingredients.append(cheese)
        print(ingredients[0].name)
        // Do any additional setup after loading the view, typically from a nib.
    }

    override func didReceiveMemoryWarning() {
        super.didReceiveMemoryWarning()
        // Dispose of any resources that can be recreated.
    }

}
```

Figure 15.9   The code required to create two ingredients, store them in an array, and display them in a table view

Concepts to remember

- *Delegate*—A way to get someone else to do the work for you; or, leaving the implementation details to another class.
- *Protocol*—A class that wants to implement the delegated methods must conform to the protocol defined in the main class.
- *Index path*—An item that lets you access the exact location of an object in an array, or an array of arrays. For table views, you use `IndexPath.Row` to get the row location.
- *Data source*—The data the table view uses to display content.
- `UITableViewDataSource`—The protocol definition that a ViewController must conform to in order to display data for the table view.

15.5   *Summary*

Wow! What a dense chapter, right? It had a lot of content. As you've seen in this chapter, table views take a lot to explain but not a lot to implement. In order to understand them, though, you had to learn about delegates and protocols. You'll use delegates, protocols, and table views a lot in your coding career, so make sure you understand the underlying concepts. You'll see table views, delegates, and data sources again in the next part of the book, when you work on LioN.

Patterns: learning to sew 16

This chapter covers

- Best coding practices
- Model-View-Controller pattern
- Delegate pattern

Some of you are probably worried that this chapter is about sewing, but relax. It's about coding patterns. What in the world are *coding patterns*? Honestly, they're kind of like sewing patterns, hence the analogy. In my goofy mind, there was some guy a million or so years ago (yes, I'm exaggerating) who wanted to make a shirt. He got a roll of fabric (or went and shaved his sheep first) and set about cutting it up to make the required pieces. After trial and error, he finally found the best combination of pieces to sew together to make a shirt. If he was smart, he probably then made a copy of the pieces and set those aside so he could trace those patterns the next time he wanted a shirt and he wouldn't have to go through the trial and error again. Pretty smart guy!

Well, some pretty smart folks have done the same thing in the coding world. Let's learn about that now (no sheep were harmed in the writing of this manuscript).

16.1 Design patterns, defined

The guy who made a shirt probably saved his patterns so he wouldn't have to go through the pain of trial and error again. That's great for him, but what about his neighbor who wants to make a shirt too? He could do the same thing—cut a bunch of fabric until he found the right pattern to make his shirt, or the first guy could be neighborly and share his pattern with the neighbor. In the coding world, some smart people figured out solutions to common problems in software design and coding, and they created reusable *patterns* or templates to help the rest of us out. These patterns make it easier to write code that's clean, understandable, maintainable, and extensible. That's a lot of "ables," so let's walk through them.

16.1.1 Clean code

Clean code is the term programmers use to define code that is well written, is well documented, and doesn't include old, commented-out code. When you're coding an app, you'll find that at times you try different methods to figure out what works best—or what works, period. When you find a line that may be causing problems, sometimes you'll comment it out and write a different line to see if that works better.

Once your app is complete and you're ready to either file it away or give it to someone, you should clean it up first. Remove all the commented lines of code that aren't needed, add comments to the lines that need them, and make sure it follows best practices. We'll talk about best practices as we continue in this chapter.

16.1.2 Understandable

There are many ways to accomplish certain tasks when you're programming. Some ways are more "elegant" than others, and some are more "kludgy" (pronounced *clue-jee*) than others. When you're coding, the most important thing to accomplish is to make your code work. It may not be the prettiest way it could be done, but it works. That's step 1. As you get better and better at coding, you'll learn better ways to do things in your code. As you're finishing your app and you have time, you need to go back in the code and make it more understandable and more elegant (clear and succinct).

For example, tell me what this this code is doing:

```
var x = .555555
var y = 32
var z = 75

var a = x*(z-32)
```

You might be able to tell me what the code is doing programmatically, but what am I trying to *do*? It's not clear. Here, let me change my variable names:

```
let fraction59 = .555555 // this represents 5/9
let constant32 = 32
var fahrenheit = 75

var FarToCelcius = fraction59 *(fahrenheit-constant32) //the formula is 5/9
➥ *(fahrenheit - 32)
```

Now anyone who reads my code will know exactly what its intent is as well as that the formula is to convert Fahrenheit to Celsius. This makes my code much more understandable.

16.1.3 *Maintainable*

I can't think of any app that I've ever written where I didn't have to go back and update something. I might have fixed a bug or implemented a new feature, or upgraded it to make it compatible with the latest version of iOS. No matter why I had to maintain my code, I had to. That's why it's so important to document your code and make it as readable, understandable, and elegant as possible. It will make your life easier down the road. If you ever work with another programmer, you'll learn to love or hate that person depending on their coding practices. When you have to follow behind a sloppy programmer, it takes a lot more time and energy to figure out what they're doing, what they intended, and how they did what they did. When you follow behind a conscientious programmer, it takes much less time to understand their intent, what they were doing, and why they did it that way.

I've mentioned *intent* a few times now, so let me explain what I mean by that. Let's assume you're writing an app that needs to retrieve weather data from the web and display it in your app. You've configured the app to get data from different data sources depending on the user's location. It makes perfect sense to you because data source A has much better data for the eastern part of the country, and data source B has better data for the western side of the country. But a year or two later, you find that there is a defect in the code, and you need to go back in and fix it. You've worked on a bunch of other apps in those intervening two years, so you need to refresh your memory when you go in. You begin reading the code and see that you're calling two different data sources based on user location. That doesn't make any sense to you because everyone knows that data source C has the best data for the entire country (things have changed). You have no idea why you would have programmed it that way. Now, what if you had written some comments in the file that explained the intent of having two data sources and the intent of the actual functions? You would remember why you wrote it with two data sources, and you could check the code to make sure the actual implementation matched the intent. I find this approach is helpful when working with math issues. A parenthesis in the wrong place changes the entire formula, and if you don't have the intent of the formula written down, you'll spend a lot more time debugging your app.

16.1.4 *Extensibility*

Extensibility allows the programmer to add new features or to respond to a change without having to completely re-architect the app. If you define a good architecture up front (by using patterns that we'll discuss shortly), you should be able to add a new feature to your app without having to completely rewrite entire sections of it.

NOTE   Don't confuse the *extensibility* of your app with the Swift keyword *extension*. Those are two different concepts. You don't need to understand extensions right now.

Extensibility helps you write *loosely coupled* code—so you can change or replace components without too much hassle.

Imagine you wrote an app that allows someone to order pizza. You wrote it so the user could configure their pizza, add it the cart, and pay for it. Great job! The client is so happy with the app that now they want you to write an app that will allow someone to order a hamburger from their other restaurant. Well, if you had planned ahead to make your app *reusable* and *extensible*, you wouldn't have to make many changes to it. But if you only wrote it with the idea that you needed to get this app out the door, and future enhancements didn't matter as much as getting the current functionality in, you'd be in a world of hurt. You'd have to change a lot of code in the app in order to handle hamburgers. You might even have to start over.

It's important to think about where you might want to take the app in the future so you don't paint yourself into a corner to the extent that you have to rewrite a lot of it. You'll get a better sense of this from the rest of this chapter and as you code more.

16.2   *Types of design patterns*

There are three main categories of design patterns:

- *Creational*—Ways to create objects
- *Structural*—Ways to structure your code
- *Behavioral*—Ways to control the behavior of your code

We're not going to cover creational or behavioral patterns in this book, because they're more advanced topics. We'll cover structural patterns, because they're important for your beginning programming career and for your upcoming LioN app. *Structural design patterns* are design patterns that make it easier to create and maintain relationships between objects. They make it easier to create code that is loosely coupled and with all the "able" properties mentioned earlier (clean, understandable, maintainable, and extensible). Let's start with the Model-View-Controller design pattern.

16.2.1   *Model-View-Controller design pattern*

The Model-View-Controller (MVC) design pattern is a key design pattern that you've used already but didn't know it. MVC classifies objects in your app based on the role that they play within the app. Let's break it down:

- *Controller*—You've seen this already numerous times; in your apps, it's called the ViewController. This role is the mediator between the view and the model. Remember back when you created buttons on the view in the storyboard? You made the buttons and then had to wire them to the ViewController. Then, when the user tapped the button on the view, the ViewController could take action.

Imagine if you created a calculator app and had 12 buttons on your view. You'd wire those buttons on the view and then create all the code in the View-Controller to handle the actions of the button tap. But then say you want to completely change the view of the calculator. You want to delete all 12 buttons and create 12 different ones. The only action you'd have to take is to delete the buttons, create new ones, and then wire them to the correct functions in your ViewController. You wouldn't have to recode all the functions because nothing changed for them. That's because you separated out the *view* and the *controller.* Pretty cool, huh?

- *View*—Imagine for a moment that you're creating the calculator app and you have 12 buttons on your iPhone view. Now you want to make an iPad view with 12 buttons. There are ways you can do this without creating another view (you'll learn that in the next chapter), but you could optionally create another view for the iPad. You could then wire all 12 buttons to the same functions in your class without having to rewrite code again. Again, pretty cool!

- *Model*—You haven't seen much of the model yet, but you definitely will in the next chapter with LioN. In chapter 15, you created a data source for the data (ingredients) that you wanted to display in the app. In other words, you modelled the data in the form of an array. The model role holds your application data and defines the different ways to manipulate it. You haven't created a class with the model role yet.

I mentioned that the ViewController was a mediator of sorts between the model and the view. As you can see in figure 16.1, there are three distinct roles within the app: the view, the controller, and the model. In this instance, the user performs an action, the controller tells the model to do something with the data based on that action, the model notifies the controller that it did something with the data, and the controller then updates the view.

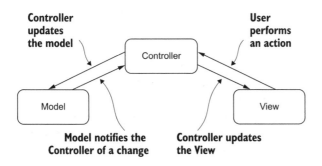

Figure 16.1 The MVC design pattern allows the controller to act as a mediator between the view and the model.

Figure 16.2 shows an example to make this easier to understand. As you can see, the user decides to delete a row from the table. The controller receives that action request from the view and tells the model to delete the row. The model deletes the row and notifies the controller that the row was deleted. The controller then updates the view, and the row is no longer visible. You can see from this example how much easier it is to maintain the code when all the data is in the model, the controller mediates between the view and the model, and the view is responsible for displaying.

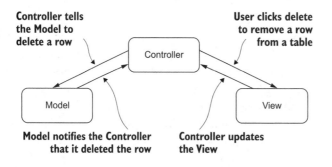

Figure 16.2   **MVC pattern in action. The user deletes a row, and the controller mediates the action.**

I mentioned the pizza and hamburger apps earlier. If you had used this MVC design pattern when you created the pizza app, you'd only have to change your model to hamburger and change the view images and labels to hamburgers. The controller would still control the interaction between the two. Amazeballs.

For the MVC design pattern to work, you need to think about the design of your app before you start coding. The more thought you give to the design before you start coding, the more organized your code will probably be (does that sound like Yoda?). I'll show you how I think about the design when we get to the next chapter and start work on LioN.

16.2.2 *Delegate pattern*

Hmmm… *Delegate*, you say? That sounds awfully familiar, doesn't it? Yes, you've already used the Delegate design pattern. It allows one object to act in conjunction with or on behalf of another object. I showed you this in the last chapter when you implemented the `UITableViewDataSource` delegate. Apple uses the Delegate pattern in a lot of its UI elements, so it's important that you understand the concept. I used a pizza restaurant analogy in chapter 15. I'll stick with that here.

As a programmer, you're pretty busy writing, testing, and commenting your code, and you don't have time to make dinner. You wish you could delegate that to someone else. Oh, wait—you can! You can call your local pizza restaurant and ask them to make you a pizza. You know that they'll do this because they implement the Pizza Restaurant functions. In other words, you are confident ordering a pizza from the restaurant because you know it conforms to the Pizza Restaurant protocol. You know you'll get some sort of pizza back when you call its `makePizza()` function, even though the implementation details might be different than those of other pizza restaurants. The Delegate pattern provides this type of functionality: you want to make sure a class implements certain methods, but you don't care how exactly they're implemented, as long as they are. This is a popular pattern and is used in many apps—including the LioN app, coming in the next chapter.

16.2.3 *The Memento pattern*

The Memento pattern kind of does what it sounds like—it saves the data (like saving a memento, get it?). This saves your stuff somewhere that you specify. One of the ways Apple implements the Memento pattern is through archiving. Guess what? Archiving also does exactly what it sounds like. *Archiving* converts your data into a stream that is then saved and can be restored later. You'll use this in LioN, too. The Memento pattern serves another purpose as well: it saves the object for you, and you can restore that object at any time without having to use several undo commands.

When you start coding the LioN app in the next chapter, you'll create a LioN object, which will include the name of the item, a description, and whether you like the item. Every time the user creates a LioN object, you'll need to save it so they can see it the next time the app loads. You'll use the Memento design pattern to save the LioN object and load it when the user wants to see it. Imagine, too, that the user goes into a LioN item, edits it, and then decides not save their edits. The original object will still be saved, so you won't have to implement any undo logic in your code. Your code will also be clean because there will be a class whose only purpose is to save and load the LioN object, instead of putting all the code into one big class. The Memento pattern supports the idea of extensibility mentioned earlier—classes should have a *separation of concerns* (SOC) so that if you want to change how or where the LioN object is saved, you can.

Concepts to remember

- Plan your app before you begin coding anything.
- Many, many smart people out there have already solved some of the most common issues in Swift programming. Learn from them, and follow their patterns.
- It's important to write good, solid, clean code. Take the time to go back and clean it up when you're finished coding. You'll thank yourself later.
- The MVC pattern is one of the most common patterns in Swift programming, and you will use it to create good code.

16.3   Summary

You may be wondering why I told you about patterns in this chapter and then several times told you that we'll get to the implementation details later. Well, if you'll remember from the beginning of the book, I explained that I wanted to give you *just-in-time* instruction so you wouldn't be overwhelmed. I want to introduce you to these concepts now, and then we'll go into more detail in later chapters. There are a lot of patterns available for you to use, and many books are devoted to nothing but patterns. I encourage you to learn more about different types of patterns as you grow as a developer, but other patterns are too dense for this book.

Part 3

Creating the Like it or Not app

Part 3 is where the magic starts to happen. You'll take everything you've learned in parts 1 and 2 and create the Like it or Not app. You can download the app from the App Store to see what you'll build at http://mng.bz/en3e. You'll be building the LioN app exactly as it is in the App Store, with the exception of the ads available at the bottom of the screens and the notes.

17

Putting it all together: the LioN app

This chapter covers

- Planning the LioN app
- Navigation controllers
- The `override` keyword

You learned a lot of new concepts in parts 1 and 2 of this book, and now you're going to put all those concepts together to build an app called LioN: Like it or Not. You'll learn some new concepts as well, but mostly you'll be putting to practice what you've learned. This is exciting, isn't it?

17.1 Like it or Not

What is the LioN app, anyway? The best way to understand the app is to go download it from the App Store on your iPhone. Search for *LioN—Like it or Not,* and tap Get to install it (it's free). Figure 17.1 shows it running. I created this app because I tend to be a bit forgetful about certain details of my life—such as which kind of toothpaste makes me throw up a little, and which one I like. (I know, you'd think I'd remember that, but for some reason it seems to be a real mental block for me.) I'd go into the grocery store, head to the toothpaste aisle, and look at the boxes. I'd then pick up the one that looks most familiar to me, thinking that because it looks

Figure 17.1   The LioN app

familiar, it must be the one I like. Next thing you know, I'm throwing up a little when I brush my teeth because I picked up the wrong one. Again. This also happens to me in restaurants. I order the chicken dish because I know I've had it before and have a strong memory of it, only to find out that it was a strong *dislike*, not strong like. I may or may not use it to remember my favorite beer, too.

Enter LioN! The LioN app lets me add items that I need to remember, and I can mark that I like or dislike them. I can easily search on items so I don't have to scroll through the entire list to find toothpaste, thus saving me that little bit of throw-up every time I brush my teeth. If you've downloaded the app, play with it and add your own items to the list. You can add, edit, delete, and add notes. I added a lot more functionality to the published app than you will create, but your LioN app will still be able to add, edit, delete, and add notes.

17.2   *Getting started*

You learned about using design patterns to create good code in the last chapter, and we're going to focus on creating that kind of code throughout the rest of the book. This means you'll create something that works, and then you might go back and redo it (called *refactoring*) to make it better. Don't be frustrated by this. It's how most coders do it. It's a process: create, test, refine, test, refine, test, and so on.

Here are the steps you'll take in this chapter:

1 Create the app, and save it.
2 Add a Navigation Controller to the storyboard.
3 Add an iPhone Simulator to Xcode.
4 Connect the data to the table view.

17.2.1 *Creating the app*

In Xcode, create a new app and call it LioN. In the Project Settings screen, change the targeted device from iPhone to Universal, as shown in figure 17.2. This means you want this app to run on both the iPad and the iPhone. Deselect Include Unit Tests and Include UI Tests.

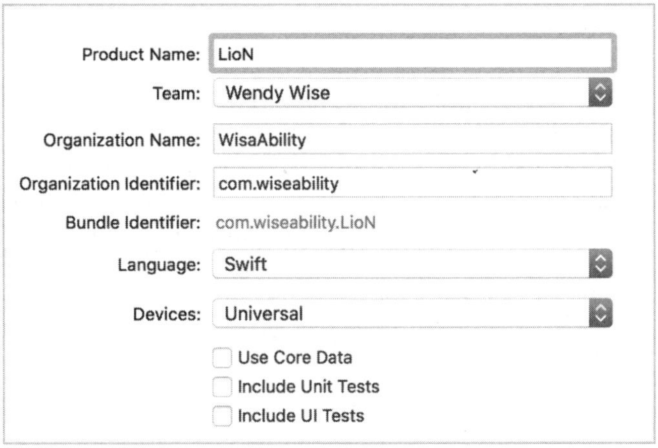

Figure 17.2   Uncheck the Include Unit Tests and Include UI Tests options.

Save it to your dev folder, as you normally do. When the project loads, you'll see the General tab. Make sure Device is Universal and Deployment Target is set to 10.0 (as of this writing, this is the latest version of iOS), as shown in figure 17.3. If there's a later version of iOS released, use 10.0 anyway.

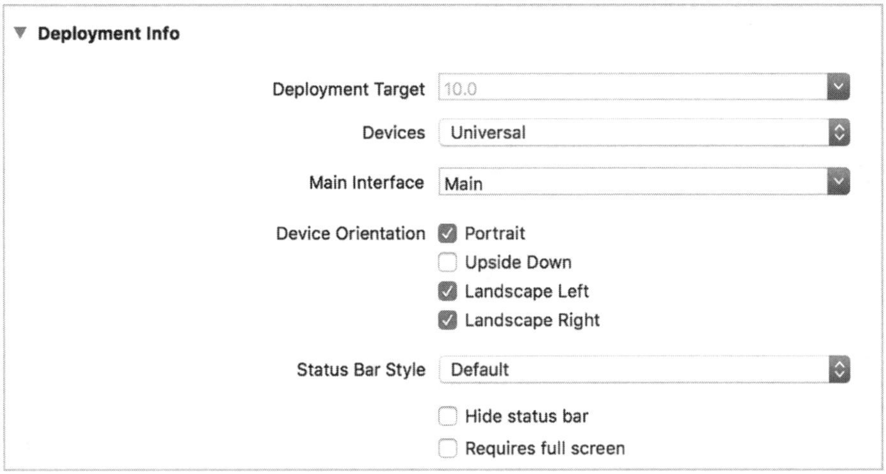

Figure 17.3   The deployment section of the General tab

17.2.2 *Adding a Navigation Controller*

In the Project Navigator, click the Main.Storyboard file to open the Storyboard Editor. Click the View Controller window in the Editor, and press Delete. You should have an empty storyboard now (don't panic—you can add something to it). Go to your Object Library, and drag a Navigation Controller onto your storyboard. The first thing you should notice is that Xcode added what look like two frames onto the storyboard, even though you only dropped one object. This is normal—let's talk about Navigation Controllers so you understand what you did.

The Navigation Controller is a container view, like the tab view we talked about back in chapter 14. This means it contains other views but doesn't display anything itself (again, like the Tab Bar Controller from chapter 14). Let's set the Navigation Controller to be the initial ViewController so you can see what it looks from here. You'll do the same thing you did with the Tab Bar Controller, except this time you'll set the Navigation Controller as the initial ViewController.

In Xcode, select the Navigation Controller (the scene on the left) that you added, and then open the Attributes Inspector panel. In the View Controller part of the panel, click the option Is Initial View Controller. You should be able to run the app now. Other than the words Root View Controller (figure 17.4), this app shouldn't look

Figure 17.4   At launch, the Navigation Controller shows a Root View Controller with a table.

that foreign to you. Grab your iPhone, and launch the Contacts app. They look similar already, don't they?

The Contacts app is using a Navigation Controller to control the flow of the app, as you will with LioN. You set the initial ViewController, which lets Xcode know that the Navigation Controller was the first scene that should be displayed. The Navigation Controller is a container view, which means it can display multiple views itself. So the Root View Controller is essentially the initial view that Navigation Controller should show: root view, or first view.

Displaying the words *Root View Controller* doesn't mean anything to the LioN app, so change them to the acronym *LioN*. Back in Xcode, make sure your storyboard is showing in the Editor window. Now, in the storyboard Document Outline, select the Root View Controller, which has an icon pointing to the left, as shown in figure 17.5.

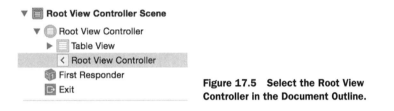

Figure 17.5   Select the Root View Controller in the Document Outline.

Once the Root View Controller is selected, open the Attributes Inspector in the Utilities panel and change the title to *LioN*. Now run the app again, and you should see the acronym LioN at the top of the window.

17.2.3   *Adding an iPhone 4s Simulator*

Back in step 1, when you created the project, you selected the option for the app to run on Universal devices, meaning it should run on both iPads and iPhones. In order to test your app on an iPhone 4s Simulator and various iPhone Simulators, you'll need to add those Simulators to your device lists. In the Xcode top menu bar, click Window > Devices. You'll notice two sections on the left side of the window that pops up: Devices and Simulators. The Simulators section shows all Simulators that you've used so far and lets you add new ones. It's important to run your app on all kinds of different simulated devices with different operating systems to make sure it runs successfully and looks good. For now, though, you'll add an iPhone 4 running iOS 8.4.

> **NOTE**   You're adding this older model phone with an older Simulator just as an example, so you'll know how to add Simulators in the future. Apple is an innovative company and launches new devices and new operating systems frequently, so you need to know how to test on those simulated devices and operating systems. It's important to make sure your app is compatible with various devices and operating systems so you don't disappoint your users.

At the bottom of the window, click the + button to add a new Simulator, as shown in figure 17.6. Add a new Simulator named iPhone 4s, with a device type of iPhone 4s and iOS version of 8.4. See figure 17.7 to verify your settings.

Figure 17.6   Click the + button at bottom left to add a new Simulator.

Figure 17.7   Create a new Simulator for an iPhone 4s running iOS 8.4

Once your new Simulator is created, go back to the main Xcode window. You now want to run the app on the iPhone 4s Simulator to see how the table view looks. At the top of Xcode, to the right of the Run and Stop buttons, you'll notice an icon that looks like three pencils in the shape of an A with the word *LioN* next to it. This is the place where you can select which *schema* you want to run the app on.

If you click the right side of the button, you'll get a list of schemas to select from. But the iPhone 4s isn't there! You just created the Simulator, but it doesn't appear. This is because you set up the iPhone 4s to run on iOS 8.4, and this project is configured to run on iOS 10 and above only. You can either change the app settings to allow it to run on a lower iOS version, or test on other Simulators that have a newer iOS version. When creating an app, you need to decide which operating system version you want to target. The lower the version number, the higher the likelihood that most people have either that version or something newer. The downside of targeting older operating systems is that you'll miss out on new functionality, bug fixes, and features that new operating systems offer. In this case, you want to use newer operating systems instead of older ones—so let's not test on the newly created iOS 8.4 device. Instead, select iPad Pro, as shown in figure 17.8.

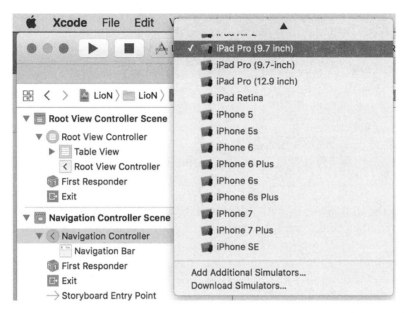

Figure 17.8   Select the iPad Pro schema to run the app on an iPad Pro Simulator.

Once you've selected the iPad Pro schema, run the app again to see what it looks like on the iPad Simulator. It will take a moment to run the first time, and you'll see the screen that looks like a device is powering on. That's normal. You can see that the app looks pretty good on the iPad, too, which is exciting!

Let's move on to hooking up your UITableView to the ViewController like you did in chapter 16.

17.2.4 *Connecting the data to the table view*

Before you hook up the table view, take a minute to make the application code a little more readable and intuitive. Start by renaming your ViewController to MainView-Controller so you know this is the main one. Go to the Project Navigator (left panel), click ViewController once, and then click it again (but not as fast as a double-click) so that the word *ViewController* is highlighted (you can also Option-click it if you find that easier). Change the name of the file to MainViewController.swift. Open that file so it shows in the Standard Editor panel, and change the class definition as well. Change ViewController to MainViewController and then change the type from UIView-Controller to UITableViewController. Your class definition should now look like this:

```
class MainViewController: UITableViewController {
```

Do you remember what this means? You're defining the class MainViewController and saying it is of type UITableViewController. Now you need to tell your storyboard that MainViewController is the controller class for the frame it created. Open the storyboard again, and select the frame that now has LioN at the top. Open the Identity Inspector on the Utilities panel (right panel) to change the class, as shown in figure 17.9. The Identity Inspector is the third button from the left.

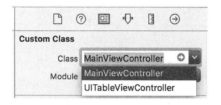
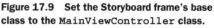

Figure 17.9   Set the Storyboard frame's base class to the `MainViewController` class.

Now run the app again to make sure everything still works as expected (which it should). You're going to add the data source to the controller class so the table has something to load. If you worked through chapter 16, you'll remember that you had to tell Xcode that the ViewController conformed to the `UITableViewDatasource` protocol, and yet this `MainViewController` isn't explicitly doing that. Let's find out why. In Xcode, click `MainViewController` so it's active in the Editor pane. Next, Option-click the word `UITableViewController` and look at the Quick Help panel that pops up, shown in figure 17.10.

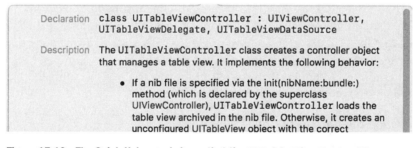

Figure 17.10   The Quick Help panel shows that the `UITableViewController` conforms to the `UITableViewDelegate` and the `UITableViewDataSource` protocols.

The `UITableViewController` class conforms to the `UITableViewDelegate` and the `UITableViewDataSource` protocols, so your class doesn't need to explicitly state that it conforms to these—because it already does. Your `MainViewControllerClass` is inheriting from the `UITableViewController` class, so you inherit all the delegations that are implemented in the base class. Isn't this neat? If you remember back in chapter 16, though, you got an error when you didn't add the required functions for `UITableViewDataSource`. This hasn't thrown any errors, which seems weird. Ahhh, inheritance to the rescue! The `UITableViewController` base class has already implemented the required methods. So your `MainViewController` is inheriting functions from the `UITableViewController`. How cool is that? Except now you want to load data into your table, and the `UITableViewController` implemented the methods, so how do you load the data? I'm so glad you asked.

17.2.5 *Implement the functions for table views*

If you remember back in chapter 16, you had to add required functions to your class so you could conform to the `UITableViewDataSource` protocol. You'll do the same thing now. In order to get the specifications for those methods, first Command-click the word `UITableViewController` in your `MainViewController` class definition (at the top of the file). This opens the definition of the `UITableViewController` class in Xcode, as shown in figure 17.11.

```
@available(iOS 2.0, *)
open class UITableViewController : UIViewController, UITableViewDelegate, UITableViewDataSource {

    public init(style: UITableViewStyle)

    public init(nibName nibNameOrNil: String?, bundle nibBundleOrNil: Bundle?)

    public init?(coder aDecoder: NSCoder)

    open var tableView: UITableView!

    @available(iOS 3.2, *)
    open var clearsSelectionOnViewWillAppear: Bool // defaults to YES. If YES, any selection is cleared in viewWillAppear:


    @available(iOS 6.0, *)
    open var refreshControl: UIRefreshControl?
}
```

Figure 17.11 Command-clicking the `UITableViewController` in the `MainViewController` class opens the class definition in Xcode.

That's pretty cool, but you really want to know the definition of the `UITableViewData-Source`; so, Command-click the word `UITableViewDataSource` in the class definition of the `UITableViewController` class (at the top of the file). This opens the class definition for the `UITableViewDataSource`, which is exactly what you were looking for. There are two function definitions here that you require: copy them by highlighting them and then pressing Command-C so they're on your clipboard. Next, click the Back button at the top of the Editor twice to get back to the `MainViewController` file. Paste the definitions right below your `viewDidLoad` function so your code looks like figure 17.12.

```
public protocol UITableViewDataSource : NSObjectProtocol {

    @available(iOS 2.0, *)
    public func tableView(_ tableView: UITableView, numberOfRowsInSection section: Int) -> Int


    // Row display. Implementers should *always* try to reuse cells by setting each cell's reuseIdentifier and querying
        for available reusable cells with dequeueReusableCellWithIdentifier:
    // Cell gets various attributes set automatically based on table (separators) and data source (accessory views,
        editing controls)

    @available(iOS 2.0, *)
    public func tableView(_ tableView: UITableView, cellForRowAt indexPath: IndexPath) -> UITableViewCell
```

Figure 17.12 Copying the function definitions into your `MainViewController` so you don't have to type the function definition again

Delete the word `public` from the function definitions. You should still get several errors in Xcode because these lines don't look like functions. Do you remember why not? You have to put brackets around the functions so Xcode knows they're functions. At the end of the `numberofRowsInSection` definition, after the `-> Int`, put an open curly bracket `{`. Press Enter, and Xcode should automatically add another one to close the function. Now do the same thing for the `cellForRowAtIndexPath` function. That should clear out a few of the errors you were seeing, but there still seem to be two errors. What gives?

Click the red exclamation button at top right in your Editor panel to display the messages that Xcode is providing, as shown in figure 17.13. Notice that the first two error messages say "Overriding declaration requires an 'override' keyword". This goes back to the awesome topic of inheritance. I told you before that the `UITableView-Controller` already implemented the required `UITableViewDataSource` functions, right? That means `UITableViewController` "declared" those functions in its class definition, and because you're inheriting from `UITableViewController`, you have access to those classes. This means you can't "re-declare" those functions unless you tell Xcode that you're overriding the `UITableViewController` function definition so you can implement our own. The superclass `UITableViewController` already declared the functions that you want to use in your class, so you can load data into your table.

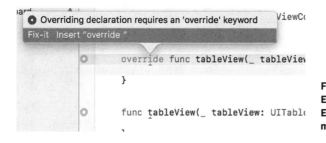

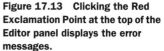

Figure 17.13 **Clicking the Red Exclamation Point at the top of the Editor panel displays the error messages.**

To correct the error, you need to tell Xcode that yes, you know these functions are declared in the superclass, but you want to override those definitions so that your functions will be used instead. How do you do that? Well, sit back and relax, because it's going to take a while to override the functions. Nah, I'm kidding. It's quick and easy. All you have to do is add the keyword `override` in front of your function declarations. Yep—it's that easy. Awesome! Now those two errors are gone. You've successfully overridden a function definition.

But wait. If you click the red exclamation point again, you'll see that there are different errors now. It looks like you declared your functions and said that they should each be returning something—the arrow to the right defines what the function should return. The `number of rows in section` is expecting an `Int`, so put `return 1` between the brackets. Now you're down to one error.

The `cellForRowAtIndexPath` is expecting a `UITableViewCell` to be returned, so you need to create a cell like you did in chapter 16. Add the following code between the curly brackets of the function `cellForRowAtIndexPath`:

```
let cell = tableView.dequeueReusableCell(withIdentifier: "lionCell", for:
    indexPath);
cell.textLabel?.text = "my first cell"
return cell
```

Do you remember what this code does? The first line creates a constant cell (using the keyword `let`) and tells the table view to reuse a cell if one is available. It specifically wants to reuse the cell that's identified as `lionCell`. Uh oh. Did you identify any cells as `lionCells`? Nope. Let's go fix that before we keep walking through the code.

Go back to your storyboard, and click the `TableViewCell` (use the Document Outline panel to make it easier). Then, in the Attributes Inspector panel, add `lionCell` to the row asking for an Identifier. Whoo! Sidestepped that error, didn't you?

The next line sets the text label's text to "my first lion". This isn't reusable because you're hardcoding the value, but remember that you want to take little steps, test, refactor, little steps, test, refactor, and so forth. Finally, you're returning the cell to the `tableView` to be displayed.

Run the app and check the output. You should see a single cell with the words "my first lion". You can run the app on the iPad Simulator or an iPhone Simulator, and it looks good on both devices. If your app doesn't show the cell with "my first lion" on it, there are three things to check:

- Make sure you used the same cell identifier in the code as you set in the Attributes Inspector for the cell. I generally copy/paste the name because I've mistyped enough that it drives me crazy.
- Make sure you copied the correct two functions into the code. You want the `cellForRowAtIndexPath` and the `numberOfRowsInSection` functions. It's easy to accidentally copy `numberOfSectionsInTableView` instead—not that I've ever done that.
- Make sure you set the class for `LionScene` to the `MainViewController`.

17.3 Summary

You're well on your way to creating the LioN app. I'll continue to introduce new concepts in each chapter. I introduced the keyword `override` in this chapter, which lets you (the programmer) override an existing function declaration so you can implement your own code. This is a powerful feature of Swift that you'll use a lot in your programming career. You also learned how to look at the class definitions of the classes you're using by Command-clicking the class in your code. It's not a super-exciting app yet, but it's getting there! If you want to see your app running on your iPhone or iPad, check out appendix B.

Adding data to your LioN app

18

This chapter covers

- Adding hardcoded data to your LioN app
- Refactoring to be MVC compliant
- Showing the description on the cell

You created the foundation of the LioN app in the last chapter, and you're going to add more functionality to it in this chapter. I told you about my approach in chapter 17: you'll code, test, refactor, and then do it all over again. You may want me to show you the final output, but this iterative development is part of the process. If you try to code a big chunk of functionality all at once, you won't know which parts work and which don't when you test it. You'll have to walk through everything you wrote to find the error. It's much easier to start small, test, refactor, and add more.

In this chapter, you're going to continue with this process by first adding some data to an array and displaying it in the table, and then refactoring the data to separate the model from the view from the controller (the MVC pattern was discussed in chapter 17).

18.1 Adding hardcoded data to your LioN

You hardcoded a single cell of data in chapter 17, and now you're going to hardcode several cells of data so you can wire up your data source. You'll do the following:

1 Create an array.
2 Hardcode some data.
3 Create a LioN object to store data.
4 Make the array the data source for the table, and then test it.

Ready? Let's get to it!

18.1.1 Creating an array of dummy data

This is the first time I've used the term *dummy data*, but it's common in the programming world. It doesn't mean the data has an intellect inferior to that of other data; it means it's placeholder data. Programmers often use dummy data to test their code to make sure it works before wiring it up to real data. It's a perfectly acceptable practice to do this, but you need to make sure your dummy data is structured the same way the real data is structured, or you'll have a lot of rework on your hands. You'll see more of this as you continue to create a model later in this chapter.

Open your LioN project again, and navigate to `MainViewController` so you can edit it. The first thing you need to do is to create an array of dummy data. You need to create the array at the class level so it's available to all the functions. Do you remember how to create an array of strings at the class level? I added the following line below my class definition line:

```
var lionData = ["lion1", "lion2", "lion3", "lion4", "lion5", "lion6", "lion7"]
```

You can make your `lion` data say whatever you want and add as many or as few items as you want, as long as it's in an array called `lionData` and it contains strings. Now you need to do something with this data.

18.1.2 Wiring lionData to the table view with hardcoded data

You need to connect the array of strings to your table view. You did this in chapter 16, so it shouldn't be new to you. The first thing you want to do is change the `numberOf-RowsInSection` function to return the actual number of strings instead of the hard-coded value 1. Delete the `return 1` code in this function, and return the number of strings in the array. Remember how? I added the following line within the `numberOf-RowsInSection` function:

```
return lionData.count
```

This returns the count of objects in the `lionData` array. It doesn't matter what kind of objects they are (strings, `Int`s, and so on). Every time an object is added to or removed from the array, the count will change, so this method will always return the correct number of objects. Go ahead and run the app to see what happens.

You should see "my first lion" repeated numerous times. The number of times it repeats will depend on how many strings you added to you `lionData` array. You haven't told the cells to use your array of strings yet, so it's repeating your hardcoded value `"my first lion"`. Make sense? Let's fix it.

You need to wire the strings in your array to the title label in the cells. This will require a change in the `cellForRowAtIndexPath` function. You hardcoded the value `"my first lion"` for the `cell.textLabel?.text` line, so that's probably the best place to start. You need to change the hardcoded value to the value of the string in your array, but you have to do it for each string in the array so it doesn't repeat one value over and over again like your hardcoded line.

You learned about the index path and rows in chapter 17, so this part shouldn't be new to you, either. As a refresher, the index path is like an arrow pointing to a specific location in a collection of collections. The index path in this case should be 0 because you have only one array in the collection (remember, you start counting at 0) and the `row` of that index path will be the actual row in your array. Fortunately, Xcode takes care of knowing all about the index path and row.

As mentioned in chapter 17, the `cellForRowAtIndexPath` function is called once for every row in the table. The first time it's called, `indexPath.row` should be 0 because it's the first cell in your table. In this case, the `cellForRowAtIndexPath` function will be called `lionData.count` times, because `lionData.count` is the number of strings in your array.

Next, you'll update the code to remove the hardcoded value and instead use the row of data in your array. I changed the line to look like this:

```
cell.textLabel?.text = lionData[indexPath.row]
```

Run the app and see what happens. You should see all the strings that you added to your array displayed in the table. Good job!

So now you have the LioN application with a table view that's populated with an array of strings. This is a great start. Next, you're going to add a LioN model to the app so you can follow the MVC pattern we talked about in chapter 17.

18.2   Adding a model to the mix

As you may remember from chapter 17, it's a good practice to separate out the view (front end) from the model (the data) from the controller (the go-between). This allows the separation of concerns (SOC) so the view isn't concerned with what data it will show, and the model isn't concerned with how the data will be presented.

You're going to add a model to your app that will represent the LioN data. You'll take the following steps:

1 Add a new Swift file to project.
2 Model the data.
3 Create a new LioN entry.

18.2.1 *Adding a new Swift file to the project*

You need to add a new file to your project, something you haven't done before. It's easy, though, so let's walk through it. In Xcode, click File > New > File. A new window will pop up. Notice at the top of the window that there are groupings of template types: iOS, watchOS, tvOS, and macOS. (There may be more than this in your version of Xcode, but there are only four in my version today.) You can use Xcode to create apps for iOS, the watch, and a Mac—but you're working with iOS now. The Source part of the window of the iOS Category shows you all of the different file type templates that are available to you (figure 18.1).

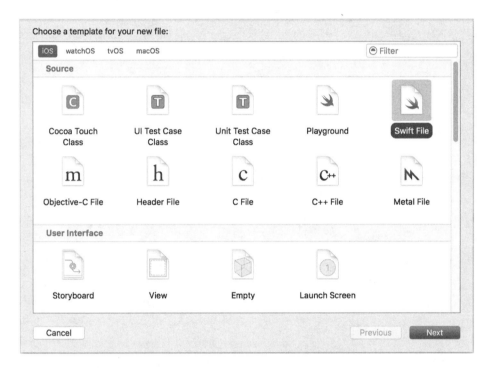

Figure 18.1   Click Source under the iOS category, and then select the Swift File template to create a new file in your project.

The only one you need to worry about right now is Swift File, which will create an empty Swift file for you. Click Swift File, and then click Next. Another dialog will open, shown in figure 18.2, where you can name the file and choose its location and target.

Name the file *LioN*, and make sure to leave the extension as .swift. Leave the "where" set to the LioN folder—this defaults to the location where you stored the project on your hard drive. You can leave Group set to the LioN folder as well, and make sure Targets is set to the LioN project. Click Create. The dialog box should

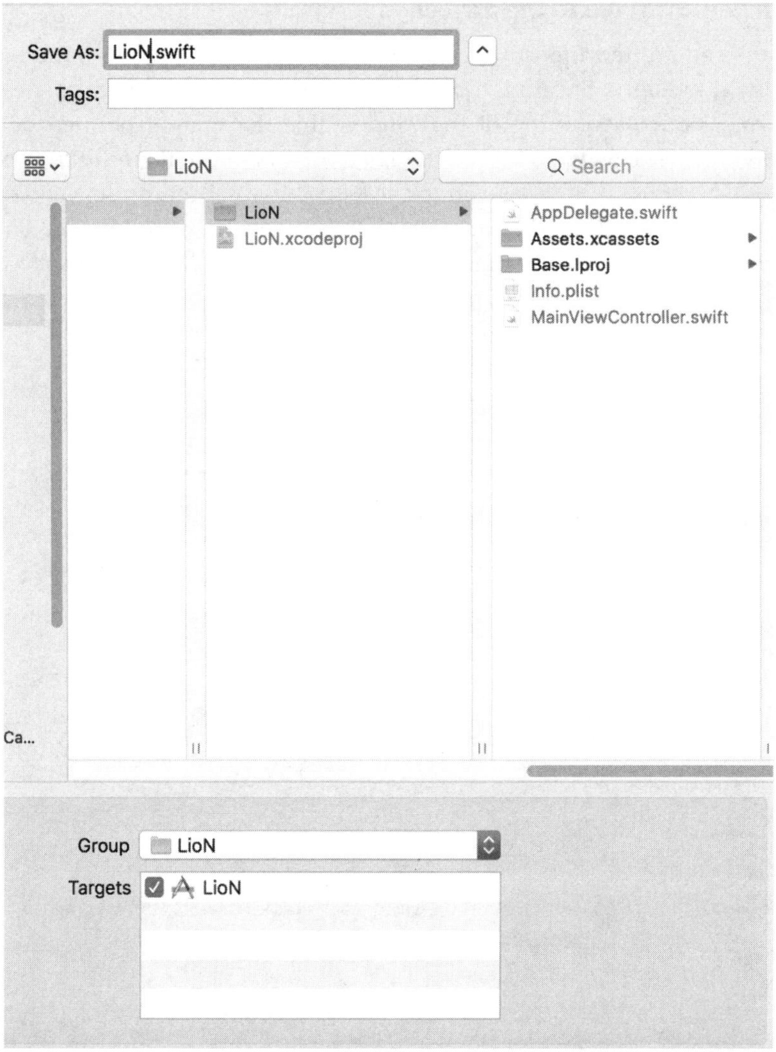

Figure 18.2   Name the file *LioN*, and make sure the LioN project is the target.

close. The new LioN.swift file should be in your Project Navigator list, and it should be open in the Editor.

Let's add the object to the file now, shall we?

MODELING THE DATA

If you remember, back in chapters 1 and 2 we talked about the pen object and how it might have a color, it might or might not have a cap, and so on. You're going to describe your LioN object in the same way but with its own properties. The first thing you need to do is create the `Lion` class so you can add properties to it. In your Lion.swift file, add the following below the `import Foundation` line:

```
class Lion {

}
```

As usual, Xcode is helpful. Once you type `class Lion` and the opening bracket, all you need to do is press Enter, and Xcode will add the closing bracket.

Your LioN object will have a name and a description, and it will have a `like` or `not-like` designation. Let's think about the best way to store this data. The `Name` property should be a string that users can add something meaningful to, like `"Wendy's toothpaste"`. Let's make that one a string. Add the following line below your class definition but between the brackets:

```
var lionName = ""
```

What is this line doing? You create a variable named `lionName` and set the initial value to a blank. Adding the two `""` tells Xcode that you plan to store a string in that field. Now you'll add the description below the name. Add a new line with this code:

```
var lionDescription = ""
```

Next, you need to add a variable to store whether you like this LioN. You'll use a *Boolean*, which stores `true` if you liked something and `false` if you didn't. Go ahead and create a Boolean to store your `like` value:

```
var like = true
```

I'm setting the default value of the `like` property `true`, because I'm a positive person like that. Your whole Lion.swift file should look like figure 18.3.

```
import Foundation

class Lion {
    var lionName = ""
    var lionDescription = ""
    var like = true
}
```

Figure 18.3   Create a Lion class with variables to hold the values for `lionName`, `lionDescription`, and `like`.

This is great work! Now you need to use this new model in your ViewController. Make sure you save the `Lion` class (press Command-S).

CREATING A NEW LION ENTRY

Remember I told you that you were going to code, test, and refactor repeatedly? Great— so don't be annoyed with me when I tell you to go delete something you've already done. Okay, go delete something you've already done. In your `MainViewController`, delete the array you created at the top of your class, and replace it with this line:

```
var lionData : [Lion] = []
```

Instead of creating the array of strings as you did before, you're telling Xcode that you want to create an empty array (hence the [and] with nothing between them) but that you'll fill it with LioN objects (hence the [Lion] definition).

Xcode should be giving you an error in the `cellForRowAtIndexPath` function. Your array isn't storing strings anymore; it's storing `Lion` objects. Xcode doesn't know how to set the cell's `textLabel` text equal to a `Lion` object. Let's fix that.

You still want the array `lionData`, and you still want to point to the right row (`indexPath.row`), but you need to tell it which value in the LioN to point to. This is the cool part. Make sure the project is saved (Command-S), and then add a period after the closing bracket of the line `cell.textLabel?.text = lionData[index-Path.row]`. You should see that Xcode provides three code-complete options for you—the three properties found in the LioN object, as shown in figure 18.4. How cool is that? Select `lionName`.

```
override func tableView(_ tableView: UITableView, cellForRowAt indexPath: IndexPath) -> UITableViewCell{
    let cell = tableView.dequeueReusableCell(withIdentifier: "lionCell", for: indexPath);
    cell.textLabel?.text = lionData[indexPath.row].
    cell.detailTextLabel?.text = lionDa    V   Bool like
    return cell                              V   String lionDescription
}                                            V   String lionName
```

Figure 18.4 Xcode's auto-complete function shows you the three properties you created for the LioN object. Select `lionName` to display on the cell.

Run the app again to make sure it works. Don't be surprised that the table view doesn't have data in it—you deleted the hardcoded values, so the `lionData` array is empty. But you'll fix it.

You finally get to use the `Lion` class to add data to the array. This is exciting, isn't it? You need to create a new LioN object, set its properties, and then add it to the `lion-Data` array. You're going to create the new LioN in the `viewDidLoad()` function, because this function is called before the table view gets set up (go back to chapter 13 if you need a refresher on the ViewController lifecycle).

Add the following code within the `viewDidLoad` brackets:

```
let toothpasteLion = Lion()
toothpasteLion.lionName = "Wendy's toothpaste"
toothpasteLion.lionDescription = "the one in the blue box"
toothpasteLion.like = true
```

The first thing you do is create a new LioN object—I called mine `toothpasteLion`, but you can name yours whatever you'd like. The next line sets the `lionName` value, followed by the `lionDescription`, followed by the `like` Boolean. So now you have a LioN object with values. Next you'll add it to your array so it will show up on the table view. Do you remember how to add something to an array? I'll give you a hint—you want to append it to the end of the array:

```
lionData.append(toothpasteLion)
```

Run the app again to see if your toothpaste shows up in the table view. Ahhh, man, this is cool, isn't it? Go ahead and create a few more LioN objects in the `viewDid-Load()` function so your table has more rows. Don't worry, I'll wait. I added another toothpaste to my array with the following:

- *Variable name*—`toothpasteLion2` (I know, not too imaginative)
- `lionName`—`Bad toothpaste`
- `lionDescription`—`The one in the red box`
- `like` = false

I have two LioN objects in my array, and you may have more than that, which is fine. You know what would be good, though? If the cell in the table showed the description of the LioN object, too. Let's make it so.

18.3   *Changing the layout of the table cell*

Right now, the table cell shows the `lionName` value for each LioN in your array. I think it would be nice to show the description of the LioN as well. Let's go back to the drawing board, er, storyboard. You're going to do the following:

1 Change the cell in the storyboard to show the description.
2 Update the function to show the description.

Let's go!

18.3.1 *Changing the cell in the storyboard to show the description*

I've said several times throughout this book that Swift is easy to learn and Xcode is your friend, and this part will demonstrate that yet again. Open your Main.storyboard file so it's showing in the Editor panel. Change your real estate by hiding the Project Navigator panel, and make sure the Document Outline panel is showing to the left of the Editor. If it isn't, click the button at the bottom of the Storyboard Editor panel that looks like a box with a vertical line on the left side of it. Your document outline should look similar to figure 18.5.

Notice in the Document Outline that you have the main LioN navigator at the top (the yellow circle—you renamed the navigator to LioN in chapter 17). Below the LioN navigator, you have the table view, which has a `lionCell` below it. The `lionCell` is the identifier that you gave the cell (for your reuse of the cell) in the last chapter. If you expand `lionCell` by clicking the triangle, you'll see the Content View. Expand

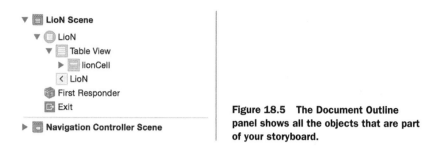

Figure 18.5   **The Document Outline panel shows all the objects that are part of your storyboard.**

it again, and you'll see the title label. You can tell it's a label because the icon next to it has a big blue *L* (like the monogram on Laverne's sweater in *Laverne and Shirley*). Xcode set all that up for you, and you only changed the title on the navigator and the identifier on the cell. Amazing.

I want to show the description on the cell, though, and there isn't a label there for a description. What to do? Never fear—Xcode is here. Select `lionCell` in the Document Outline panel. Make sure the Attributes panel is showing on the Utilities panel (right panel) so you can see which attributes are available to change on the cell. The first attribute is Style. Change that to Subtitle, as shown in figure 18.6.

Figure 18.6   **Change the cell style to Subtitle so it will show both a title and a subtitle on each cell.**

Once you change the style to Subtitle, you should see the cell in the Editor change to include the words *Title* and *Subtitle*. If you look back at your Document Outline, you should see a second label on the Content View. The second label also has a big blue *L*, because it's a label. Run the app again to see the subtitle. If the cells in your table appear under the top navigation bar, or they're slightly hidden by the navigation bar, go back to your storyboard, select the `UITableViewController` (the one you named LioN), and uncheck Extend Edges Under Top Bar (see figure 18.7).

Figure 18.7   **Deselect the Under Top Bars option.**

Well, I did say that you would see the subtitle, and that's all you see—the word Subtitle. Can you guess why? You haven't wired anything up to the subtitle label yet, so

Xcode displayed the value of the subtitle label, which is *Subtitle*. That won't do, so let's wire it up.

18.3.2 *Updating the function to show the description*

You saw in the last few paragraphs how easy it is to add a subtitle to a cell, because Swift and Xcode make it so easy. There are still some things that may make you scratch your head, though, and this section is about one of them. You set the cell title to `lionName` earlier, and it's so easy because you set the cell's title label to `lionName`. It's almost that easy to set the subtitle, but looking for the right label to update isn't intuitive.

Let's look at the `cellForRowAtIndexPath` function again:

```
cell.textLabel?.text = lionData[indexPath.row].lionName
```

You set the cell's text label equal to `lionName`. If you try to use Xcode's wonderful auto-complete function to set the subtitle text, you'll be looking for a long time. The subtitle label on the cell is `detailTextLabel` rather than `subtitle`—which is used on the storyboard. It isn't intuitive, but it's not that big of a problem once you know this. Next, add a line where you set the `lionName`:

```
cell.detailTextLabel?.text = lionData[indexPath.row].lionDescription
```

This should be pretty understandable, because you set the `lionName` earlier. Now run the app again. Oh man, oh man, this is so cool!

18.4 Summary

You accomplished a lot in this chapter. You refactored your code to use the Model-View-Controller pattern, and then you displayed the LioN description on the cell. You're going to add more and more functionality in each chapter, so make sure your code works at this point before moving on.

Displaying details of your LioN

This chapter covers

- Optionals
- Typecasting
- Optional binding

If you open the Contacts app on your iPhone, you'll notice that your contacts are displayed using a table view, and individual contacts are in a `tableView` cell. If you select one of those cells, another page loads with the details of that contact, and you can edit the contact if you choose. You're going to add the same type of functionality to your LioN app now.

19.1 Capturing the tapped row index

The first thing you need to do in order to display the details of a specific row is to capture which row the user tapped. If only there was a function that already captured this information! Oh, wait—there is. Open your `MainViewController` again, and start typing (outside of any other functions but still within the class) the following:

```
override func tableV
```

Xcode's auto-complete function will now display the functions that are available for you to select, as shown in figure 19.1. Let Xcode fill in the auto-complete data and add the didSelectRowAtIndexPath function to your code.

```
override func tableV
        M  tableView(_ tableView: UITableView, didSelectRowAt indexPath: IndexPath)
override    M  tableView(_ tableView: UITableView, didSelectRowAt indexPath: IndexPath)
    super   M  tableView(_ tableView: UITableView, didDeselectRowAt indexPath: IndexPath)
    let 
    tooth   M  tableView(_ tableView: UITableView, didDeselectRowAt indexPath: IndexPath)
    tooth   M  tableView(_ tableView: UITableView, didHighlightRowAt indexPath: IndexPath)
    tooth
    lion    M  tableView(_ tableView: UITableView, didHighlightRowAt indexPath: IndexPath)
    let     M  tableView(_ tableView: UITableView, didEndEditingRowAt indexPath: IndexPath?)
    tooth   M  tableView(_ tableView: UITableView, didEndEditingRowAt indexPath: IndexPath?)
    tooth  Tells the delegate that the specified row is now selected.
    tooth
```

Figure 19.1   Xcode uses auto-complete to display the available functions for the tableView. **Select the** didSelectRowAtIndexPath **function.**

Next you'll add a line to print out which row the user tapped to make sure you're capturing it correctly. Add the following line:

```
print(lionData[indexPath.row].lionName)
```

Run the app again, and tap several different rows. Your console should print out the name of your LioN objects. Mine looks like figure 19.2 after I tap a few rows.

```
Wendy's toothpaste
bad toothpaste
Wendy's toothpaste
bad toothpaste
```

All Output ◇

Figure 19.2   Adding the didSelectRowAtIndexPath **method lets you capture which row the user tapped.**

Now you know which row was tapped, so you can print the corresponding name stored in the LioN array. That's a good step, but you want to display the details of the LioN on another screen.

19.2   *Adding a detail page to the storyboard*

We're getting into the fun stuff. In this section, you'll add a new ViewController that will display the details of the LioN object, and you'll also add the code to wire it up. Here are the steps:

1   Add a ViewController to the storyboard, and create a segue.
2   Add a detail ViewController file.

Let's get to work!

19.2.1 *Adding a ViewController to the storyboard*

In order for your app to show the details of the LioN object, you need to create a new view for the user to interact with. The view will be where all the details are displayed, and the coding norm is therefore to call the view `DetailViewController`. You'll start by creating the view first.

ADDING THE NEW VIEW CONTROLLER

Open Main.storyboard in Xcode again, and make sure you set your real estate so you can work easily in the Editor. You've done this numerous times in previous chapters, so you should have a sense of what works for you as you show and hide panels. The first thing you want to do is add a ViewController to the storyboard. This will be the view that displays the details of the LioN. The ViewController is usually near the top of your Object Library, so grab one and drag it to the right of the table view with the prototype cell on it.

Now you need to connect the new prototype cell to the new ViewController so that when the cell is clicked, the new view will show.

CREATING A SEGUE

You connected two views together back in chapter 12, so you've done it before, but let's walk through it anyway. On the scene with your table view on it, click once on the prototype cell (it's called `lionCell`) so it's the active object. Control-click the cell, hold down the Control key, and drag your mouse pointer over to the new view. Once the new view turns blue, release the mouse button and the Control key. A new dialog will pop up, and you can select the kind of segue you would like to use (*segues* are the transitions between scenes). In this case, you want to select Show in the Selection Segue section at the top, as shown in figure 19.3.

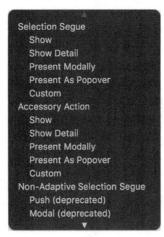

Figure 19.3   Choose the Show option in the Selection Segue section when this dialog pops up. This will connect your `lionCell` to your new view.

Run the app. Did you notice that Xcode automatically added the navigation bar at the top of the view? This means you can easily get back to the full list of `lions` by hitting the back button. You may be wondering where the word "LioN" came from on the back button. Xcode used the navigation bar title label for the back button label. If you change the navigation bar title label to something else, the back button will be updated. You can find the Navigation Bar Title attribute in the Attribute Inspector for the navigation bar. Pretty cool, huh?

RENAMING THE SEGUE

Most apps have more than one segue in them because they have more than one scene or ViewController that loads. You need to be able to tell the difference between the segues so you can take different actions depending on what the user action is. In your storyboard, click the segue—the arrow between your two ViewControllers, as shown in figure 19.4.

Figure 19.4   Click the segue between your two ViewControllers to change the Attributes Inspector panel so you can set the identifier for the segue.

Now you can change the identifier of the segue in the Attributes Inspector. Change the identifier to showLionDetail. You can run your app again, and it shouldn't look any different than the last time you ran it.

Next you're going to create a ViewController file to control what's presented on this scene.

19.2.2 *Creating a new ViewController class*

You have a ViewController for your main view (MainViewController), and you need one for the detail view. You're going to create a new file in the same way that you created the Lion.swift file. Click File > New > File, and select the Swift File template. Save it as DetailViewController.swift and leave the other fields as they are. Xcode will then load the empty file in the Editor window.

This time, instead of creating a Lion class, you want to create a DetailViewController class and have it inherit from UIViewController. Do you remember how to do this? I added the following code under the import Foundation statement:

```
class DetailViewController : UIViewController {
}
```

If you remember chapter 8, we talked about frameworks, which are a bunch of classes bundled together so we can use them when we need them. I suggested an analogy of building a house and only needing the plumbing tools. In this case, the Swift file that Xcode created for you is importing the Foundation framework. You don't need the Foundation framework—you need the framework that provides all the classes for your UI controller. Your UI classes are found in the UIKit, so you can delete the import Foundation statement and instead add import UIKit.

You'll add two functions to handle when the view loads and when the device is running low on memory. I added the two functions to my class inside the class definition (the curly brackets):

```
override func didReceiveMemoryWarning() {
    super.didReceiveMemoryWarning()
    // Dispose of any resources that can be recreated.
 }
override func viewDidLoad() {
    super.viewDidLoad()
}
```

I didn't retype these functions; I copied them directly from the `MainViewController`. I try to be as efficient as possible, and that includes copying existing code.

Now that you have your `DetailViewController` set up, you need to wire it to the ViewController on your storyboard. Right now, these are two separate objects that know nothing about each other. Open Main.storyboard, and click the top of the ViewController that you added earlier. In the Utilities panel, select the Identities Inspector (the third button from the left). You should see the panel in figure 19.5. Click in the Class field, and select the DetailViewController you created. If it doesn't show up, make sure you've saved your work.

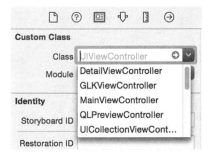

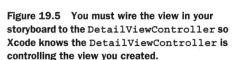

Figure 19.5   **You must wire the view in your storyboard to the `DetailViewController` so Xcode knows the `DetailViewController` is controlling the view you created.**

Run your code again, and it should work as it did before. This is great! You've created a new view in the storyboard and created the segue so it will show up when the user taps a row. You also created a `DetailViewController` and wired it to the new view. You'll use the `DetailViewController` to (can you guess?) display the details for the rows.

Next, you need to pass some data from `MainViewController` to the `DetailViewController` so it can be displayed on the new view. This is the same idea as opening the Contacts app on your iPhone or iPad and tapping one of the rows—a new view opens with the details of the contact.

19.3   *Passing data to the DetailViewController*

You have a LioN object that's stored in an array in the `MainViewController` class. When the user taps a row in the table view, you want that one LioN object to show up on the detail view with all the data present. There are two steps you need to take to implement this new functionality:

1 Prepare the `DetailViewController` to accept incoming data.
2 Update the `MainViewController` to pass the data.

19.3.1 *Preparing the DetailViewController to accept the LioN*

You have your LioN data stored in an array in the `MainViewController` class, but you want the user to be able to see it and eventually edit it when they tap a row in the table. To do this, you need to pass the `Lion` data to the `DetailViewController`.

Open the `DetailViewController` again, and add the following line under the class definition:

```
var lionDetail : Lion?
```

You're creating a variable called `lionDetail` and telling it that it will be of type `Lion`. What's with the question mark, though? This is something you haven't seen before, and it's a great feature of Swift. Let's talk about it next.

OPTIONALS

Imagine that you and I are friends and we're planning on going to a party tonight. I tell that you I'll drive my car to the party and you can drive it home (perhaps I'm staying the night). You get to the party, only to find out that I'm not there, so there's no car, and you have no way to get home. This is similar to a null pointer reference in the coding world.

You had planned to call my implementation of `rideHome()` for my car so you could drive my car; but I didn't show up with the car, so when you tried to call `wendys-Car.driveHome()`, you got an error message because my car didn't exist. Trust me—it's as rude in the coding world as it is in the real world. If you're expecting an object to be there (like a car), and you try to do something with the car—`openDoor()`, `driveHome()`, `turnLightsOn()`—and the car isn't there, you'll get what's called a *null pointer exception*. You can't call a function on an object that doesn't exist, even if you think it should exist.

Null pointer references have probably happened to every developer at some point in their career. Even when they created all the code, they expected that an object would be there to use, but for some reason, it wasn't. Apple created a way to handle this situation with the *optional*. The optional is the question mark ?, also known as an *interrogation point, query,* or *eroteme*. The preceding line of code is declaring a variable named `lionDetail`, which is of type `Lion`, and it may or may not be null. As you continue to add more code to the `DetailViewController`, the ? will tell Xcode to follow your instructions if `lionDetail` isn't null, or disregard the instruction if it is null.

> **Syntax alert!**
> The ? can be added to a variable definition to let Xcode know that the variable might be null.

Back to my extremely rude behavior. I told you I'd be at the party, so you made plans to drive my car home. With the optional, I would have told you that I *may or may not* be at the party. With *that* knowledge, you probably would have made a backup plan to get home in case I didn't show. I'm not nearly as rude as before—I have commitment issues.

PRINTING THE PASSED DATA

Now your `DetailViewController` has an optional variable named `lionDetail` (which you know may or may not be null). You'll take small steps to make sure it's getting passed correctly and print the value of the variable to the log. Add the following line within the `viewDidLoad()` function:

```
print(lionDetail?.lionName)
```

Notice the optional again. This line is telling Xcode, "If lionDetail is not null, then print the lionName." You have to use the ? each time you refer to `lionDetail` because you defined the variable as optional. If you run the app now, the `DetailViewController` won't print what you want because `lionDetail` is in fact null. You're going to fix that by editing the `MainViewController` to pass data into the `DetailViewController`.

19.3.2 *Updating the MainViewController to pass data*

Back in section 1.2.1, you named the segue used to transition between the `MainViewController` and the `DetailViewController`, and now you get to find out why. Remember what you're trying to do here: when you tap a row in the table view, you want the app to show the detail screen and show the details from the LioN object that was tapped. When the user taps a row, the segue is used to move to the next screen—so let's see what we can do with segues, shall we? Add the followings lines to your code in `MainViewController`—and remember that Xcode will try to use auto-complete to predict the function that you're trying to add:

```
override func prepare(for segue: UIStoryboardSegue, sender: Any?) {
```

This function is overriding the implementation of the superclass (hence the `override` keyword) and the function `prepare(for segue` gives you the opportunity to do things before the segue occurs. You can see the parameters for this function are `segue`, which is of type `UIStoryboardSegue`, and `sender`, which can be any kind of object but may also be null. The `Any?` is the object that's calling the function, and this is saying that anything can call it.

Most scenes on a storyboard will have more than one segue going between them, so it's a good idea to make sure you're responding to the correct segue. You're going to create an `if` statement to make sure that your code will run only when the show-LionDetail segue occurs.

Add the following code inside the `prepare(forSegue:...)` function:

```
if (segue.identifier == "showLionDetail"){
}
```

Remember, earlier you changed the segue's identifier attribute to `showLionDetail`. Now you're checking to see whether the identifier is equal to `showLionDetail`. Add the following line inside the `if` statement you wrote:

```
let controller = segue.destinationViewController as! DetailViewController
```

This line creates a new variable named `controller` and sets it equal to the segue's destination ViewController. You're telling Xcode to create a variable named `controller` and set it equal to whatever ViewController the segue is pointing to on the storyboard. Back in section 1.2.2, on the storyboard, you set the new ViewController equal to the class `DetailViewController`. That's what the segue is pointing to, right? You're saying to set the variable controller equal to the segue's `destinationViewController`, which in this case is the `DetailViewController`. But what's the deal with that `as!`, you may be wondering? I'm glad you're wondering, because I'm going to tell you.

THE AS!

Let's start by looking at `segue.destinationViewController`. In Xcode, Option-click the word `destinationViewController`, and a Quick Help pop-up window should appear, as shown in figure 19.6.

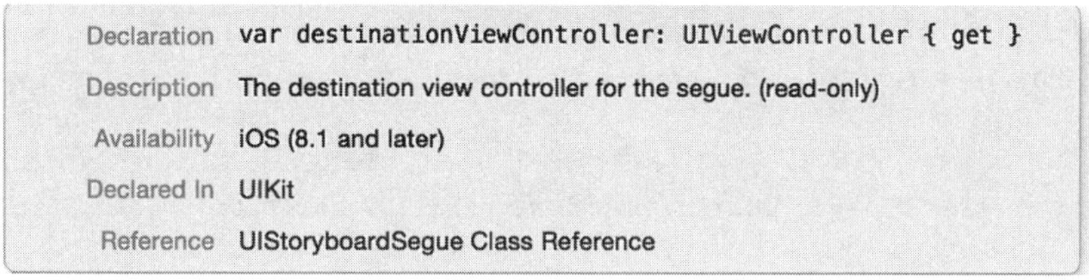

Declaration	`var destinationViewController: UIViewController { get }`
Description	The destination view controller for the segue. (read-only)
Availability	iOS (8.1 and later)
Declared In	UIKit
Reference	UIStoryboardSegue Class Reference

Figure 19.6   Option-clicking `destinationViewController` will load the Quick Help window.

As you can see in the first line (the declaration), `destinationViewController` is of type `UIViewController`. You created a variable (`controller`), and you're setting it equal to the `segue.destinationViewController`, which is a `UIViewController`. Great! This is all working out nicely, because your `DetailViewController` is a subclass of UIViewController (you can see this if you open the class DetailViewController and look at the class definition line). Again, you set your new controller variable equal to whatever the segue is pointing to (destinationViewController), which is of type UIViewController, but you want to specify that you want it to be the Detail-ViewController. Enter the as!.

> **Syntax alert!**
> The as? and as! keywords are ways to tell Xcode that one object should be treated as another object. as? lets Xcode know that the objects *might* be in the same class hierarchy, and as! tells Xcode to force the typecast, even if it might be wrong. The as! will create an error at runtime if the two aren't in the same class hierarchy.

The as! keyword is a way of typecasting one object to another. *Typecasting* allows you to treat something as if it were of a type of something in its class hierarchy. You know that your DetailViewController is of type UIViewController, and that the UIView-Controller is the superclass of the DetailViewController. The class hierarchy looks like figure 19.7.

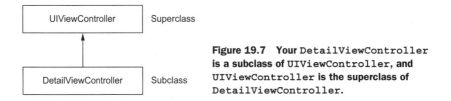

Figure 19.7   Your DetailViewController is a subclass of UIViewController, and UIViewController is the superclass of DetailViewController.

Because you're sure that the DetailViewController is a type of UIViewController, you can typecast UIViewController to DetailViewController. The as keyword lets you typecast from one to the other. If you weren't positive that the two were in the same class hierarchy, you could check by using the ? again. So the statement would be like this:

```
let controller = segue.destinationViewController as? DetailViewController
```

This is telling Xcode to set your controller variable to the segue's destinationView-Controller, and *if* it's in the same class hierarchy, typecast it to the DetailView-Controller. This is a safe way to go because you might not always know that the classes are in the same hierarchy, but in this case you're sure, so you use as!. This tells Xcode that you're absolutely sure the two are in the same class hierarchy and you're forcing the typecast even if it isn't right. If the two classes weren't in the same class hierarchy, this would cause an error in your app.

Now that you have a reference to your `DetailViewController`, you need to pass the data to it from the row the user tapped. Add the following lines below the `let controller` line:

```
if let indexPath = tableView.indexPathForSelectedRow{
}
```

You haven't seen the `if let` statement before, so let's talk about that now.

THE IF LET STATEMENT

In previous chapters, you created `if` statements to check the value of a variable, and you then executed some code (if x = y, then do something). The `if let` statement allows you to do the same thing but using less code and making the code more precise. If I were to write out the preceding code in longhand, it would look like this:

```
let indexPath = tableView.indexPathForSelectedRow
if indexPath != nil{
}
```

Again, I'm setting a new variable called `indexPath` equal to the `tableView`'s index-Path for the cell that the user tapped (typecast as a `UITableViewCell`). Then I'm checking to see whether the `indexPath` variable is null. (Apple uses the keyword `nil` for values that are null, so don't use *null, nada,* or *zippo* in your code—use `nil`.) This is a long way of doing it. Instead, I can shorten it to this:

```
if let indexPath = tableView.indexPathForSelectedRow {
}
```

The two statements do the exact same thing, but one is much more concise. The `if let` statement is known as *optional binding*—if the item isn't null, then set it equal to your variable.

Let's recap what you've done so far. You added a new function (`prepare(for-Segue:...)`) that will run after the user taps a row but before you segue to the next scene. Within that function, you added an `if` statement to check to make sure you were operating on the correct segue (`showLionDetail`).

> **Syntax alert!**
> The `if let` statement is known as *optional binding* and is a more concise way of check-ing a variable to make sure it isn't null and then setting it equal to another variable.

Within that check, you created a new variable called `controller`, a reference to the new `DetailViewController` scene. The preceding line is getting the `indexPath` (the loca-tion) of the row within the `tableView` that the user tapped. Now that you have the location of the cell, you can use that location to get the data from your array and pass it to the `DetailViewController`. Add this line within the `if let` statement:

```
controller.lionDetail = lionData[indexPath.row]
```

This line is taking the controller (your `DetailViewController`) and setting the variable `lionDetail` (that you created earlier in section 1.3.1) equal to `LionObject` in the array of `lionData` at the `indexPath.row` location.

Your entire `prepare(forSegue:...)` function should look like this:

```
override func prepare(for segue: UIStoryboardSegue, sender: Any?) {
    if (segue.identifier == "showLionDetail"){
        let controller = segue.destination as! DetailViewController
        if let indexPath = tableView.indexPathForSelectedRow{
            controller.lionDetail = lionData[indexPath.row]
        }
    }
}
```

Run the app again, and you should see the printout of the row you tapped. In my case, I tapped the first row and then went back and tapped the second row. This is what my console looks like:

```
Optional("Wendy\'s toothpaste")
Optional("bad toothpaste")
```

Remember that you made the variable `lionDetail` optional, so Xcode is printing that the optional variable contains "Wendy's toothpaste" and then "bad toothpaste".

19.4 *Summary*

You did quite a bit in this chapter. At a high level, you created the code necessary to pass data from the `MainViewController` to the `DetailViewController`. To do this, you created a new optional variable in the `DetailViewController`. Then, in the `MainViewController`, you captured the row the user tapped and passed that data to the `DetailViewController`.

You learned several new concepts in this chapter:

- *Optionals*—These are variables that can have a value or might be nil.
- *Typecasting*—This allows you to cast one class as another class, as long as the two classes share a hierarchy.
- `if let`—The `if let` statement shortens the code by checking to see whether the variable has data in the same line as setting it equal to a variable.

Remember that if you have a problem with this chapter, you can always download my source code from www.manning.com/books/anyone-can-create-an-app or https://github.com/wlwise/AnyoneCanCreateAnApp. Make sure your app runs before moving on to the next chapter. You're going to display the details of your LioN object in the `DetailViewController` in the next chapter, so this should be fun!

Creating the details of the detail view

This chapter covers

- Adding a detail screen to display the `lion` details
- Using `Int` values as a string
- Deleting `lion` objects from the list

You created the `DetailViewController` in the last chapter, and you were able to pass a `lion` object from the `MainViewController` to the `DetailViewController` and print the `Lion` name to the console. In this chapter, you'll add labels to the `DetailViewController` scene so you can display the `lion` object for the user.

20.1 Adding some labels to your detail screen

The first thing you're going to do is create three labels on the detail screen and connect them to your code through `IBOutlets`. You've done this several times in the book, so it shouldn't be new. Go into your storyboard, and drag three labels from the Object Library onto the `DetailViewController` scene. Drop them toward the top-left corner for now, and make them a little longer so they can display the `lion` details when you wire them up.

Next, open the Assistant Editor view (click the button at top right that looks like two interlocking circles). Control-click a label, drag it over to the DetailViewController .swift file, and drop it right under the class definition. Do this for each of the three labels, and name them like this:

- lblName
- lblDesc
- lblLike

I named them with the prefix lbl because they're labels and it will make my code easier to read in the future, because I know that all variables that start with lbl will be labels. Now that the three labels are on the scene and they're connected to your code, you'll set the values to the values of your Lion object that you passed in. If you think about how to do this, you want to set the text of label to the lionDetail object's lion-Name. How would you do that? Where would you do it? Here's how I did it; I put it inside in the viewDidLoad() function:

```
lblName.text = lionDetail?.lionName
```

Do the same for the description label:

```
lblDesc.text = lionDetail?.lionDescription
```

The like label won't work the same way as the description and the name. Do you know why? You defined the like property as an Int when you created the Lion object, and the label's text field is expecting a string. You could go back and change the Lion object's like type to a string if you wanted to, but I want it to stay as an Int. There are many ways to get the Int value into a string value, and some programmers have strong feelings about the proper way to do it. I'm of the opinion that if it works and it doesn't break any coding conventions, then it's considered proper.

20.1.1 *Converting an Int to a string using the description*

One way to get a string value of an Int is to use the Int's description. The *description* is what it sounds like—a textual description of the variable. You could do something like this:

```
lblLike.text = lionDetail?.like.description
```

This will return the value of either 1 for like or 0 for dislike.

20.1.2 *Converting an Int to a string using String*

Another way to get the string value of an Int is as follows:

```
lblLike.text = "\(lionDetail?.like)"
```

This is called *string interpolation.* You're creating a new string value by including the values inside a string literal (the \ () portion). This is probably the most accepted way of converting an Int to a string value; but again, there are many different ways of doing it, and my goal is to teach you how to do it so it works. From there you can build your knowledge about the other ways as you become more and more comfortable with the coding language. I'm going to use the first option, though, because the description function doesn't print out the word Optional like the string interpolation method does. In this case, I want the value 0 or 1 to show up.

Run the app, and you should see cells load like they did in the last chapter; but when you click the cells, the new view will load with the details of the lion object. This is pretty cool, I have to say. My DetailViewController looks like figure 20.1 right now.

```
import UIKit

class DetailViewController : UIViewController {

    @IBOutlet weak var lblLike: UILabel!
    @IBOutlet weak var lblDesc: UILabel!
    @IBOutlet weak var lblName: UILabel!
    var lionDetail : Lion?

    override func viewDidLoad() {
        print(lionDetail?.lionName)
        lblName.text = lionDetail?.lionName
        lblDesc.text = lionDetail?.lionDescription
        lblLike.text = lionDetail?.like.description
    }

    override func didReceiveMemoryWarning() {
        super.didReceiveMemoryWarning()
        // Dispose of any resources that can be recreated.
    }
}
```

Figure 20.1   The DetailViewController code up to this point includes three labels that are displayed based on the Lion object values.

To recap where you are with the app: you've created the new app with a tableView to hold the data. The data in the table is still hardcoded, but when you click the row, it opens the detail view, which displays the details of your Lion object. You can also click Back to go back to your view of all the Lion objects. This is a lot of functionality without writing a lot of code. Apple tries to make it as easy as it can for programmers by doing a lot of the plumbing behind the scenes so we don't have to.

You still have a lot of work to do on the app—like adding items to the list, making sure the list saves, and not hardcoding the values. In the next section, you'll add the functionality so you can add new items to the lion list.

20.2   *Adding new LioNs to the list*

You're going to add the Add button to the top bar (your navigation bar) so when a user taps it, it will open a new view for the user to enter the details of the new LioN item. This is like adding a new contact in your Contacts app on your iPhone. From the All Contacts screen in the Contacts app, you click the + button at top right, and you're presented with the form to create a new contact. You'll be doing the exact same thing, except you'll add LioNs instead of contacts.

The steps look like this:

1   Add the + button to the view.
2   Create a function to handle the action, and link the two together.
3   Hardcode values to add to your LioN list to test the functionality.
4   Add the ability to delete the items.
5   Change the code so the user can add their own LioN item (you'll do this in chapter 21).

This is a lot of new functionality. Let's get started.

20.2.1   *Adding the + button to the view*

You need to add a button to your navigation bar at the top of the view so users have a way to add new items. You won't believe how easy Apple has made this. Go back to the storyboard, and select the main LioN scene with the `TableViewController` on it. In the Object Library, search for *button* again, as you have many times before in this book. This time, however, you're adding a Bar Button Item instead of a regular Button, as you can see in figure 20.2.

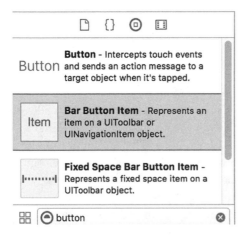

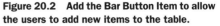

Figure 20.2   Add the Bar Button Item to allow the users to add new items to the table.

Drag the Bar Button Item to the top of the LioN view, and drop it on the right side of the navigation bar. Your view should look like figure 20.3.

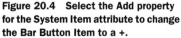

LioN   Item

Prototype Cells

Title
Subtitle

Figure 20.3   Drop the Bar Button Item on the top of the navigation bar on the LioN view.

Now you have a button on your navigation bar, but you want it to show a + sign so users can add items. With the Bar Button Item selected, open the Attributes panel, and you'll see the Style, System Item, and Tint attributes Click the System Item attribute, and you'll see all the different types of properties that can be set for this button. Change the attribute to Add (figure 20.4), and you'll see that your button changes to a + button.

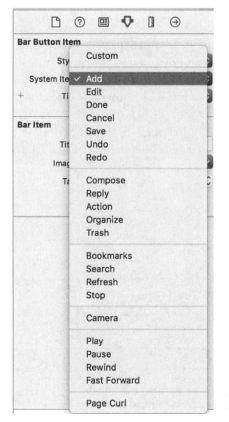

Figure 20.4   Select the Add property for the System Item attribute to change the Bar Button Item to a +.

You can click through the different options to see how they change the icon on the button—remember to set it back to Add when you're done. One thing to note here: the only thing that happens when you change the System Item attribute is the icon change. Apple isn't adding the code behind the scenes for the add functionality.

20.2.2 Creating a function to handle the action and link the two together

You have a + button on the view, and you need to create a function for that button to call. Open the `MainViewController` file so you can add a new function. Add the following code to the class file:

```
@IBAction func addItem(_ sender: AnyObject) {
print("add clicked")
}
```

You should know exactly what this does by now: when this function is called, it will print out the line `"add clicked"`. Next, you'll wire the + button to the `addItem` function on the storyboard. You should know how to wire the + button to the `addItem` function because you've done similar actions throughout the book, but I'm going to show you a different way to do it here.

In the past, you changed your real estate in Xcode to the Assistant Editor view so you could see both the storyboard and the ViewController. You then Control-clicked or right-clicked the item in the storyboard and dragged to the ViewController to create the link. You did it this way because the act of dragging and dropping to create the link created the function at the same time. In this case, though, you've already created the function `addItem()`, so there's an easier way.

In your storyboard, Control-click or right-click the + button, and drag to the top of the view, to the yellow circle with a square in it, as shown in figure 20.5. This is the icon that represents the `MainViewController`.

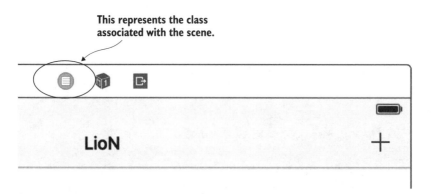

Figure 20.5   The yellow icon with the square in it represents the class that's associated with the scene. In this case, it's the `MainViewController` class.

If you hover your mouse pointer over the button, you'll notice that it says LioN, because that's the title you have on the Navigation Controller itself. When you release the button or the Control key, the black box pops up with the options to create the link between the storyboard button and the function in the `MainViewController`. Notice the add-Item() function in the list (figure 20.6). Connect the button to this outlet.

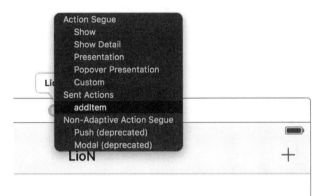

**Figure 20.6 Connect the +
button on the storyboard to
the `addItem` function in the
`MainViewController`.**

Once you've made the connection, run the app again and click the + button to make sure it's connected correctly. If all works well, you should see the words "add clicked" in the console. Great! Now you have a function that's called when the + button is clicked. Next you'll make it add something to your `Lion` array.

20.2.3 *Adding hardcoded values to the LioN list*

You need to replace the `print` statement in the `addItem()` function with code that will add values to the list of LioN objects. Delete the `print` statement to start with so you don't clutter up the code. To add a new row to the table, you need to know how many rows are in the table. If you remember back to chapter 11, when we talked about arrays, it's easy to add an object to the end of the array by using the `append()` function. Adding rows to a table isn't that easy, even though your data source for the table is an array. So you need to know how many rows are in the table and then add an object to the end of the table.

The `lionData` array in the `MainViewController` holds the LioN objects you've created so far ("Wendy's toothpaste" and "bad toothpaste," in my case). You know that there are exactly the same number of LioN objects in this array as there are in the table, because the array is the data source for the table. So the `tableView` created one row for each LioN in the array `lionData`. This means you know the number of rows in the table by counting the number of objects in the `lionData` array. Add this code to the `addItem()` function in your `MainViewController`:

```
let currentIndex = lionData.count
```

Next, create a new LioN object to insert into the array. See if you can create the object and set the properties without looking at how I did it. Set the properties as follows:

```
Like = 1
lionDescription = "hardcoded description"
lionName = "hardcoded name"
```

How did you do? This is how I created the new LioN and set the properties:

```
let newLion = Lion()
newLion.like = 1
newLion.lionDescription = "Hardcoded description"
newLion.lionName = "hardcoded name"
```

You need to add this new LioN object to the `lionData` array. I've already hinted about how to do this—see if you remember how to do it yourself.

This is how I did it:

```
lionData.append(newLion)
```

Now you know the number of rows in the `tableView`, you've created a new LioN object with hardcoded values, and you've added it to the `lionData` array. You need to insert a new row at the end of the `tableView` to display your new LioN object.

You may remember that back in chapter 17, we talked about an index path and how it was a pointer to a row in the table view. Table views have an array of index paths that hold pointers to the rows for each section of the table view. You only have one section of data in the table view, so you only have one index path in the array of index paths. So you need to create a new variable to point to the row you want to insert. Add the following line to your code:

```
let indexPath = IndexPath(row: currentIndex, section: 0)
```

Here you create a constant variable named `indexPath` that's an `NSIndexPath`. The arguments for creating the index path are `forRow:`, which takes an `Int` value, and `inSection:`, which also takes an `Int` value. You may be wondering why you aren't creating the `indexPath` as one value larger than the array count, rather than the array count itself. If you remember, the count of the `lionData` array is 2, meaning there are two LioN objects in the array. You start counting your values at 0, though, remember? If I wanted to print the values in the array, I'd do so by using index 0 and index 1, not index 1 and index 2. When you create your `indexPath` using the count of the objects in the array (2), you're indexing a new row. This is the same reason you're using 0 as the `inSection` value—because there's only one section in your table, and it resides at the first index, which is 0.

Now you have a new `indexPath` variable that points to the new row that you want to create in your table view, and you need to insert the data. You have one more step before you can do this, though. Again, as I mentioned in chapter 17, tables use an array of `indexPaths`—so you'll need to do that here. Add the following line of code to the function:

```
let indexPaths = [indexPath]
```

This line creates a new constant variable called `indexPaths`, which is an array with only one object in it (the `indexPath` variable). You know it's an array because it has the square brackets around it.

You have everything you need to insert a row in the table. The `lionData` array, which is the data source for the table, has a new object called `newLion`. You have the `indexPath` for the table view that you want to insert the data into, and you created an array to hold the `indexPath` variable so you could pass in the expected arguments to the function you need to call.

Let's call it. Add the following line of code:

```
tableView.insertRows(at: indexPaths, with: .automatic)
```

Not surprisingly, you're calling the `insertRowsAtIndexPaths` function of the `table-View` and passing in two arguments: `indexPaths` and the type of animation you want. You pass in the row animation type, which is an animation of how the row appears when it's inserted. Many options are enumerated for you (figure 20.7)—you can see these when you type the entire line of code up to the `.Automatic` and let Xcode show the values that are available. You can set the animations to the different options to see what they do, but I recommend using Automatic.

Figure 20.7 The Xcode auto-complete function will show you the different animation options for adding a row to the table view.

My complete `addItem()` function looks like this:

```
@IBAction func addItem(){
    let currentIndex = lionData.count
    let newLion = Lion()
    newLion.like = 1
    newLion.lionDescription = "Hard coded description"
    newLion.lionName = "hard coded name"
    lionData.append(newLion)
    let indexPath = NSIndexPath(forRow: currentIndex, inSection: 0)
```

```
    let indexPaths = [indexPath]
    tableView.insertRowsAtIndexPaths(indexPaths, withRowAnimation: .Automatic)
}
```

You can run the app now and click the + button, and you should see one row added for each time you click the button. You can click the button as many times as you want, and the app will keep adding rows. You'll also notice that the new rows aren't saved when you close the app and open it again. That's because you haven't added the code to save your data yet, so it's working as expected. You do want to be delete items from the list, though, so you'll do that next.

20.2.4 *Deleting LioNs from the list*

Apple provides a function that will allow you to easily delete your row, but the name of the function isn't as intuitive as you'd expect. If I were to think up a name for it, I'd call it something like `tableView delete row`, but alas, I'm not the queen, so we'll have to go with Apple's implementation. Add the following function to your code in the `MainViewController`:

```
override func tableView(_ tableView: UITableView, commit editingStyle:
➥ UITableViewCellEditingStyle, forRowAt indexPath: IndexPath) {
}
```

Although the name of this function doesn't seem intuitive (at least, to me), it allows the table to go into editing mode. If you run the app, you'll notice that when you swipe from right to left on a cell (click the mouse button, hold it down, and move it to the left), you're presented with the option to delete the row. You haven't coded anything yet to tell it what to do, but adding this function to your code enables the delete action on the table.

You'll fix that now and add the code to delete an item from the list. Remember that earlier, when you added a new row, you first had to add it to the array (which is the data source for the table) and then add it to the table itself. You need to do the same thing for deleting a row: remove it from the array and the table.

Add the following line to remove it from the array:

```
lionData.remove(at: indexPath.row)
```

And remove it from the table as well:

```
let indexPaths = [indexPath]
tableView.deleteRows(at: indexPaths, with: .automatic)
```

As with `insert row`, you first have to create an array of your one index path because the `delete row` function is expecting an array as an argument, not a single index path. My `commitEditingStyle()` code looks like this:

```
override func tableView(_ tableView: UITableView, commit editingStyle:
➥ UITableViewCellEditingStyle, forRowAt indexPath: IndexPath) {
```

```
    lionData.remove(at: indexPath.row)
    let indexPaths = [indexPath]
    tableView.deleteRows(at: indexPaths, with: .automatic)
}
```

Run the app, and see that you can delete a row, and it's removed from the table. It's amazing that all you had to do was use one of the functions that Apple provided and then add three lines of code in order to delete items from the table.

20.3 Summary

You accomplished a lot in this chapter. You added a new detail screen with three labels to display the name, description, and like value of each of the LioN objects. You then passed the LioN object to the detail screen so you could display the details. Next, you added the code to create new LioN objects and add them to the table. Finally, you added the code necessary to delete items from the table.

If you think back to chapter 1, you didn't know how to write any code, and now you have an app that can display rows of data, add new data, and delete data. Pretty amazing, if you ask me.

Where do we go from here? In the next chapter, I'm going to show you how to add a new LioN that isn't hardcoded. You'll implement the functionality to edit an existing LioN, and then you'll learn how to save the data so it reloads every time the app is launched. Remember, make sure your code is working at this point before moving on to the next chapter. If you can't get it working, post on the book forum, and I'll help you out, or download my source code at www.manning.com/books/anyone-can-create-an-app) or https://github.com/wlwise/AnyoneCanCreateAnApp.

The AddEditView scene

This chapter covers

- Adding functionality to add new LioNs
- Adding keyboard behaviors
- Adding gesture recognizers

You have a good start on the LioN app, and it's time to add some more functionality. Remember that a lot of programming is adding a bit of functionality, testing it, editing it, adding more functionality, and so on. It's generally a good idea to add small bits of functionality so you can test it and make sure it's working. If you find an error, it's relatively easy to figure out because you only added a few lines of code. Why am I telling you this again? Because it's sometimes hard to delete work that you've already completed, but that's how we're going to start this chapter.

21.1 Creating a new detail view

You have several steps to follow now, so I'll list them here:

1 Add a new `TableViewController`.
2 Add a new `AddEditViewController`.
3 Hook up the Cancel and Done buttons.

21.1.1 *Adding a new Table ViewController*

You'll start by deleting the existing `DetailViewController` from the storyboard. Select the entire detail view, and click Delete. Don't worry; you'll be adding a new one. Go to the Object Library, and search on *table*. Grab the top item returned—Table-ViewController—and drop it next to the main scene (the LioN screen). Next you'll connect the row of the `MainViewController` to a segue which will show the detail view, just like you did when you created the first `DetailViewController`. On the storyboard, Control-click the table row in the `MainViewController`, and drag it to the new scene. Use the Show Detail option for the action segue type.

In chapter 20, you added an identifier for the segue from the `MainViewController` to the `DetailViewController`, and you also added a function in the `MainView-Controller` to handle the segue. The function is `prepareForSegue`, and you no longer need it. You can delete the entire function from the `MainViewController`—so delete these lines:

```
override func prepareForSegue(segue: UIStoryboardSegue, sender: AnyObject?) {
    if (segue.identifier == "showLionDetail"){
 let controller = segue.destinationViewController as! AddEditViewController
        if let indexPath = tableView.indexPathForCell(sender as!
        UITableViewCell){
           controller.lionDetail = lionData[indexPath.row]
       }
    }
}
```

Now connect the action of the Add button to the new `TableViewController`, and select Present Modally as the action segue type. You should have two segues from the `MainViewController`: one from the table row (Show Detail) and one from the add button (Present Modally). Run the app to make sure the new table shows correctly when you click the Add button. What did you notice? There's no way to get back to your main scene—you're stranded. It's never good to leave a user stranded anywhere in your app, so you definitely need to change that. You need to add a navigation bar at the top of the screen so you can add buttons for the users to navigate back to the previous view and to click Done when they're finished adding an item. Your first instinct might be to look in the Object Library for a navigation bar, but there's an easier way.

Click the new `TableViewController` scene first; then, in the Xcode menu, select Editor > Embed In > Navigation Controller. This automatically adds the navigation bar at the top and a controller to control the actions. Very convenient! If you run the app again…there's no change. Well, that was a little anticlimactic. You have the navigation bar, but you need to add the buttons to perform the back and done actions. You did this in the last chapter when you created the Add button (+ button)—do you remember how?

Search on *button* in the Object Library, and select Bar Button Item. Drag one to the top left of the navigation bar on your `TableViewController` and one to the top right of the `TableViewController`. Your `TableViewController` should look like figure 21.1.

Figure 21.1   The `TableViewController` scene should have two bar button items on the top—one at the right and one at the left—after you add them from the Object Library.

Change the left bar button item to Cancel and the right bar button to Done. As you may remember from chapter 20, you select the button on the scene and then change the System Item attribute in the Attribute Inspector panel.

Now, run your app again, and test the new buttons, and…anticlimactic again! (Does it feel like I keep setting you up for this?) You haven't added any code yet to connect the buttons to, so you'll do that now.

21.1.2 Adding a new AddEditViewController class

You don't have a class to connect this to yet, but you do still have the `DetailView-Controller` class in the project. You don't need it anymore, so select the class (`DetailViewController.swift`) in the project navigator and press Delete. Xcode will ask if you want to remove the reference or delete the file (Move to Trash). You want to delete the file, sending it to the Trash on your Mac. If you remove the reference, it will remove the file from your Xcode project, but the file will still be in the project files on your computer. You won't need this in the future, so it's safe to completely delete this one.

Create a new file by going to File > New > File; when the dialog box pops up, select iOS, Source, Swift File. Like last time, be careful in this dialog box, because there are several different Swift files to choose from: the iOS Source Swift file, the watchOS Swift file, the tvOS Swift file, and the macOS Source Swift file. You obviously want the iOS Source Swift file.

When you get to the naming dialog, name it `AddEditViewController`. I happen to know (because I'm writing the book, after all) that we can use the same ViewController for adding and editing LioNs, so I'm naming the file for both the `Add` and the `Edit` functions. If you didn't do this here, you could rename the file later, but I decided to make it easier in this case.

In previous chapters, when you added new files to your project, the first thing you needed to do was import the proper framework. You can delete the `import Foundation` line at the top of the file and instead add `import UIKit` so you'll have the right tools available to you. Next, you need to create your class definition, so add the following class definition under the `import` line:

```
class AddEditViewController: UITableViewController{
}
```

You're defining the `AddEditViewController` class and saying that it inherits from the `UITableViewController` class. If you don't remember details about the ViewControllers or inheritance, go brush up on it in chapter 13. You need to add your `View-DidLoad()` function too, so add the following lines in the class:

```
override func viewDidLoad() {
    super.viewDidLoad()
}
```

You also need to add the `didReceiveMemoryWarning()`, so add these lines below the `viewDidLoad()` function:

```
override func didReceiveMemoryWarning() {
        super.didReceiveMemoryWarning()
    }
```

Now you need to let the storyboard know that the `AddEditViewController` class is the controller for your new scene. Do you remember how to do this? Go into your storyboard again, select the new scene, and open the Identity Inspector panel on the top right (figure 21.2). You want to select the `AddEditViewController` from the drop-down list for the `Class` property. If you don't see it there, go back to your code and make sure you defined the `AddEditViewController` as a type of `UITableViewController`, and not just a `UIViewController`, and make sure you saved your code.

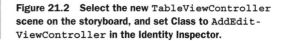

Figure 21.2 **Select the new `TableViewController` scene on the storyboard, and set Class to `AddEdit-ViewController` in the Identity Inspector.**

If you run the app now, there aren't any errors—which is a good thing. You need to hook up your Done and Cancel buttons, though, so users can get back to the main screen. Let's do it!

21.1.3 *Hooking up the Cancel and Done buttons*

You need the `AddEditViewController` scene to dismiss when you're done with it so the main scene will show up again. You're going to add two action outlets, one for the Cancel button and one for the Done button. Add the following two functions to the `AddEditViewController` file:

```
@IBAction func doneClicked(){
}

@IBAction func cancelClicked(){
}
```

You want to dismiss the `AddEditViewController` when either button is clicked, so the user will be taken back to the `MainViewController` scene, and fortunately there's an easy way to do this. Add the following line to both functions:

```
dismiss(animated: true, completion: nil)
```

Finally, you'll hook up the buttons to the new functions. Go back to your storyboard, Control-click the Cancel button, and drag it up to the yellow icon at the top of the scene (it represents the `AddEditViewController` object). When you let go, you should see both the `doneClicked` and `cancelClicked` functions available to connect to. If you don't see them, it means you didn't set the scene to be the `AddEditViewController` (see section 21.1.2) or you didn't save the file before moving back to the storyboard. Do the same thing with the Done button. Once the buttons are connected, you can run the app again to test it, and both the Cancel and Done buttons should take you back to the main view.

21.1.4 *Checkpoint*

Let's pause for a moment and review where you are and what you just did. First, you deleted the `DetailViewController` class from the project navigator, and you also deleted the scene from the storyboard. You then added a new `TableViewController` to the storyboard and embedded a navigation controller into the `TableViewController` so you could add Done and Cancel buttons to the scene. If you can't get the app working at this point, make sure you added a `TableViewController` to the storyboard, and not a table view.

You then added a new iOS Source Swift file to the project, named it `AddEdit-VicViewController`, and made it inherit from the `UITableViewController` class. This makes sense because you added a `TableViewController` to your storyboard, doesn't it? You then set the class identifier of the `TableViewController` scene on the storyboard to your new `AddEditViewController` class so Xcode knows that they're tied together.

Finally, you hooked up your Cancel and Done buttons so the `AddEditView-Controller` would be dismissed when either button is clicked. Take a good, deep breath now. You've made it this far. You've implemented the basics for adding and editing an actual LioN object. Let's get back to it, shall we?

21.2 Adding new LioNs

In this section, you're going to build out the Add New Lion screen so it looks like figure 21.3. Go back to your main storyboard, and click the `AddEditViewController`'s table view so it's the active item. Change the TableView Content attribute to Static Cells (figure 21.4), and you'll see three rows appear on your table view. Next, change the table view style to Grouped. This will group the cells together and add a little color to the background. Your table view should look pretty good now—make sure it looks like figure 21.5 before you continue.

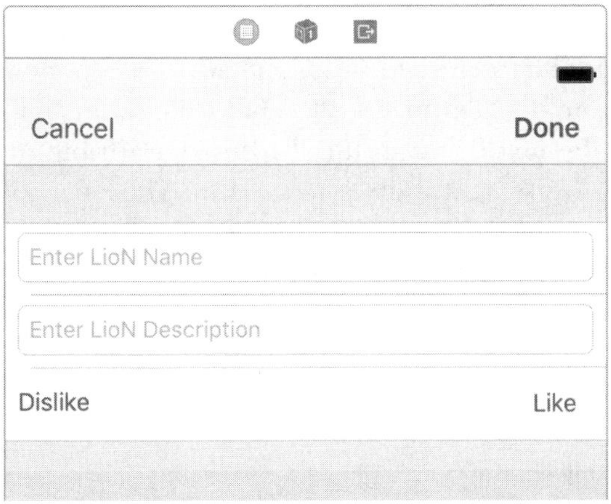

Figure 21.3   The Add New Lion scene will have two text boxes and two buttons.

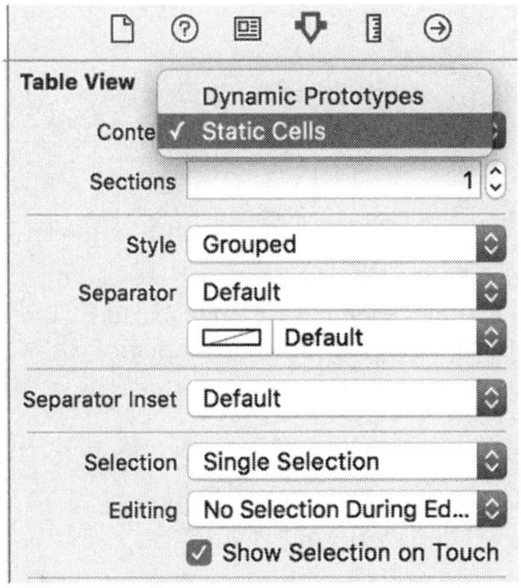

Figure 21.4   Change the table view Content to Static Cells, and Style to Grouped.

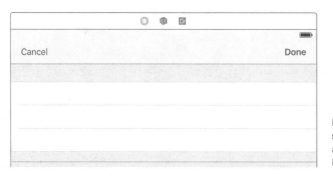

Figure 21.5   The table view should have three static cells, and it should be grouped so it looks like this.

Search the Object Library for *text*, and the top result will be Text Field (make sure you grab the Text Field and not the Text View). Drag one text field to the first row, and size it so it takes up most of the row. Drag a second text field to the second row, and size it the same as the first. Click the first text field so it's the active component in your view, and then add some placeholder text in the Placeholder field in the Attribute Inspector. Make sure to enter the text below in the Placeholder attribute (the sixth attribute from the top) and not the Text attribute (figure 21.6). The Placeholder attribute displays text that disappears when the user taps the field, and the Text attribute puts text in the field that the user must delete before they can type something in. I entered the following in the Placeholder attribute:

- *For the first text box*—Enter a Lion Name
- *For the second text box*—Enter a Lion Description

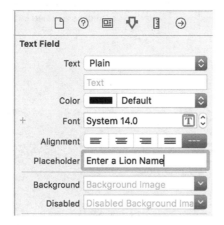

Figure 21.6   Enter placeholder text for the first and second text fields for the LioN name and the LioN description.

Next you'll add the Like and Dislike buttons to the third row. Search the Object Library for a button, and drag two buttons to the third row. Make sure you select the Button object and not a bar button item. One button should be on the far right, the other on the far left. Double-click each button to change the titles. The one on the far left should be Dislike, and the one on the far right should be Like.

Run the app, and make sure it looks like mine does in figure 21.3. If you can't see the Like button and the text boxes are cut off on the right side, go back to the storyboard, make the text boxes smaller, and move the Like button to the left. You'll fix the alignment in later chapters so it looks good on all different devices. Click one of the text fields, and your keyboard should pop up for you to enter text. Notice that the keyboard doesn't go away, no matter where you tap the scene after you've clicked in the text box. You'll fix that in a minute. Click the Like or Dislike button, and then click somewhere on the cell between the two buttons. The cell is now selected, and you can't deselect it, either. Let's see how to fix both of these problems.

21.2.1 *Don't allow the cell to be selected*

The table view default is to allow the cells to be selected, so you need to change that. If you run the app right now and select a row, you'll notice that the row looks selected—it changes color to show it's selected. You don't want that. Open your AddEditView-Controller file, and add the following code:

```
override func tableView(_ tableView: UITableView, willSelectRowAt indexPath:
    IndexPath) -> IndexPath? {
        return nil
}
```

This function is part of the TableView delegate—the user taps a cell, and the table view calls this function, but you're returning nil, telling the table view not to select the row. If you run the app, you should see that you can click between the Like and Dislike buttons, and the row briefly turns gray and then back to white. This is the time it takes for the table view to call the function above and return the nil. This flicker of gray doesn't look good, so you'll fix that, too.

Go back into your storyboard, and click the cell with the two buttons. Change the Selection attribute to None (figure 21.7). Run the app again, and the behavior of the cell is much cleaner when you click in it.

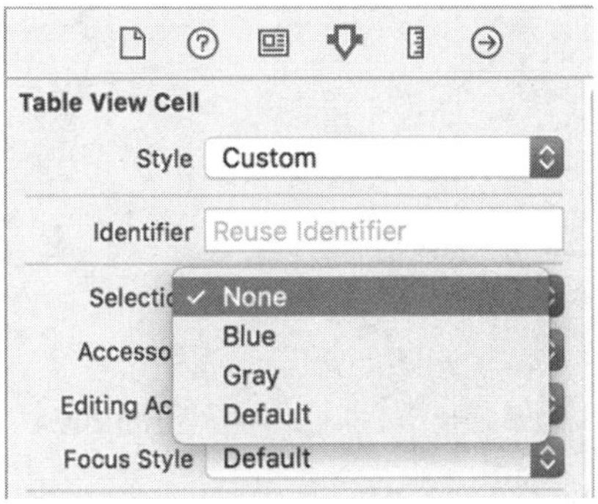

Figure 21.7 Change the third cell's Selection property to None so the user can't tap the cell and select it.

21.2.2 *Setting the keyboard behaviors*

It's a good practice to dismiss the keyboard when the user taps out of the text field. This is especially important when you only have so much room on your scene and the keyboard hides a portion of it so the user can't take action on items hidden by the keyboard. Although you don't have that problem with your current real estate, you're going to implement it anyway because it's good practice and you need to know how to do it.

The UITextField components have functions to control most of their behavior already, so you just need to use those functions. How? How can you make use of the text field functions without implementing everything yourself? Our friend the delegate steps in from stage left to help you out. The UITextField component has a lot of functionality as part of its definition, so you just need to become delegates of it in order to access some of it. Do you remember how?

Open the AddEditViewController file again, and look at the class definition. Ring any bells? All you need to do to be a delegate for any UITextField component is add the delegate to the class definition. Change the definition to this:

```
class AddEditViewController: UITableViewController, UITextFieldDelegate{
```

Isn't that amazing? You have access to the functions of the text field component just by conforming to the protocol. You have to tell the text fields themselves that your class will be the delegate, so go back into the storyboard, Control-click the text field, drag it to the yellow square at the top of the scene, and connect the delegate outlet for each text field (figure 21.8). You'll have to do this for each text field, so you should remember how to do this.

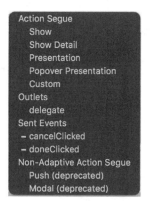

Figure 21.8   Connect the text field to the AddEditViewController's delegate outlet.

Now all you have to do to dismiss the keyboard is to implement a function:

```
func textFieldShouldReturn(_ textField: UITextField) -> Bool {
        resignFirstResponder()
        return true
    }
```

This function is called by the textField when the user taps the Return key. It asks the delegate whether the text field should process the Return key press, so you return true. What about that resignFirstResponder() thing, though? What's that? It basically tells the app that it's relinquishing *focus*—or it shouldn't be the active component on the view. Test your app again, and you should notice that the keyboard is dismissed when the user taps Return. This is great behavior for when the user taps Done after they enter text in the description field, but it's annoying when the user presses Done after entering text in the name field. It would be much nicer if the focus moved from the name field to the description field when the user presses Done, don't you think? Let's fix that next.

You'll first add some outlets for the text fields so you can access each of them in your code. You've done this numerous times before. You just need to Control-click the text field box, drag it into the AddEditViewController code, and name the outlet for each one. I named mine as follows:

- nameTxt
- descTxt

I have the following two lines at the top of my AddEditViewController class:

```
@IBOutlet weak var descTxt: UITextField!
@IBOutlet weak var nameTxt: UITextField!
```

Great! Now I can manipulate these components in my code. You're going to edit the textFieldShouldReturn function so when the user is finished entering the name of the LioN and presses Enter, the description field has focus; and when they press Enter on the description field, the keyboard hides itself. This sounds like it's going to be a lot of code, doesn't it? Nope! It's pretty easy now that you have the textFieldShould-Return function and you have outlets to your two text fields.

If the text field that's calling textFieldShouldReturn is equal to nameTxt, then make the descTxt field the first responder. Otherwise (else), if the text field is the descTxt field, dismiss the keyboard. This is my pseudocode—can you implement it without looking at the following code?

Here's my code:

```
func textFieldShouldReturn(_ textField: UITextField) -> Bool {
    if (textField == nameTxt){
        nameTxt.resignFirstResponder()
        descTxt.becomeFirstResponder()
    }else {
        descTxt.resignFirstResponder()
    }
    return true
}
```

How did you do? Run the app, and test it out. Clicking in the Name field should bring up the keyboard, pressing the Return key should move the focus to the Description field, and then pressing the Return key again should dismiss the keyboard. Pretty cool, huh? You still have one problem, though: iPhones and iPads are touch-enabled, meaning the user can touch anywhere on the screen. You really want the keyboard to dismiss if the user taps anywhere on the screen, not just when they press the Return key. You can see this behavior when you open the Safari app on your device. If you tap into the address bar, the keyboard pops up so you can enter a URL. If you tap out of the address bar, the keyboard is dismissed. You're going to add this functionality to your app next.

21.2.3 *Dismissing the keyboard on user tap*

iOS was developed specifically for devices in which the user can tap the screen and expect a response, like iPhones and iPads. This means Apple must have a way to know when those taps occur. There are classes that handle all the different kinds of actions the users can make on a screen:

- UITapGestureRecognizer
- UIPinchGestureRecognizer
- UIRotationGestureRecognizer
- UISwipeGestureRecognizer
- UIPanGestureRecognizer
- UIScreenEdgePanGestureRecognizer
- UILongPressGestureRecognizer

You can see from this list that you can capture every kind of gesture a user makes. In this case, you only want to capture the tap gesture (the first in the list). You're going to create a variable of type UITapGestureRecognizer so that when a tap occurs, you dismiss the keyboard. Add the following lines inside the viewDidLoad() function:

```
let tap = UITapGestureRecognizer(target: self,
    action: #selector(dismissKeyboard))
 view.addGestureRecognizer(tap)
```

The first line creates the variable named tap, which is of type UITapGestureRecognizer, and sets the target of the tap to the view itself. The action: argument is new, but it's essentially saying, "When a tap occurs, call a function named dismissKeyboard." The next line adds the tap gesture recognizer to the view. All you need to do to complete this is add a dismissKeyboard function to your code! Add the following lines to your code as a new function:

```
func dismissKeyboard(){
    view.endEditing(true)
}
```

This function is called anytime the user taps the screen. If you want to add a print line to see that, feel free! When this function is called, endEditing(true) resigns the first responder (or loses focus), and `true` forces the view to resign first responder, whether it wants to or not.

> **Important note**
>
> I've spent a lot of time debugging apps because the action argument name that I specify in the gesture recognizer doesn't exactly match the function I've created. It's important that the action function is identical to the function you create—in this case, `dismissKeyboard`. If you want to see what error it generates when it can't find the right function, change a single letter in the `dismissKeyboard` declaration to see the error you get. You'll get an "Unrecognized selector" error, and you'll probably be confused because you just *knew* you implemented the function correctly. Make sure your `#selector:` argument always matches the function you create for it to call.

If you want to implement different types of gesture recognizers to test them out, feel free. It's kind of fun capturing those events, because you can actually do it. Run the app, and test it out. You should be able to tap into the Name field, press Return, get to the next text field, and then tap anywhere to get rid of the keyboard.

But there's still one piece missing that a user will find rather annoying if they use the app. When the scene first launches, you know the user will want to add a name for the LioN as the first action. You currently require them to tap in the Name field in order to start typing, and that's a tap they shouldn't have to make. This may seem like a small thing right now, but you'll get complaints about your app when you make users click and tap things that they shouldn't have to. How do you think you can make the first text field focus when the scene launches?

I hope you thought of the `viewDidLoad()` function, because that's where you can make the Name text field the first responder so it has focus when the scene first loads. You need to have the `nameTxt` field become the first responder, so add that now:

```
nameTxt.becomeFirstResponder()
```

Run the app, and it should behave like a well-thought-out app. It's important to think of the user when you design and create your app, not just how you—the developer—would use the app. Nobody likes apps that require them to do more than they should have to do, and the reviews in the App Store will definitely let you know that you didn't think of the user as you designed it.

21.3 Summary

Wow! You added a lot of cool stuff in this chapter. You created a new class—the Add-EditViewController class—and connected it to a new view. You created the new view with three rows for the LioN properties and then added text boxes and buttons to show and edit those properties. More important, you learned about controlling keyboard functionality, how to make different fields have focus, how to move focus between fields, and how to recognize gestures. These items will probably be used in every app you ever create—because apps are meant to be interacted with, after all.

In the next chapter, you'll create new LioNs and store them in your array. More fun awaits! As usual, make sure your app works up to this point. If you're having problems, download my source code (www.manning.com/books/anyone-can-create-an-app or https://github.com/wlwise/AnyoneCanCreateAnApp) or drop me a note on the Author's Forum or Twitter, and I'll check it out.

Delegates are everywhere

This chapter covers

- Adding new LioNs
- Implementing the Delegate pattern
- Adding the `like` and `dislike` properties

You added a lot of functionality in the last chapter, but you still haven't added the functionality you need to let a user create a new LioN. You're going to do that in this chapter, but you're also going to use delegates again. You learned about delegates in chapter 16, so refer back there if you need a refresher.

22.1 Connecting your views

As you know, you've created the functionality that allows a user to tap the + button and open the `AddEditViewController` scene; and when the user taps Done or Cancel, they're returned to the main screen. You want to add functionality that will allow you to save the text that the user has entered in the text fields and pass that back to create a new LioN object. If you think about it, though, in order to pass data between two views, you need to have references to those views. You could have your `AddEditViewController` set the LioN property in the `MainViewController` by doing something like this:

1 Create a variable called `mainVC` that is of type `MainViewController` in your Add-EditViewController.
2 Add a function to create a new LioN (`addLion`) in the `MainViewController`.
3 Call the `mainVC.addLion` function from `AddEditViewController`.

This would work, but it isn't the right way to do things. That may have been your first instinct, but I want you to try to think more about protocols and delegates. Here's why: in apps with many views, you may want to call the `addNew` function from numerous different places in the app. If you think about the Contacts app on your device, you can create a new contact by tapping the + button on the top-right corner. You can also create a new contact from a phone number when someone calls you. This is the same New Contact screen, but it's called from two different places. If you hardcoded the Done button on the New Contact screen, you wouldn't know which scene to return to when it's tapped. Do you return to the Add New Contact scene or the Phone Number scene? This is where our friend the delegate steps in (figure 22.1).

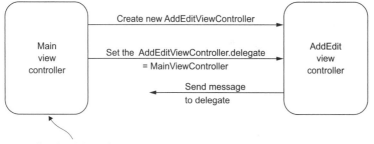
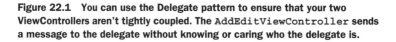

Figure 22.1   You can use the Delegate pattern to ensure that your two ViewControllers aren't tightly coupled. The `AddEditViewController` sends a message to the delegate without knowing or caring who the delegate is.

When the `MainViewController` creates the `AddEditViewController`, it sets itself as the delegate, so when the user taps Done on the `AddEditViewController` scene, the `AddEditViewController` sends a message to the delegate—and it doesn't care who the delegate is. This ensures that any scene that conforms to the `AddEditViewController` protocol can call it, set itself as the delegate, and know that the `AddEditViewController` will return control to it when it's done. This is called *loosely coupled* code, and it's much easier to maintain in the future if and when you want to add more functionality and allow other scenes to call the `AddEditViewController` scene.

Okay, enough explaining. Let's implement the code already.

22.1.1 *Implementing the protocol*

You need to create a protocol for the `AddEditViewController` that will handle two different actions: when the user Cancels out of the scene, and when the user taps Done. The protocol is created outside the class, so add the following lines between the import `UIKit` statement and the class definition:

```
protocol AddEditViewControllerDelegate: class {
    func addItemViewControllerDidCancel(controller: AddEditViewController)
    func addItemViewController(controller: AddEditViewController,
    didFinishAddingItem lionItem: Lion)
}
```

As you can see, you're creating a protocol called `AddEditViewControllerDelegate`, which has two functions: `didCancel` and `didFinishAddingItem`. This is saying that any class that wants to be a delegate of your `AddEditViewController` class *must* conform to this protocol. Protocol names are generally pretty long because you want them to be readable and you want what they do to be clear.

The `didCancel` function will pass the `AddEditViewController` back to the delegate so the delegate can dismiss it, but the `didFinishAddingItem` function passes the ViewController and the new LioN that will be created. You'll learn more as you continue implementing.

22.1.2 *Updating your Cancel and Done actions*

In your cancel and done functions in the `AddEditViewController` class, you're currently dismissing the ViewController. You don't want to do that anymore, though. You want to send a message to the delegate to let it know that one of the two functions is called and let the delegate handle dismissing the view. But to tell the delegate to handle it, you need to have a reference to the delegate.

Add the following line under your class definition:

```
weak var delegate: AddEditViewControllerDelegate?
```

This line creates a variable named `delegate`, which is of type `AddEditViewController-Delegate`, and it's an *optional*. The weak keyword is used for memory management—which we won't go into in this book. (If you're interested in reading up on the topic, search the Apple documentation for *Automatic Reference Counting*.)

Delete both lines for the `dismissViewControllerAnimated` functions in the `cancel-Clicked` and `doneClicked` actions. Delete both of these lines:

```
dismiss(animated: true, completion: nil)
```

Add the following line to the `cancelClicked` function:

```
delegate?.addItemViewControllerDidCancel(controller: self)
```

If you let the auto-complete try to finish the statement, you'll see that both delegate functions are available, as shown in figure 22.2.

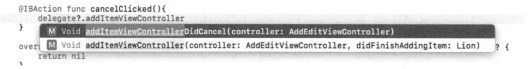

Figure 22.2   You created the protocol definitions so Xcode can auto-complete the definitions when you implement the `cancelClicked` **functionality.**

You need to implement the `done()` function using your delegate method as well, but it's expecting you to pass in the LioN object, and you don't have one yet. Add the following to the top of the class, under the `class` definition:

```
var newLion: Lion?
```

Now add the `didFinishAddingItem` to the `doneClicked` function:

```
delegate?.addItemViewController(controller: self, didFinishAddingItem: newLion!)
```

You haven't created a new LioN yet—you have the placeholder for it. You do know, however, that every time a user taps the + button on the `MainViewController` scene, you'll need to create a new LioN, so add the following line to the `AddEditView-Controller viewDidLoad()` function:

```
newLion = Lion()
```

This ensures that a new LioN object is created every time the view loads.

22.1.3   *Capturing the user input*

You now need to capture whatever the user types into the Name and Description fields so you can add it to the `newLion` object. Where do you think you should add this code? You could add it to the `dismissKeyboard` function so every time the keyboard is dismissed you save the text to the LioN, but the user might not be done entering the text, and they might tap back into the field. This wouldn't be a problem, except you'd be saving the text to the LioN object more often than necessary, and that would make it slightly slower. You should add it to the `doneClicked` function, because the user taps Done when they're done editing. You'll do that now. Add the following code above the delegate message:

```
newLion?.lionName = nameTxt.text!
newLion?.lionDescription = descTxt.text!
```

Fantastic! Run the app to make sure it all works. What happens when you click the Done and Cancel buttons? Nothing. Why doesn't the app respond anymore when you click these buttons? You implemented the code for the AddEditViewControllerDelegate so it would send a message to the delegate, but you don't have any classes that are listening for that message yet. You need to make MainViewController conform to the AddEdit-ViewControllerDelegate so it will listen for messages coming from the AddEditView-Controller. Look back at figure 22.1—you haven't completed the middle arrow code, so when the third arrow at the bottom executes (the AddEditViewController sends a message to the delegate), nobody is waiting for the message. Let's turn our attention to the MainViewController to make it conforms to your new protocol.

22.2 *MainViewController conformance*

Open the MainViewController file, and make it conform to the protocol. Do you remember how to do this? You did it recently when you made the AddEditViewController class conform to the UITextField protocol. Change the MainViewController class definition to the following:

```
class MainViewController: UITableViewController, AddEditViewControllerDelegate {
```

As soon as you finish adding this to the class definition, you should see an error in Xcode. Click the red exclamation point, and you should see the error indicating that MainViewController doesn't conform to protocol AddEditViewControllerDelegate. Why do you get this error? Remember what protocols and delegates do for you. By saying that your class conforms to the protocol, you're saying that it implements the required functions, which you defined as the didCancel and didFinishAdding functions. So you need to add these functions to your MainViewController class to make it conform to the protocol.

Add the following code to your MainViewController class and see how auto-complete helps you with the function:

```
func addItemViewControllerDidCancel(controller: AddEditViewController) {
}
func addItemViewController(controller: AddEditViewController,
➡ didFinishAddingItem lionItem: Lion) {
}
```

The Xcode error should go away, because you conform to the protocol. Good! Now you have all three errors completed in figure 22.1. You need to add some code to these functions to do something. First, you need to dismiss the AddEditViewController scene when these functions in the MainViewController are called. Add the following line to both the didCancel and the didFinish functions:

```
dismiss(animated: true, completion: nil)
```

This line should look familiar to you. You originally had this in the AddEditView-Controller done() and cancel() functions. You've transferred the responsibility to the MainViewController now. Pretty cool, huh?

You can run your app, but the Cancel and Done buttons still won't work. You have one more thing to do first. You need to add the `prepareForSegue()` function back to the `MainViewController`. Add the following code, and then we'll walk through it:

```
override func prepare(for segue: UIStoryboardSegue, sender: Any?) {
    if segue.identifier == "add" {
        let navigationController = segue.destination as!
➡ UINavigationController
        let controller = navigationController.topViewController as!
➡ AddEditViewController
        controller.delegate = self
    }
}
```

This may seem like a lot of code, but you've done most of this already. You already know that the `prepareForSegue` function is called before the segue transition occurs, and you know that you can have identifiers for your segues so you can tell which one is being used. In this case, you're looking for the segue that's identified as "add". You haven't added an identifier to your segue yet, so go do that now before you forget.

Open the main storyboard again, select the transition that exists between the + button on the `MainViewController` scene (figure 22.3) and the `NavigationController` scene, and add the identifier "add" in the Attributes Inspector. Make sure you use the exact same identifier here as you added in the code, or it won't work.

Figure 22.3   Update the segue to ensure the identifier is "add".

Now, back to the code (in `MainViewController`) that you added earlier (the prepare-ForSegue function). The `let navigationController` line is new, and you haven't seen it before. Remember back in chapter 21 when you embedded a Navigation Controller in the `AddEditViewController` scene? This is the Navigation Controller you're referring to on this line. You're grabbing a reference to this Navigation Controller so you can then grab a reference to the scene that it's navigating you to. If you look back at your storyboard, you can see that the `MainViewController` segues to a Navigation Controller, which segues to the `AddEditViewController`. To communicate with the `AddEditViewController`, you have to go through the Navigation Controller; hence the reference to the Navigation Controller, then the `AddEditViewController`. The final line in this function tells the `AddEditViewController` that the `MainViewController` is its delegate. This is the blue bubble in figure 22.1 ("Hey, I'm the delegate"). Okay. Now that you have all that set up, run it and see how it works.

If you tap the + button, you get the `AddEdit` scene pop-up, and if you click the Cancel or Done button, it goes away. The same is not true if you click one of your rows in the main view. The `AddEdit` scene opens, but the Cancel and Done buttons don't work. Why? Walk through your code (review it line by line), and see if you can figure out why before I tell you.

Did you figure it out? The prepareForSegue function is checking to see whether you're using the segue that you identified as "add" and is then setting the AddEdit-ViewController delegate property to the MainViewController (self). You aren't setting the delegate property for the other segue yet, and you don't have an identifier for it. Let's see how to fix that while you're here.

Open your storyboard again, and add the identifier "edit" to the segue that exists for the rows in the MainViewController to the Navigation Controller. Now go back to the code in the MainViewController, copy the entire if statement, and paste it right below the other if statement. Change the identifier in the second statement to "edit", and then change the second if to else if. Your entire prepareForSegue function should look like this:

```
override func prepare(for segue: UIStoryboardSegue, sender: Any?) {
      if segue.identifier == "add" {
          let navigationController = segue.destination as!
➡ UINavigationController
          let controller = navigationController.topViewController as!
➡ AddEditViewController
          controller.delegate = self
      }else if segue.identifier == "edit" {
          let navigationController = segue.destination as!
➡ UINavigationController
          let controller = navigationController.topViewController as!
➡ AddEditViewController
          controller.delegate = self
      }
   }
```

There's some redundant code in here, which we generally don't like, but you'll fix that later. Right now, test the app again and make sure the Cancel and Done functions work for both adding a new item and tapping an existing row. Great! Next you need to add the LioN object to the lion array.

22.3   *Adding the LioN object to the lion array*

You created the new LioN object in the AddEditViewController. You captured the user input and stored it in the new LioN object, and you're already passing it back to the MainViewController. Make sure it's getting back to the MainViewController by adding a print line to didFinishAdding function. In the MainViewController, add this line inside the addItemViewController didFinishAdding function:

```
print(lionItem.lionName)
```

Run the app again, and see if what you typed in the Name field is printed to the console when you click Done. Sweet! The LioN object is getting passed from the AddEdit scene to the MainViewController, and you need to add it to the array. You already did most of the work when you coded the `addItem()` function in chapter 20, so you'll edit that function so you can pass in the LioN object. The `addItem()` function is also not an `@IBAction` anymore because it isn't connected the scene, so you can remove the `@IBAction` keyword for the function definition while you're at it. Delete the `@IBAction` keyword and add an argument for `lionItem` of type `Lion`. This is what my function definition looks like now:

```
func addItem(lionItem: Lion){
```

You still have the code in the function that creates the hardcoded LioN objects, so you're going to delete that code. Remove these three lines:

```
newLion.like = 1
newLion.lionDescription = "Hard coded description"
newLion.lionName = "hard coded name"
```

Change the `lionData.append` line to append the `lionItem` that you're passing into the function:

```
addItem(lionItem: lionItem)
```

Now, in the `MainViewController`, go to the `didFinishAddingItem` function; you can call the `addLion()` function and pass in the `lionItem`. Add this line to the `didFinishAddingItem` function:

```
addItem(lionItem)
```

The functions should look like this now:

```
func addItemViewController(controller: AddEditViewController,
  didFinishAddingItem lionItem: Lion) {
      addItem(lionItem: lionItem)
      dismiss(animated: true, completion: nil)
  }
func addItem(lionItem :  Lion) {
      let currentIndex = lionData.count
      lionData.append(lionItem)
      let indexPath = IndexPath(row: currentIndex, section: 0)
      let indexPaths = [indexPath]
      tableView.insertRows(at: indexPaths, with: .automatic)
  }
```

Run the code in the Simulator, add a new LioN, and see what happens. Oh my goodness! You can click the + button and type in a name and description: the app saves it to the array, and it shows up in the table. Wow! This is starting to look good, isn't it? Now you can delete your dummy rows, too. Delete everything from the `viewDidLoad()` function except the `super.viewDidLoad()`. The app should behave as before but without the toothpaste cells.

What happens when you click the + button and then tap the Done button when the AddEdit scene opens? An empty LioN object is added to the table. Try it yourself. You can't see the empty row after you do it, but if you swipe left on the area where the top cell should be, you can delete the empty row. This isn't good behavior for the app, so you need to fix that.

22.3.1 *Changing the Done button properties*

Open the AddEditViewController file, and set the Done button property enabled to false in the viewDidLoad function. Oh, wait—you don't have a reference to the Done button; you only have a function to respond when it's tapped. Open the storyboard in the Assistant Editor view, Control-click the Done button, drag it into the AddEdit-ViewController, and name the outlet doneButton. This should add the following line to your AddEditViewController class:

```
@IBOutlet weak var doneButton: UIBarButtonItem!
```

Now you can set the doneButton to disabled when the scene first loads:

```
doneButton.isEnabled = false
```

While you're editing the viewDidLoad() function, move the line that creates a new LioN object and put it where it belongs: in the doneClicked() function.

My doneClicked() function looks like this:

```
@IBAction func doneClicked(){
      newLion = Lion()
      newLion?.lionName = nameTxt.text!
      newLion?.lionDescription = descTxt.text!
      delegate?.addItemViewController(controller: self,
  didFinishAddingItem: newLion!)
   }
```

Now your code is a little cleaner. When do you think you should enable the Done button again? It should happen when there's text in the LioN Name field. You know what you should also do while you're here? Allow the user to paste text into both fields. There's a function that's called every time the user changes the text, either by entering letters from the keyboard or pasting into the field. It's part of the UITextField-Delegate (those delegates are everywhere, aren't they?). Add the following function to the AddEditViewController class:

```
func textField(_ textField: UITextField, shouldChangeCharactersIn range:
  NSRange, replacementString string: String) -> Bool {
      let oldText : NSString = textField.text! as NSString
      let newText : NSString = oldText.replacingCharacters(in: range,
  with: string) as NSString
      doneButton.isEnabled = (newText.length > 0)
      return true
   }
```

Let's walk through this to see what it does. The first line (`let oldText ...`) gets the text from the text field in case the user already has something typed into it. The second line (`let newText ...`) replaces any of the characters in the range that the user pasted over. Finally, the Done button should be enabled if the `newText` text length is greater than 0. You don't need to fully understand the first two lines—they're standard lines that are used in this function, but you can research more about them in the Apple docs if you're interested.

Test it out, and you can see that the Done button isn't enabled when the scene first loads but is enabled as soon as you type even one character in the Name field. Pretty slick, right?

22.4   *Setting the like and dislike properties*

Now you can add a new LioN with a name and a description, but you still haven't set the `like` and `dislike` properties. Time to fix that. The first thing you need to do is hook the Like and Dislike buttons up to the code as actions (not outlets). Open the main storyboard, and use the Assistant Editor to Control-click and drag each of the buttons into the `AddEditViewController` class. You've done this many times throughout the book. Remember to set the outlet type to `IBAction` instead of `IBOutlet`.

My code looks like this:

```
@IBAction func likeClicked(_ sender: AnyObject) {
}
@IBAction func dislikeClicked(_ sender: AnyObject) {
}
```

Next you'll create a class-level variable to store whether the LioN is a like or dislike. At the top of the class, add the following line:

```
var likeVar: Int = 1
```

This creates a variable called `likeVar`, of type `Int`, with a default value of 1. This means if a user doesn't set the `like` or `dislike` value by tapping one of the buttons, it will automatically be saved as a like (I'm an optimist, what can I say?). Now that you have your `like` variable, set it to 1 or 0 depending on which button the user tapped. In the `likeClicked` function, set the variable equal to 1, and in the `dislike` function, set the variable equal to 0:

```
@IBAction func likeClicked(sender: AnyObject) {
   likeVar = 1
 }
@IBAction func dislikeClicked(sender: AnyObject) {
   likeVar = 0
 }
```

Next, update the `doneClicked()` function in `AddEditViewController` to set the new-Lion's `like` property. Here's what my code looks like:

```
@IBAction func doneClicked(){
        newLion = Lion()
        newLion?.lionName = nameTxt.text!
        newLion?.lionDescription = descTxt.text!
        newLion?.like = likeVar
        delegate?.addItemViewController(controller: self,
    didFinishAddingItem: newLion!)
    }
```

The `mainViewController` doesn't have a way to display whether the item is liked or not, so print the value until you add the functionality to display it in the cell. Back in the `MainViewController`, add a line to the `didFinishAddingItem` function to print the value of the `like` property of the LioN:

```
print(lionItem.like)
```

Run the app again, and see what happens when you don't click a button and save the item, and then when you do click a button and save the items. You should see ones or zeros printed out in the console, depending on which button you clicked.

You can now add a LioN and save it to your array with all three properties set. In the next chapter, you'll update the code so you can edit the LioNs.

22.5 Summary

You added a lot of functionality in this chapter, and I hope you feel good about it. Remember that you can always download my code from www.manning.com/books/anyone-can-create-an-app or https://github.com/wlwise/AnyoneCanCreateAnApp if you run into any problems. It's definitely better for you do all the work and then check it against mine, though, so you become more familiar with how to do things. Remember that there are five steps to making a delegate work. The following steps assume you have two classes, class 1 and class 2:

1 Create a delegate protocol in class 2.
2 Create a weak optional delegate variable in class 2.
3 Have class 2 send a message to the delegate when needed (Cancel or Done button tapped, for example).
4 Make class 1 conform to the protocol by adding the name of the protocol in the class definition (`AddEditViewControllerDelegate`, for example).
5 Have class 1 set the delegate property of class to itself (using the `delegate` variable you created in step 2).

In the next chapter, you'll add the functionality to edit the LioN. I know—this is exciting, isn't it?

23

Editing LioNs

This chapter covers

- Optional binding
- Editing LioNs
- Adding another function to the AddEditViewControllerDelegate

You've built out the functionality to create new LioN objects, but you don't have the ability to edit them yet. You'll add all the functionality to edit LioNs and display the edited cells in this chapter. You'll also add functionality to show whether the user liked or disliked the LioN by changing the background colors of the Like and Dislike buttons.

23.1 Editing existing LioNs

You're now going to add the ability for users to edit the LioNs they've already created. Based on what you know now, what specifically do you need to do to make this happen?

1 Set up the AddEditViewController to accept a LioN object to edit.
2 Fill in the text boxes with the existing LioN name and description.

3 Show whether the LioN is liked or disliked.

4 Pass the LioN object to the `AddEditViewController`.

5 Save the LioN when the user taps Done, but don't create a new LioN.

Let's get to it.

23.1.1 Setting up the AddEditViewController to accept a LioN object to edit

When the user taps a row in the main LioN scene, they're expecting another scene to open with the LioN data so they can edit it. In order for this to happen, you need to know which LioN they tapped so you can pass it to the Edit scene and then pass that object to the `AddEditViewController`. The first thing you need to do is to create a variable in the `AddEditViewController` for the LioN that will get passed in. Add the following line to the top of your `AddEdit` controller:

```
var lionToEdit : Lion?
```

Why did you add the ? at the end of the LioN? Remember that the ? signifies to Xcode that this variable is optional, and it may or may not be nil. You know this variable will be nil when the user creates a new LioN and this class is called; but you want it to not be nil when the user wants to edit a LioN, so optional is the perfect solution.

Now that you have a variable in the `AddEdit` controller for the LioN object that you want to edit, you need to know whether there's something in that variable. If there isn't anything in the variable (the main controller didn't pass an object in to be edited), then you know the user tapped + so they could create a new LioN. If there's something in the object, then you know the user tapped a row in the table and you should be editing that object. Add the following code to the `viewDidLoad()` function:

```
if let item = lionToEdit {
    title = "Edit LioN"
 } else {
    title = "Add LioN"
 }
```

In the preceding code, you're using a feature of Swift called *optional binding*. This statement can be read as "If there is a value in the variable `lionToEdit`, set it equal to a new variable called `item`. Then set the title of the scene to Edit LioN. If there isn't a value in the variable `lionToEdit`, set the title of the scene to Add LioN." Run the app again, and you should notice that the Add/Edit scene has the title Add LioN when you add the LioN or edit it. Because you're not passing the LioN into the Add/Edit controller yet, it makes sense that `lionToEdit` will always be nil at this point, right?

Let's go ahead and plan for the time when `lionToEdit` isn't nil and see how to fill in the text fields with the code so it can be edited.

23.1.2   *Filling in the text boxes with the LioN name and description*

Now you need to populate the two text fields on your Add/Edit scene so the user can edit them. In the `if let` statement you added earlier, add the following two statements:

```
descTxt.text = item.lionDescription
nameTxt.text = item.lionName
```

Here you're setting the text of the description text field to the `lionDescription` of the `item` variable. You may be wondering why you didn't use the `lionToEdit` object to fill in the text fields—why didn't you use the following code instead?

```
descTxt.text = lionToEdit!.lionDescription
nameTxt.text = lionToEdit!.lionName
```

Although it's absolutely possible to use the `lionToEdit` object to populate your text fields, it isn't good practice. The variable `lionToEdit` will be set by the main controller when the user taps a row to edit it, so that variable is somewhat out of your control. You don't know if that variable may be changed by some other part of the app while you're trying to use it—you aren't finished coding the app yet, so there's a possibility that another function might change that variable at any time.

There are many times in a programmer's coding career when they expect a variable to contain a certain object and are confounded when it doesn't. They don't realize that another part of the app is changing the variable behind the scenes. Because they didn't make a *local copy* of the variable, it can change without their knowing it. So it's good practice to make a copy of the variable for your class to use that you know can only be changed by you in that class. Your `if let` statement should look like this now:

```
if let item = lionToEdit {
    title = "Edit Lion"
    descTxt.text = item.lionDescription
    nameTxt.text = item.lionName
} else {
    title = "Add Lion"
}
```

You have the two text boxes set to show the values of the `lionDescription` and the `lionName` fields when the object is passed into the `AddEdit` controller, but what about the Like/Dislike buttons? Let's work on that next.

23.1.3   *Showing whether the LioN is liked or disliked*

You're eventually going to add some images to your buttons so they look nicer than having Like and Dislike on them (in chapter 26). For now, you want to give the user some visual cue for which option they chose. You're going to set the background color of the buttons based on the user selection to green for like and red for dislike. When the user taps Like, the Like button should turn green, and the Dislike button shouldn't show any color. When the user taps the Dislike button, it should turn red, and the Like button shouldn't show any color.

You set the default value for your like variable to true, which means like. You did this near the top of the AddEdit ViewController class:

```
var likeVar: Bool = true
```

This means when a user creates a new LioN, the default is like and they must tap the Dislike button to change the value. This also means that when the Add/Edit scene first loads, the LioN object default is like, which means you should show that to the user by having the background color of the Like button set to green. In order to set the properties of the Like and Dislike buttons, you need a reference to them. You already created action outlets when each of them is tapped, but you didn't create reference outlets so you could change the properties of the button. Open the storyboard again, drag from the likeButton to the AddEditViewController, and create an outlet named likeButton. Do the same for the Dislike button, but name the outlet dislikeButton.

Back in the viewDidLoad() function, under the title = "Add Lion" line, add the following line:

```
likeButton.backgroundColor = UIColor.green
```

Run the app again, and you should see the Like button with a green background when you add a new LioN. The problem is that the green doesn't go away when you tap Dislike. You haven't set the Dislike button background to red anywhere—but you can fix that. You created a dislikeClicked function earlier, and this seems like the perfect place to change the background to red, don't you think?

In the dislikeClicked function, add the following line:

```
dislikeButton.backgroundColor = UIColor.red
```

Perfect! Run the app again, and let's see what happens. Not quite right, is it? You want the green color on the Like button to disappear and the red color to stay. In the dislikeClicked function, you also need to add the following line:

```
likeButton.backgroundColor = UIColor.clear
```

Great. Now when you click Dislike, the Dislike button turns red and the Like button is clear. You need to add the code to turn the Like button green when it's tapped and turn the Dislike button clear. Change the likeClicked function so it looks like this:

```
@IBAction func likeClicked(sender: AnyObject) {
    likeVar = true
    dislikeButton.backgroundColor = UIColor.clear
    likeButton.backgroundColor = UIColor.green
}
```

Have you noticed that you seem to be repeating the code for setting colors in several different places in the app? This isn't a good coding practice and can definitely lead to problems when you forget to set the color for one condition. It also makes it more difficult to maintain the code in the future—if you want to change the behavior of the buttons (say you want to change the Dislike background color to orange instead), you have to search through your code to find all the different places that you set the background color. There's a better way to do this to make your code easier to read and to maintain.

You're going to create a new function in the `AddEdit` controller class called `toggleLike`. Add the following code in your class:

```
func toggleLike() {
}
```

In this function, you need to check what the `likeVar` is set to and toggle the buttons' background colors based on that variable. You can take the code out of your like and dislike click functions and move it to the `toggleLike()` function.

Add the following code to your `toggleLike()` function so it looks like this:

```
func toggleLike() {
    if likeVar == true {
        dislikeButton.backgroundColor = UIColor.clear
        likeButton.backgroundColor = UIColor.green
    } else {
        dislikeButton.backgroundColor = UIColor.red
        likeButton.backgroundColor = UIColor.clear
    }
}
```

This code evaluates the `likeVar` variable and, if it's equal to `true` (`like`), sets the background color of the `likeButton` to green and the background color of the `dislikeButton` to clear. If the `likeVar` variable isn't equal to `true`, it must mean `dislike`, so the code sets the background color of the Dislike button to red and the background color of the Like button to clear.

Now that you have this function, you can call it anytime either the Like or Dislike button is tapped and when the scene first loads. Clear out the code you put into the `likeClicked()` function and the `dislikeClicked()` function, so they look like this:

```
@IBAction func likeClicked(_ sender: AnyObject) {
    likeVar = true
    toggleLike()
}
@IBAction func dislikeClicked(_ sender: AnyObject) {
    likeVar = false
    toggleLike()
}
```

Run your app, and see what happens. It looks great, doesn't it? The only thing you need to fix is to toggle the button colors when the scene first loads. Add a call to the `toggleLike()` function at the end of the `viewDidLoad()` function, and remove the line where you set the `likeButton` background to green. This will take the value of the `likeVar` and toggle the buttons accordingly. There's only one problem left: what happens when the user wants to edit a LioN? The buttons should be set based on the value of the LioN—set to green/Like if they liked the LioN or to red/Dislike if they didn't like the item. You need to set the value of `likeVar` based on the LioN object that's being passed in. Add the following line of code to the `if let item = itemToEdit` function, after you set the text field value for the `lionName`:

```
likeVar = item.like
```

Your entire `viewDidLoad()` should look like this now:

```
override func viewDidLoad() {
        super.viewDidLoad()
        if let item = lionToEdit {
            title = "Edit Lion"
            descTxt.text = item.lionDescription
            nameTxt.text = item.lionName
            likeVar = item.like
        } else {
            title = "Add Lion"
            likeButton.backgroundColor = UIColor.green
        }
        toggleLike()
        doneButton.isEnabled = false
        nameTxt.becomeFirstResponder()
        let tap = UITapGestureRecognizer(target:
    self, action: #selector(dismissKeyboard))
        view.addGestureRecognizer(tap)

    }
```

Run the app again, and the Like button should be green when the Add/Edit scene first loads because the default is 1 or `like`.

You're definitely making progress. Now you need to add in the functionality that will set the `lionToEdit` variable with the LioN object that you want to edit.

23.1.4 *Passing the LioN object to the Add/Edit controller*

Let's check in on what you've done before you add more functionality, shall we? Remember that you want the user to be able to tap a row in the main LioN scene and have the Add/Edit scene open with the LioN data that they want to edit. To do this, you need the main scene (`MainViewController`) to pass the LioN data to the `AddEdit-ViewController` so it can display the data for editing.

You already set up the `AddEditViewController` to accept the incoming LioN object by creating a variable called `lionToEdit`. You then populated the text fields based on the data in that object and toggled the Like/Dislike buttons based on the lionToEdit data. To tie it together, you need to pass the LioN object from the Main-ViewController to the AddEditViewController. Fortunately, you've already done most of the work.

Open the MainViewController file, and look at the prepareForSegue function. You already have the code for "If segue identifier is equal to edit," so you only need to pass the LioN object that the user tapped when this function is called. Pretty cool, huh? The first thing you need to know is which row the user tapped. You already figured this out when you added the delete functionality in the last chapter, so this shouldn't be new to you. You need to get the index path (the pointer to the row that we want) of the cell in the table view.

Add the following code inside the prepareForSegue function and inside the if segue == Edit part:

```
if let indexPath = tableView.indexPath(for: sender as! UITableViewCell) {
}
```

We talked about optional binding earlier (the if let statement), and you're using it again here. In English, this reads, "If the index for the path that the user tapped in the table view is not nil, then set it equal to this new variable indexPath." Now you have an indexPath, which will give you the row number for the tapped row. You have an array of LioN data called lionData (appropriately named, don't you think?) that you'll use to get the object that the user wants to edit. Add the following line inside the if let statement that you created:

```
controller.lionToEdit = lionData[indexPath.row]
```

This will set the lionToEdit variable in the AddEditViewController equal to the row of data in the lionData array. Run the app again, add a new LioN object, and then click it to edit it. You should see the text fields populated with the LioN data and the Like/Dislike buttons set based on your choice. Here's the prepareForSegue function in case you need to see the whole thing:

```
override func prepare(for segue: UIStoryboardSegue, sender: Any?) {
    if segue.identifier == "add" {
        let navigationController = segue.destination as!
➡ UINavigationController
        let controller = navigationController.topViewController as!
➡ AddEditViewController
        controller.delegate = self
    } else if segue.identifier == "edit" {
        let navigationController = segue.destination as!
➡ UINavigationController
        let controller = navigationController.topViewController as!
➡ AddEditViewController
        controller.delegate = self
        if let indexPath = tableView.indexPath(for: sender as!
➡ UITableViewCell) {
```

```
                        controller.lionToEdit = lionData[indexPath.row]
                    }
                }
            }
```

Run the app again, and see if you can edit the LioN object. Great—you can! One annoying thing, though: the Done button isn't enabled in the details scene until after you edit text in one of the text fields. You're going to fix that next.

You'll add one line in the `viewDidLoad()` function of the `AddEditViewController`. Inside the `if let item = itemToEdit` section, add the following line:

```
doneButton.enabled = true
```

Now the entire `viewDidLoad()` function should look like this:

```
override func viewDidLoad() {
    super.viewDidLoad()
    doneButton.isEnabled = false
    if let item = lionToEdit {
        title = "Edit Lion"
        descTxt.text = item.lionDescription
        nameTxt.text = item.lionName
        likeVar = item.like
        doneButton.isEnabled = true
    } else {
        title = "Add Lion"
        likeButton.backgroundColor = UIColor.green
    }
    toggleLike()
    nameTxt.becomeFirstResponder()
    let tap : UITapGestureRecognizer = UITapGestureRecognizer(target:
    self, action: #selector(dismissKeyboard))
    view.addGestureRecognizer(tap)

}
```

If you run your code and try to edit a LioN object, you should notice that your edits are saved as a new LioN instead of being saved to the original LioN. That won't work. You need to overwrite the values of the original LioN when the user is finished editing them.

23.1.5 *Saving the LioN when the user taps Done, but not creating a new LioN*

How do you think you can send the updated LioN object back to the `MainView-Controller` so it can be edited instead of saved as a new object? Right now, when the user taps Done, you're using the delegate pattern for `didFinishAddingItem` and passing the data for the new LioN back. If you thought of using a delegate to pass the edited item back, you get a cookie. (I can't give you a cookie, but consider this permission to go eat a cookie.)

You're going to add a new function definition to the protocol at the top of the `AddEditViewController` for passing back the edited LioN. Add the following line under the `didFinishAddingItem` description in the protocol:

```
func addItemViewController(controller: AddEditViewController,
  didFinishEditingItem lionItem: Lion)
```

The entire protocol now looks like this:

```
protocol AddEditViewControllerDelegate : class {
    func addItemViewControllerDidCancel(controller: AddEditViewController)
    func addItemViewController(controller: AddEditViewController,
  didFinishAddingItem lionItem: Lion)
    func addItemViewController(controller: AddEditViewController,
  didFinishEditingItem lionItem: Lion)
}
```

Fantastic! Next you need to add the functionality in the `AddEdit` ViewController for `didFinishEditingItem`. Where do you think you should put it? How about the same place you put the `didFinishAddingItem` functionality: in the `doneClicked()` function.

If you look at the `doneClicked()` function, you can see that it creates a new LioN, sets the properties based on the user input, and then sends a message to tell whatever delegate is listening that you're done adding the item (or `didFinishAddingItem`). You need to change this to check whether you're editing an item and then send the appropriate delegate message. Sounds like you need to use optional binding again, don't you think?

Add the following lines inside the `doneClicked()` function:

```
if let item = lionToEdit {
{ else }
}
```

As a reminder, this says, "If `lionToEdit` isn't `nil`, then set it equal to this new variable called `item`. Otherwise, do something else." Now you can move all the existing code inside the `doneClicked()` function in the `else{}` section—because you know you're adding a new LioN. Your function should look this now:

```
if let item = lionToEdit {
{ else }
    newLion = Lion()
    newLion?.lionName = nameTxt.text!
    newLion?.lionDescription = descTxt.text!
    newLion?.like = likeVar
    delegate?.addItemViewController(controller: self, didFinishAddingItem:
    newLion!)
  }
```

If you run the app, adding a LioN should still work, but saving the edited LioN doesn't because you don't have any code in the first part of your `if` statement. You can definitely fix that—you should be able to do this yourself because you did it earlier. Where do you think you should do it? You're checking whether `lionToEdit` has a value that would indicate the user is editing a LioN, so add the code in the `if let item = liontoEdit{}` section above the `{ else }` line.

Set the properties of the `item` object equal to the values that the users entered on the scene. My added lines look like this:

```
item.like = likeVar
item.lionDescription = descTxt.text!
item.lionName = nameTxt.text!
```

You've set the values of the object `item`, so you need to send it back to the delegate to save it. Look at how you sent a message for saving the object to the delegate (`didFinish-AddingItem`), and see if you can code the line for saving the object for editing to the delegate (`didFinishEditingItem`). My added line looks like this and is under the lines I previously added:

```
delegate?.addItemViewController(controller: self, didFinishEditingItem: item)
```

Wonderful! But you have a problem: Xcode generated a new error (the red exclamation point). The `MainViewController` doesn't conform to the protocol for the `AddEditViewControllerDelegate` anymore because you added a new function to it. You need to go back into the `MainViewController` and handle the message when it's sent (`didFinishEditingItem`). Add the following function to your `MainView-Controller`:

```
func addItemViewController(controller: AddEditViewController,
➡ didFinishEditingItem lionItem: Lion) {
}
```

Now the `MainViewController` conforms to the `AddEditViewControllerDelegate` protocol, so the error message is gone. You need to do something with the LioN object that was passed back in this message.

You're going to save the LioN back to the LioN array in the same row that it was already in—otherwise you'll create another object again or overwrite an object you didn't mean to. You need to know which row of data you sent over to the Add/Edit scene, which you don't know right now. So go back and fix that by creating a new variable at the top of the `MainViewController` called `editIndexPath`. You'll store the `indexPath` of the row the user tapped in this variable so you can use it to figure out which row needs to be edited.

At the top of the `MainViewController` class, add this variable declaration:

```
var editIndexPath: NSIndexPath?
```

You need to set this variable before you pass control to the AddEditViewController, so edit the prepareForSeque function to include the following line, in the segue .identifier == Edit section:

```
editIndexPath = indexPath
```

I put this inside the if let indexPath code, so it looks like this:

```
} else if segue.identifier == "edit" {
        let navigationController = segue.destination as!
UINavigationController
        let controller = navigationController.topViewController as!
AddEditViewController
        controller.delegate = self
        if let indexPath = tableView.indexPath(for: sender as!
UITableViewCell) {
            controller.lionToEdit = lionData[indexPath.row]
            editIndexPath = indexPath as NSIndexPath?
        }
    }
```

Back to the didFinishEditingItem function. You need to update the cell in the table view for the cell that was edited. You know which cell was edited, thanks to the editIndexPath variable, so add the following code inside the didFinishEditing-Item function:

```
if let cell = tableView.cellForRow(at: editIndexPath! as IndexPath) {
    cell.textLabel?.text = lionItem.lionName
        cell.detailTextLabel?.text = lionItem.lionDescription
 }
dismissViewControllerAnimated(true, completion: nil)
```

This code is setting the variable cell equal to the cell in the table view that's at index editIndexPath. Then you can set the cell properties equal to the properties of the edited LioN. Finally, you have to dismiss the ViewController so the main ViewController scene will be visible. Test out the code and make sure it works. Amazing, isn't it?

You're displaying the right data to the user, but you haven't updated the LioN object in the lionData array; let's see how to do that. You have the index path for the data, so that means you know the row that you need to edit in the array. Add the following lines inside the if let cell area in the didFinishEditingItem portion of the code in MainViewController:

```
lionData[editIndexPath!.row].lionDescription = lionItem.lionDescription
lionData[editIndexPath!.row].lionName = lionItem.lionName
lionData[editIndexPath!.row].like = lionItem.like
```

You're setting the properties of the LioN object in the lionData to the properties of the LioN that was passed back by the AddEditViewController. Now the array is also updated so when you save the data in the next chapter, it will be ready to go.

Here's the entire `didFinishEditingItem` function so you can compare it to yours:

```
func addItemViewController(controller: AddEditViewController,
    didFinishEditingItem lionItem: Lion) {
        if let cell = tableView.cellForRow(at: editIndexPath!) {
            cell.textLabel?.text = lionItem.lionName
            cell.detailTextLabel?.text = lionItem.lionDescription

            lionData[editIndexPath!.row].lionDescription =
    lionItem.lionDescription
            lionData[editIndexPath!.row].lionName = lionItem.lionName
            lionData[editIndexPath!.row].like = lionItem.like
        }
        dismiss(animated: true, completion: nil)
    }
```

23.2 Summary

Can you believe how far you've come? You started out not being able to code anything for iPhones and iPads, and now you have a functioning app that can create new LioNs, edit them, and even delete them. The only thing that would be better would be if you could save those LioNs each time you exit the app so they load when you open the app again. That's coming in the next chapter.

In this chapter, you learned

- About optional binding, a way to test whether a variable is `nil` and set it equal to another variable
- How to pass data to an edit controller and pass it back to the main controller

Saving LioNs

Now you have the ability to create new LioNs and edit them, but when you close the app and open it again, all of your data is gone. You can fix that, though, so let's get to it. The purpose of this chapter is to save the `lionData` array to the iPhone so the data loads every time you load the app, and the data saves to the phone every time you close the app.

24.1 Playing in the sandbox

Saving data to your iOS device isn't that different from saving a file to your computer. When you're on the computer, you pick any location that you have access to and click Save. When you're on an iPhone or iPad, though, the programmer (you) picks the location to save the file, and it's saved automatically so the user doesn't have to. Apple put some security measures in place for the iPad and iPhone so you can only save the app file to specific locations—called *sandboxes*.

Imagine two kids, each building a sandcastle in their own sandbox. They don't want to share their space in the sand with anyone else. Little Peter doesn't want little Bridget to mess up his sandcastle any more than little Bridget wants him to mess up her sandcastle. Apps behave the same way—they each have their own sandbox to store files (or build castles), and no other apps can have access to that area. This is a great security measure. It ensures that the file you save can be accessed by your app only and not by any others.

You need to add some code to create a file in the LioN sandbox. I'm going to add the following function near the bottom of my `MainViewController` class (I tend to add utility-type functions near the bottom). Create a new function called `getData-FilePath`, and have it return a type URL. Remember how to do that?

This is what my new function looks like:

```
func getDataFilePath() -> URL {
}
```

Next, add the following two lines inside the `getDataFilePath()` function:

```
let paths = FileManager.default.urls(for: .documentDirectory, in:
    .userDomainMask)
return paths[0].appendingPathComponent("Lion.plist")
```

The first line gets a list of the directories in your sandbox area. The `FileManager` `.default.urls` function returns an array of strings for the sandbox directories. The next line returns the first path object from the `paths` array and appends the string `"lion.plist"` to the end to form a full path to save files, including the filename. lion.plist is the name of the file you'll save on the user's phone. What is a *plist* (pronounced "pea list"), anyway? It stands for *property list*, and these files can store all kinds of settings for your app, not just the data you want to save.

You're going to make a call to the `getDataFilePath()` function so you can see where the sandbox is on your computer. Inside the `mainViewController viewDidLoad()` method, print out the returned string from `getDataFilePath()`. My code looks like this:

```
print(getDataFilePath())
```

Run your app, and you should see a long string printed to your console. My string looks like this:

```
/Users/wendylwise/Library/Developer/CoreSimulator/Devices/CD3B094F-C3A9-
    44D7-A935-565FC29CEACA/data/Containers/Data/Application/9D0E98E2-0A18-
    464A-A155-B1645F9FC84D/Documents/lion.plist
```

Wow—that's a long string, isn't it? This is the behind-the-scenes look at where Xcode is saving data for your app. All the crazy letter-number combinations are random IDs that Xcode picks to make the location unique. Let's go look at the file, shall we?

Open a new Finder window on your Mac (either click the icon with the guy smiling or press Command-N in your Desktop). Once the new Finder window opens, click

Go > Go to Folder, or press Command-Shift-G. Copy and paste the long string from the console (do *not* include the lion.plist part of the string, because you haven't created the file yet) into this new prompt, and click Go. Welcome to your sandbox! It will be much neater when you create the lion.plist file, so do that and then come back and look at it again. Your lion.plist file should be empty because you haven't saved any LioNs yet.

24.2 *Saving your data*

Saving your data is pretty straightforward, although it may not seem so at first. You now know about the sandbox where your data will be saved, and you know that your data will be saved in a file called lion.plist. The question is, how do you get the data to save into that file, and, for that matter, how will you get it back it out? (Okay, I know that's two questions, but go with me anyway.) You have to take several steps (as usual), so let's get to it.

You're going to need to take the following steps:

1 Change the class definition for the LioN object.
2 Encode the data for saving.
3 Decode the data for loading.
4 Add a `load` function to the `MainViewController`.
5 Add a `save` function to the `MainViewController`, and call as appropriate.

Now that you know what you need to do, let's get started.

24.2.1 *Changing the class definition for the LioN object*

Go back to Xcode, and open the Lion.swift file. If you remember, this is the class definition for the LioN object. It states that there are three properties: `lionName`, `lionDescription`, and `Like`. If you look at the class definition on the top line, it states that the class `Lion` doesn't inherit any functionality from any other objects. You learned about inheritance back in chapter 13, but as a refresher, *inheritance* gives you access to the functions and properties of the superclass. Your LioN object isn't inheriting from anything, which means the only functions and properties it has access to are the ones you create for it. That hardly seems expedient or efficient, does it? There are a lot of classes that you could inherit from to get some of the functionality you need to save and load objects from a file.

The first class that you need to inherit from is the `NSObject` class. `NSObject` is the most basic class in programming for Apple technologies. It's used pretty heavily in Objective-C programming—the precursor to Swift programming. You don't need to know a lot about this base class other than that it's required in order to save and load data from a file. Change the class definition of the LioN object to inherit from `NSObject`. My code looks like this:

```
class Lion : NSObject {
```

The second thing you need is NSCoding. This allows you to encode data, save it to disk, and decode the data to read it from a file. This isn't a class you're inheriting from, but a protocol you want to conform to. Protocols are everywhere, aren't they? Change the class definition so it inherits from NSObject and conforms to the NSCoding protocol (don't confuse NSCoding and NSCoder—make sure you use NSCoding, or you'll get an error). This is what my Lion class definition looks like:

```
class Lion : NSObject, NSCoding {
```

If you remember what you've learned about protocols and delegates, you *must* implement certain functions in order to conform to the NSCoding protocol. Do you recall the easiest way to find out which functions you must implement? You could Command-click the word NSCoding to open the protocol definition file. The file itself is somewhat confusing because it contains several protocol definitions. The other option is to click the word NSCoding once and look at the Quick Help panel (as shown in figure 24.1). This shows that NSCoding is a protocol and gives a lot more information about the different functions and availability of the protocol (if it doesn't open automatically, click the blue question mark).

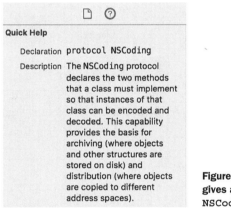

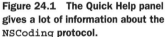

Figure 24.1 The Quick Help panel gives a lot of information about the NSCoding protocol.

It doesn't explicitly tell you which functions you must implement to conform, but keep reading: near the bottom, you'll see NSCoding Protocol Reference. Click the link, and a new window opens with the protocol information. (If a new window doesn't open, go to Xcode > Preferences, click Components, and, in the right panel, download the documentation files for Xcode and iOS.)

When the window opens, there's a headline for Initializing with a Coder. If you look inside this, you'll see that -initWithCoder: is a required function. Great! Now you know at least one required function you need to conform to. Keep scrolling down, and you'll see that encodeWithCoder: is also a required function. Now you know there are two functions to conform to the NSCoding protocol. (The other way I remember what functions are required for the protocol is to keep notes for myself so I don't have to look up the information. Believe it or not, I don't store everything in my brain—otherwise I'd be likely to forget the simple things, such as what toothpaste I like. Wait a minute...)

How you choose to find the information is up to you. But you'll still need to implement the two functions, so let's do it.

IMPLEMENTING THE INIT(CODER) FUNCTION

The first function required is the init function. You can copy the definition from the reference file or type it in. I added the following to my Lion class:

```
required init(coder aDecoder: NSCoder) {
    super.init()
}
```

This function will be used to read data from the file, which you'll implement in the next step.

IMPLEMENTING THE ENCODE FUNCTION

The next required function is the encode function, which you'll use in a few minutes to save the data to a file. For now, add the function definition. This is what my code looks like:

```
func encode(with aCoder: NSCoder) {
}
```

IMPLEMENTING THE INIT() FUNCTION

Now that you've added the required init with Coder aDecoder : NSCoder, you must have an init() statement that will be called each time a LioN object is created. You need to override the superclass's implementation, which you do with the override keyword. This is what I added to my code:

```
override init() {
  super.init()
}
```

Your entire Lion class should look like this now:

```
import Foundation

class Lion : NSObject, NSCoding {
    var lionName = ""
    var lionDescription = ""
    var like = 1

    required init(coder aDecoder : NSCoder) {
        super.init()
    }

    func encode(with aCoder: NSCoder) {

    }
```

```
    override init() {
        super.init()
    }
}
```

You have the class basics, so you can add some functionality to these functions.

24.2.2 Encoding the data for saving

Before you can save your LioN object to a file, you need to tell the system what a LioN object looks like. The coder must have this information so it knows how to save it.

Add the following lines to your encodeWithCoder function:

```
aCoder.encode(lionName, forKey: "lionName")
aCoder.encode(lionDescription, forKey: "lionDescription")
aCoder.encode(like, forKey: "like")
```

This may look strange, but all you're doing is telling the coder (aCoder) to encode an object named "lionName" that has a value of the variable lionName, which in this case is a string. aCoder can encode many different types of objects, and you can look through the documentation if you're interested in learning more.

Now that you've encoded the LioN object so that you can save it to a file, you're going to decode it so you can load it from the file.

24.2.3 Decoding the data for loading

The decode function is used when you want to load the LioN object from the file, so you need to do the exact opposite of what you did in the previous section for the encoding. You need to set the Lion values based on what's in the file.

Add the following lines to your init(coder) function:

```
lionName = aDecoder.decodeObject(forKey: "lionName") as! String
        lionDescription = aDecoder.decodeObject(forKey: "lionDescription")
    as! String
        like = aDecoder.decodeInteger(forKey: "like")
```

The first line loads the lionName property by decoding the object for LionName, which is the same key you used when encoding the object. If you don't encode and decode with the same key, you'll get errors because your app won't be able to find the object you're looking for. So you decode the object for key LionName as a string—because that's the expected type of the property lionName in your Lion class, and that's how you stored it. The lionDescription is treated exactly the same because it's also a string. The like variable is treated slightly differently again because it was stored as an Int. You'll get an error if you try to decode the like variable as a string (because it's an integer), so make sure to check your code and use decodeInteger, not decodeObject.

I can tell you from experience that it's important that the encoding key and decoding key are exactly the same; otherwise you'll get errors. That's all you have to do the Lion class to allow it to be saved to a file and loaded from a file.

Next you need to add the functionality to the `MainViewController` class to make this happen. Before you do that, though, here's the `Lion` class with all the edits:

```
import Foundation

class Lion : NSObject, NSCoding {
    var lionName = ""
    var lionDescription = ""
    var like = 1

    required init(coder aDecoder : NSCoder) {
        super.init()
        lionName = aDecoder.decodeObject(forKey: "lionName") as! String
        lionDescription = aDecoder.decodeObject(forKey: "lionDescription")
     as! String
        like = aDecoder.decodeInteger(forKey: "like")
    }

    func encode(with aCoder: NSCoder) {
        aCoder.encode(lionName, forKey: "lionName")
        aCoder.encode(lionDescription, forKey: "lionDescription")
        aCoder.encode(like, forKey: "like")
    }

    override init() {
        super.init()
    }
}
```

The first thing you need to do to the `MainViewController` class is add a new initializer. The LioN data is being saved to a file and loaded from a file, so you need to have an `init` with a decoder function so you can access the data. This `init` function will be called when the app loads, which then loads the `MainViewController`, so you can use it to load your LioN objects from the file.

Add a new function near the top of the `MainViewController` class that looks like this:

```
required init?(coder aDecoder: NSCoder) {
}
```

You need to add a line to call the super `init` function to ensure that everything is initialized properly, so add the following line within the new required `init` function:

```
super.init(coder: aDecoder)
```

Good. You're getting there. Before you can load the data from the file, you need to create the array to store the data. You already defined the variable `lionData`, which is of type `Array` and stores LioN objects (look near the top of the `MainViewController` file to see this declaration). Now you need to initialize this array in your `init` function.

Add the following line under the `super.init` line:

```
lionData = [Lion]()
```

This line creates the `lionData` array and defines it as holding LioN objects. Now you need to ready the LioN data from the file so you can load the lionData array.

Add this line under the `lionData` line:

```
loadLions()
```

This will be another function that you'll define to load the LioNs. Let's see how to create this function now.

24.2.4 Adding the loadLions() function

As I've said, I tend to add my utility type functions near the bottom of my class, so I scrolled to the bottom of my `MainViewController` class to define the `loadLions()` function. To start, add the function so your code compiles:

```
func loadLions() {
}
```

The first thing you need to do in order to load the data is to know where the data is stored. Fortunately, you already know this from the work you did earlier in this chapter. You can create a new variable called `path` and set it equal to the function you created previously (`getDataFilePath()`). This is what I added as the first line in my `loadLions()` function:

```
let path = getDataFilePath()
```

Next, you need to find out whether the file exists at the path in the sandbox—it might not, if this is the first time the user launched your app. Apple provides a class called File Manager to help you manipulate files on the device. File Manager has many properties and functions that you can use. You'll use the File Manager to get this information, so add the following `if` statement under the `let path` statement:

```
if let data = try? Data(contentsOf: path) {
}
```

`try?` is something you haven't seen before. This is a handy feature that tells Xcode to try to create the variable `data` using the contents of the path, but if it can't create the `data` object, return `nil`. You may be wondering why it would fail. What happens the first time you run the app? You know that you don't create the plist until the user creates the first LioN object; therefore, there won't be any data to load on first run. Hence `try?`.

If this statement evaluates to true, you need decode it using an *unarchiver* (who makes up these names, anyway?). Add the following line inside the `if let` brackets:

```
let unarchiver = NSKeyedUnarchiver(forReadingWith: data)
lionData = unarchiver.decodeObject(forKey: "lionData") as! [Lion]
unarchiver.finishDecoding()
```

On the first line, you create an unarchiver used for reading in the variable that you defined as `data` when you checked to see whether there was data in the file you were trying to load. The second line uses the unarchiver to decode the file using the key `lionData` and cast each object as a LioN object. Don't worry about the `forKey: "lion-Data"`—you haven't defined it yet because you haven't added the code to save your `lionData`, but you will in the next section. Finally, you tell the unarchiver to clean up after itself and `finishDecoding()`.

24.2.5 *Loading summary*

That's all there is to loading data from a file. I know it may seem complex, or like there are a lot of steps, but it isn't that complex when you break it down. You must make the class that you want to save to a file conform to the `NSCoding` protocol by implementing the two required methods. Within those methods, you need to encode the object based on the object type (`String` and `Int` in this case). You then need to implement the ability to load the object from the file within the object by decoding the object based on the object type (again, `Strings` and `Int`).

Once you've made the Lion class `NSCoding`-compliant, you need to create an initializer in the `MainViewController` class (or whatever class you need to load the data from a file) to initialize the array and load the data. To load the data, you need to get the path to the file that's stored in the sandbox, use the File Manager to determine if there is data in the file, and then use the unarchiver to decode the data.

These functions are required anytime you want to save a file to the phone—I do have a cheat sheet so I don't have to code this every time I need to save a file. And I recommend that you do the same, because it does save time.

Now that you've loaded the data, you can go back and add the functionality to save the data to a file.

24.2.6 *Adding save functionality*

Create a new function you can call every time you need to save an object. Add a new save function down near the bottom of the `MainViewController` file—this is what mine looks like:

```
func saveLionItems() {
}
```

The first thing you're going to do is create a variable you can use to store the data. Add the following line inside the `saveLionItems` function:

```
let data = NSMutableData()
```

`NSMutableData()` is another item that hails from Objective-C. Anytime you see the word `Mutable`, it means the variable is a collection type that can grow and shrink based on the size of the data that's stored within it. Because you don't know the number of

LioN objects that you're going to save, it makes sense that the data can shrink and grow as needed.

When you created the load functions earlier, you used an unarchiver to unarchive the data, so guess what you're going to use to the save the data? Did you guess an archiver? Okay, you get another cookie (again, I can't give you a cookie, so you'll have to reward yourself). Add the following line under the let data line:

```
let archiver = NSKeyedArchiver(forWritingWith: data)
```

You're going to use the archiver to encode the data for your objects, so add the following line under the let archiver line:

```
archiver.encode(lionData, forKey: "lionData")
```

Remember that in the load section, you loaded data for the keyword lionData, and I told you it would come into play later in the chapter. Well, here it is. You're encoding the array lionData using the keyword lionData. Just like when you loaded the data, you need to finish encoding it, so add the following line under the archiver.encode-Object line:

```
archiver.finishEncoding()
```

You've archived the data, but you still haven't written it to a file. Add this line under the finishEncoding() line:

```
data.write(to: getDataFilePath(), atomically: true)
```

This line writes the data to the file that you returned in the function getDataFilePath(). As you may notice, the writeToFile function takes a String as the first argument. Your getDataFilePath() function returns a String, so you use the shortcut of using the function as your argument in writing data to the file. You could instead create a new String variable and set it equal to the getDataFilePath(), and then use that String in the argument, but this is more succinct.

You've now added all the code required to save a file to the app sandbox and load that data back into the app. The only thing left is to call saveLionItems() when you need to save an item. Before we talk about that, though, here's what my entire save-LionItems() function looks like:

```
func saveLionItems() {
    let data = NSMutableData()
    let archiver = NSKeyedArchiver(forWritingWithMutableData: data)
    archiver.encodeObject(lionData, forKey: "lionData")
    archiver.finishEncoding()
    data.write(to: getDataFilePath(), atomically: true)
}
```

SAVING THE LIONS FROM THE APPROPRIATE PLACES

When do you think you should call the `SaveLionItems()` function? You should save it after you create a new LioN, so add the following line to the end of the `didFinish-AddingItem` function in the `MainViewController`:

```
saveLionItems()
```

Believe it or not, that's all you need to add to the function to save the new LioN to the sandbox. Where else should you add it? If you answered `edit`, you get another cookie. Add the same line to the end of the `didFinishEditingItem` function.

Is that it? You're still missing one place: you added functionality to delete a LioN from the list, so you need to save there, too. Add the `saveLionItems()` line to the end of the `commitEditingStyle` function to save after the user deletes a LioN.

That's it! You did it. All you need to do is test the app to make sure it all works as expected.

24.3 *Testing the load and save functionality*

Go ahead and run the app and add a LioN or two. You should still have the file path printing your console so you know where your sandbox is. If you don't, go back to the `viewDidLoad()` function in the `MainViewController` and add the following line:

```
print(dataFilePath())
```

After you've added a few LioNs to the app, stop the Simulator by clicking the Stop button in Xcode (next to the Run button). In the Finder, press Command-Shift-G or click Go > Go To Folder. Copy and paste the file path in your Xcode console into the window that pops up, and press Enter. Again, this is the location of your sandbox and plist file that you created. You can double-click the lion.plist file, and it will open in Xcode.

Take a look at figure 24.2. At first glance, this is a weird-looking file, isn't it?

If you expand the `$objects` line by clicking the triangle, you'll be presented with several items that are numbered starting with item 0. Xcode puts a bunch of stuff in the plist file that you don't need to worry about, but with the `$objects` expanded, you should see the LioNs that you created within the file.

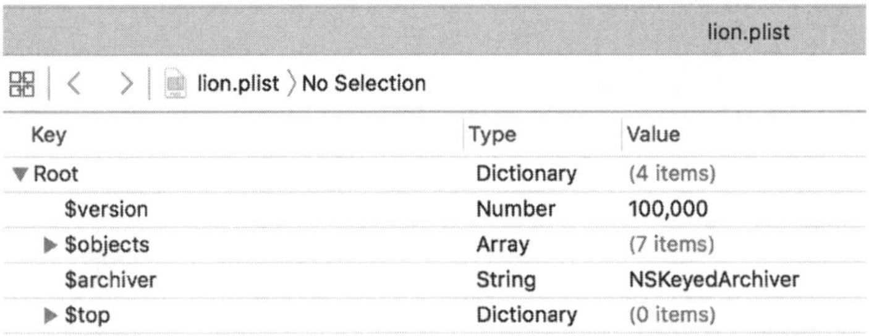

Key	Type	Value
▼ Root	Dictionary	(4 items)
$version	Number	100,000
▶ $objects	Array	(7 items)
$archiver	String	NSKeyedArchiver
▶ $top	Dictionary	(0 items)

Figure 24.2   You can open the lion.plist file in Xcode by double-clicking it in the Finder window.

Close the plist file, run the app again, and you'll see that your LioNs loaded again. Pretty cool, huh?

> **Key point**
> Make sure you don't have the plist file open when you're running your app, because this may cause the file to get corrupted. Always stop the app before opening the plist file and close the plist file before running the app.

If you want to test it again, you can delete the plist file from your hard drive and then run the app again. You'll notice that there are no LioNs in the list.

24.4 Summary

Wow, what a chapter! You accomplished a lot, and I hope you feel accomplished (and got a few cookies out of it, too). You added all the functionality required to load objects from a file and to save them off to a file. I'll reiterate that even I don't have all these functions memorized. I use a cheat sheet where I save the functions and steps required to save and load files. You can use this chapter as your cheat sheet going forward, or you can create your own sheet.

In this chapter, you learned

- How to add functionality to a class to allow it to be saved to a file
- How to conform to the NSCoding protocol
- How to load data from a file
- How to save data to a file

Your LioN app is coming along. You'll make it a little prettier in the next chapter.

25

Making your LioN prettier

The basic functionality of the Lion app is almost complete. You can do everything you need to in order to create LioNs, edit them, and delete them, but the app looks utilitarian and isn't pretty. It also doesn't look good on different sizes of devices. You'll fix that in this chapter.

25.1 Basic fixes

The first thing you need to do is make some basic fixes so the app looks a little better. Open the storyboard, and select the lionName text field on the Add/Edit scene. In the Attributes Inspector, change Border Style to None. Do the same for the lionDescription field. Run the app, and see how much better it already looks without the borders on the text fields (figure 25.1).

Figure 25.1 Changing Border Style to None for the `lionName` **and** `lionDescription` **fields will make the scene look much nicer.**

25.1.1 Creating two sections

Next, you'll add two sections to the table view so the Like and Dislike buttons have separation from the Name and Description fields. The easiest way to do this is by using sections, so click the table view (make sure to click the table view and not a table view cell) and change the number of sections to 2 in the Attributes Inspector. You now have two sections in the table, and each section has all three of the rows, as you can see in figure 25.2. That's okay. You'll fix it.

Figure 25.2　Add a second section to the Add Edit View Controller scene, and delete the duplicated cells so the final product looks like this.

You want the first section to have the LioN name and description fields, and the second section should only have the Like and Dislike buttons. Using the Document Outline (the panel to the left of the Storyboard panel—see figure 25.3), select the third row in the first section (the one with the Like and Dislike buttons) and delete it. Select the first two rows in the second section (the ones with the LioN Name and LioN Description), and delete those as well.

You deleted the third row of the first section—the Like and Dislike buttons—and these were the buttons that were connected to your code. Now you have to reconnect the Like and Dislike buttons' outlets in the second section to the code. Open the Assistant Editor view so you have the storyboard and the `AddEditView-Controller` visible.

You already have the outlets for the Like and Dislike buttons defined in the `Add-EditViewController` file, so you need to reconnect the outlets to the buttons. Notice

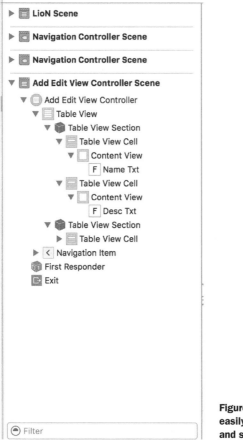

▶ 🖼 **LioN Scene**

▶ 🖼 **Navigation Controller Scene**

▶ 🖼 **Navigation Controller Scene**

▼ 🖼 **Add Edit View Controller Scene**

  ▼ 🔵 Add Edit View Controller

    ▼ 🖼 Table View

      ▼ 📦 Table View Section

        ▼ 🖼 Table View Cell

          ▼ ⬜ Content View

            F Name Txt

        ▼ 🖼 Table View Cell

          ▼ ⬜ Content View

            F Desc Txt

      ▼ 📦 Table View Section

        ▶ 🖼 Table View Cell

    ▶ ⟨ Navigation Item

    🖼 First Responder

    🖼 Exit

⊙ Filter

Figure 25.3   Use the Document Outline panel to easily delete the cells you don't need for the first and second sections of the table view.

the left margin (or gutter) in the AddEditViewController file—there are small circles that are either black or empty. The black circles signify that the outlet or action is connected to the storyboard, and the empty circles signify that the item isn't connected (see figure 25.4). Click the empty circle next to the Dislike button outlet in the file, and drag your mouse pointer over to the Dislike button on the storyboard to connect the two again. This is the opposite action of connecting the storyboard to the file. Pretty easy, huh?

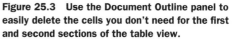

```
○   @IBOutlet weak var likeButton: UIButton!
◉   @IBOutlet weak var dislikeButton: UIButton!
    override func viewDidLoad() {
        super viewDidLoad()
```

Figure 25.4   Use the empty circles in the AddEditViewController file to reconnect the outlets to the buttons in the storyboard.

If you run the app again, it should work as it did before you split the table into two sections.

25.1.2 *Adding the Like and Dislike images*

Adding and using images is pretty easy in Xcode 7. Back in the old days, we had to do a lot of work to use images and make them look good on different kinds of devices. It was kind of like walking to school in the snow, uphill both ways. Now it's much easier. Look in the Project Navigator in Xcode, and you'll see a blue folder named Assets .xcassets. Click it, and the Standard Editor opens a new panel. At the bottom of the panel, click the plus button (+) and select New Image Set. A new item will appear in the catalog that says Image, and on the right you'll see placeholders for Universal images for 1x, 2x, and 3x.

Apple uses these universal sizes to optimize the app size for download from the App Store. Why should a user with an iPad download images that are sized for an iPhone (and vice versa)? The process of providing different sized images is *app thinning*, and the way Apple optimizes the download is called *slicing*. If you're building apps for iPads and iPhones (and any other screen sizes such as those of tvOS or watchOS), you should supply the different sized images so that Xcode and Apple can optimize the bundle size for your users.

What do 1x, 2x, and 3x stand for? They're intended to show the size differences of images. 1x represents older iPhones and iPads; 2x is for newer iPhones; and 3x represents the newest iPhones and iPads. It isn't all about screen size, though. It's also about resolution. Images are measured in *points*—a mathematical representation that most of us don't need (or care) to know about. In the old days, 1 point was equal to 1 pixel. On retina devices, 1 point is equal to either 2×2 pixels or 3×3 pixels (depending on screen size), which is why images look so much clearer. There is more data in each image. Why is all this important, you may be wondering?

If you don't provide different sized and scaled images, Xcode and Apple will upscale and downscale your images to make them work with the various sized devices. You'll usually lose a lot of clarity in the images, and processing will take longer and use more memory to complete this. That's why you should provide the different-sized assets for your app to make it look better and to improve its performance and memory usage.

This was a great (in my opinion) discussion of the different sized images you must provide, but what are the sizes, other than 1x, 2x, and 3x? The easiest way to understand the sizes is to use an example. Let's assume you have an image that you want to display on an iPad, and it's 150×150 pixels. That would be your 3x image, so it needs to have the most detail and look the best. You also need to create an image for the 2x version, so that would 100×100, and the 1x image would be 50×50. There are no set sizes for images in your app—it's based entirely on how you want to use the images. The Apple developer docs explain which devices need 1x, 2x, and 3x images; the complete list of required images and sizes is available at http://mng.bz/i0h0.

Now that you understand the 1x, 2x, and 3x image sizes and scales, I want to introduce you to a simpler way of doing things. I prefer to use *vector* images that are saved as PDF images. If you add a PDF image to your project, Xcode will do the work of scaling your images to 2x and 3x for you—it assumes your PDF is the 1x version. I know I said earlier that having Apple scale your images may have performance and quality impacts, but this is different. Vector images scale easily with minimal performance impact. In my opinion, it's easier to use PDFs so you ensure you have all the correctly sized images at the right quality, but you can make your own choices (because you're now a programmer). The graphics for the LioN app aren't detailed with various levels of shading and effects, so allowing Xcode to resize the images isn't a problem. If you use Adobe Photoshop, you can save your images as PDF files; otherwise, ask your graphic artist to provide you with the PDF files. There are also other graphic editing programs that can do this for you if you know how to use them.

Luckily, I already have the images needed for the Like it or Not app, and you can download the image file from www.manning.com/books/anyone-can-create-an-app or https://github.com/wlwise/AnyoneCanCreateAnApp. Rename the Image Set you created earlier to likeIt, and change the Scales of the image set to Single Scale (figure 25.5). Drag the LikeIt.pdf image into Xcode on the dotted square in the image set (figure 25.6).

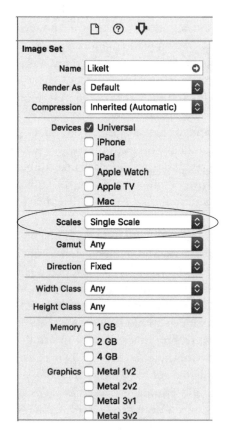

Figure 25.5   Change the Scales attribute to Single Scale for the likeIt image set.

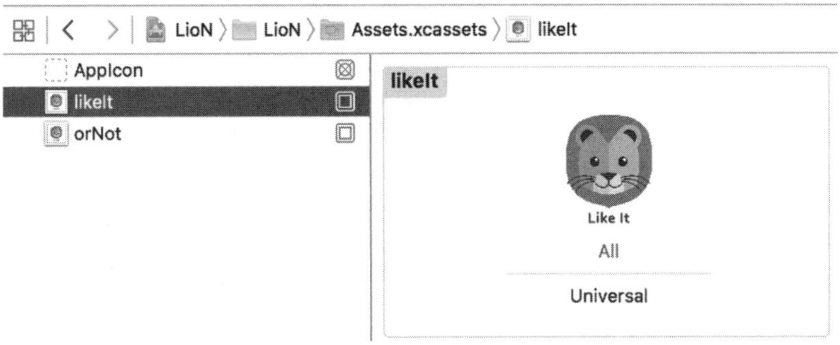

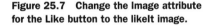

Figure 25.6 **Add the likeIt image to the likeIt image set so it looks like this.**

Next, create a second image set, name it orNot, and set it to Single Scale. Drag the orNot.pdf image into the dotted-line area labeled Universal.

Open the storyboard again, and make sure the AddEditLion scene is visible. Click the Like button, and select the likeIt image in the Image attribute on the Attribute panel, as shown in figure 25.7.

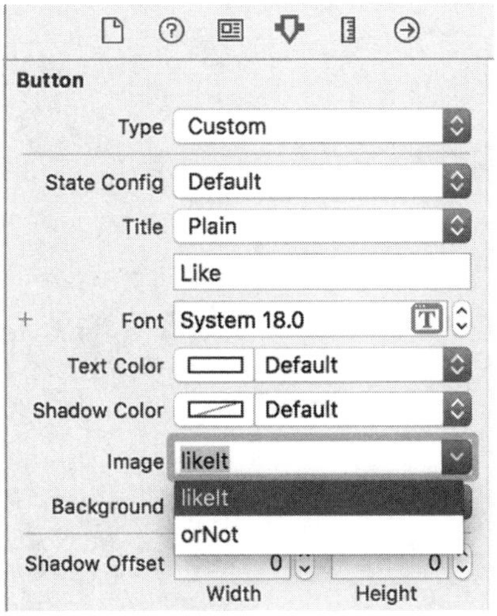

Figure 25.7 **Change the Image attribute for the Like button to the likeIt image.**

Once you set the Image attribute, note that the Like button shows the image you added. It isn't sized quite right yet, though, so drag the corners of the image and size it smaller so it fits in the cell. Do the same for the Dislike button, resizing it as well (you'll need the orNot.pdf file for the Dislike button).

You can see now that the cell shows Or Not and then Like It—which isn't correct. Drag the buttons so the Like It button is on the far left and the Or Not button is on the right. Run the app again, and make sure it still works as expected. Pretty cool, huh?

25.1.3   *Changing the table view background colors*

The Add/Edit scene still looks a bit bland, so you're going to update it to look a little more modern (and prettier). Make sure the Add/Edit scene is visible in the storyboard and then click the table view in the Document Outline, or click the table in the scene. The Attributes Inspector panel will allow you to change the background color of the table as well as the color of the separator line between the rows. For the separator, I used the color of the LioN's mane. To do this, click the drop-down arrows next to Default below the Separator attribute (figure 25.8), and then click Other at the bottom of the selection box (figure 25.9).

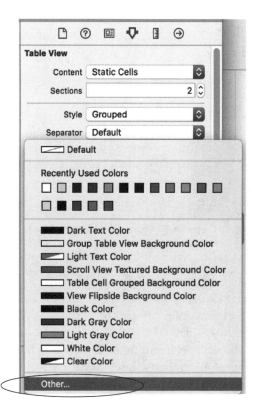

Figure 25.8   Click the drop-down arrows next to the Default color box to change the color of the line that separates the different cells.

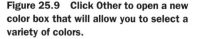

Figure 25.9   Click Other to open a new color box that will allow you to select a variety of colors.

A new color selector panel will open, and there you can choose any color on the spectrum—or use the eyedropper to select a color that's currently visible on the screen. Click the eyedropper, and a new magnifying circle pops up—this has a small square in the middle of it.

Move the circle around until the square is over the dark color of the LioN's mane on one of the button images and then click the mouse. You should see the color under the separator attribute change to the dark brown color; the separator lines in the table will change to the dark color as well (figure 25.10).

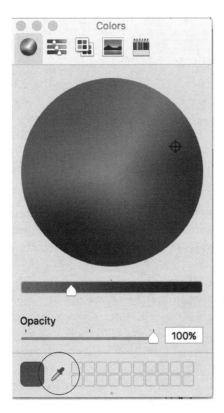

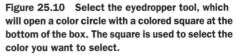

Figure 25.10   Select the eyedropper tool, which will open a color circle with a colored square at the bottom of the box. The square is used to select the color you want to select.

Scroll down the table view's Attribute panel until you see the Background attribute. You're going to select the color in the same way as you did the separator line, but this time you'll select the light area under the lion's nose. This will change the background color of the table. It's looking much better now, isn't it?

25.1.4 Toggling the images based on selection

Create two new image sets called likeItSelected and orNotSelected. Set the Scale Factor for each one to Single Vector. Next, drag the appropriate files in for each image set (likeItSelected.pdf and orNotSelected.pdf). You need to change your code to display these selected images instead of changing the background color of the buttons. Open the AddEditViewController file, and find your toggleLike() function.

Now that you have your images assets stored in the Xcode Assets folder, you can load the images by name. Add the following code to your toggle function:

```
func toggleLike() {
      if likeVar == true {
          dislikeButton.setImage(UIImage(named: "orNot"), for: .normal)
          likeButton.setImage(UIImage(named: "likeItSelected"), for:
      .normal)
      } else {
          dislikeButton.setImage(UIImage(named: "orNotSelected"), for:
      .normal)
          likeButton.setImage(UIImage(named: "likeIt"), for: .normal)
      }
   }
```

Run the app again, and see that the images toggle for the selected and unselected states. It looks pretty good, doesn't it? One thing I would like, though, is for the main page to show whether you like the item. You'll do that next.

25.1.5 *Setting images on the cells*

You can probably figure out the first few steps of getting the images to appear on the cells. First, create two new image sets named likeItCell and orNotCell. Set each of the respective Scale Factors to Single Vector. Next, you need to change the cell to show an image. Open your storyboard, and select the lionCell on the main LioN scene. You set the cell style to Subtitle back in chapter 18, but in case your cell isn't set to Subtitle, here's how. Make sure you select the cell itself and not the content view—double-check by looking at the Document Outline for the cell. When the cell is selected, look at the Attributes Inspector panel, and notice at the top that there are several cell layouts you can choose from. Select the Custom style, and you'll see that the cell changes its layout a bit.

Right under the Style selector, you can select an image. Select the likeItCell image here, and the happy lion will appear on the cell. Pretty cool, huh? It doesn't matter which cell image you select, because you're going to override it programmatically in the next step. You need the placeholder image on the cell right now. Your LioN cell should look like figure 25.11.

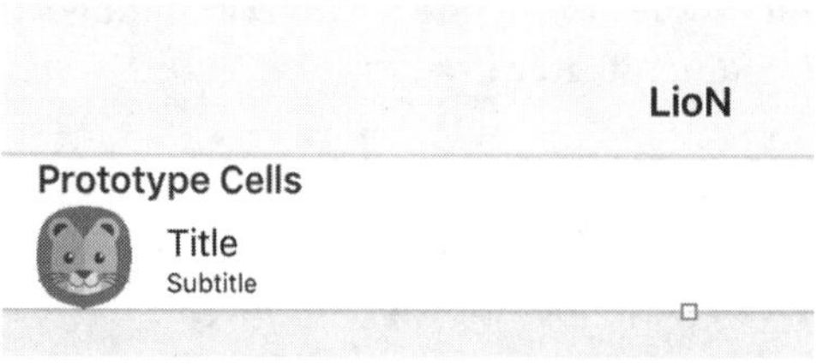

LioN

Prototype Cells

Title
Subtitle

Figure 25.11   Change the cell type
to Subtitle, and then set the image to
likeItCell.

If you run the app, you'll see that all the cells are happy lions (likeItCell) because that's the image you set for the cell. You need to have the image update based on whether the user likes the item.

Let's think about what you need to do. If the LioN is a like item, then you need the green, smiling, like lion to show up (`likeItCell`)—otherwise you want the dislike lion to appear. Which tool will work best for this? You guessed it: our friend the `if` statement. You need to add the `if` statement in several places in your code. Where do you think those places are?

If you guessed on first load, on edit, and on add, then you're correct! If not, don't worry, you're still totally awesome. You need to change the cell image when the LioN cells first load, and you need to change the image when an item is added or edited.

Add the following code to the `cellForRowAtIndexPath` function, above the `return cell` line:

```
if lionData[indexPath.row].like == true {
        cell.imageView?.image =  UIImage(named: "likeItCell")
    { else }
        cell.imageView?.image =  UIImage(named: "orNotCell")
    }
```

This should look familiar. You're checking the LioN object to see if it's a like (`true`) or dislike (`false`) and then setting the appropriate image. Make sure you use the exact image literal string that you used when you created your assets, or Xcode won't be able to find the images and will throw an error when you run the app. Run the app now, and make sure the cells and images load correctly.

Next, you'll change the add function to reload the cell correctly when it's added or edited. Add the following code to the `AddItemViewController` function inside the `if let` bracket:

```
if lionData[editIndexPath!.row].like == true {
   cell.imageView?.image =  UIImage(imageLiteral: "likeItCell")
{ else }
   cell.imageView?.image =  UIImage(imageLiteral: "orNotCell")
}
```

Run the app again, and you'll see that the lion images appear correctly on the cells for each lion item—whether the item was added or edited, or if it was reloaded.

25.1.6 *Making the MainView scene prettier*

You need to make the same type of color changes to the main view scene that you did for the Add/Edit scene. You'll change the color of the separator line and the background. See if you can do it yourself before I walk you through it. The colors will be easier to select this time because you've done it once, and you're going to use the same colors.

Select the table view so the Table View attributes are displayed in the Attributes Inspector. You should be able to select the separator line color from the drop-down because it's a recently used color. You can do the same for the table view background color, too.

25.1.7 Updating the navigation bars

The navigation bars at the top of each scene will be the same dark brown that's inside the lion's ears. You'll use white for labels so they stand out from the dark background. With the main storyboard open, make sure the first Navigation Controller scene is visible and the Main ViewController is partially visible. Click the Navigation Controller once so the Document Outline displays the navigation bar (figure 25.12).

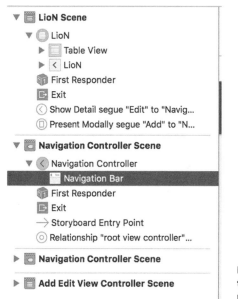

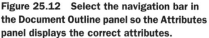

Figure 25.12   Select the navigation bar in the Document Outline panel so the Attributes panel displays the correct attributes.

Make sure you select the navigation bar in the Document Outline so the Attributes Inspector shows the right attributes. Click the Bar Tint drop-down in the Attributes selector, and then select Other at the bottom of the menu option. When the color selector box opens, click the eyedropper again, but this time select the dark color in the lion's ears as the background color. The bar should now turn dark on the Main-ViewController scene, as shown in figure 25.13.

With the Navigation Bar attributes still showing, change the Title Color attribute to white. This is looking better and better, isn't it? You may notice on the MainView-Controller scene that the + button is hard to see because it's blue. You need to change that to white. Select it on the MainViewController scene so the Attributes

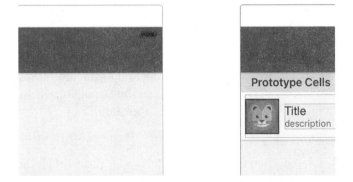

Figure 25.13   Scroll the Standard Editor Panel so the Navigation Controller scene and the `MainViewController` scene are both partially visible. You need to select the dark color of the lion's ears.

Inspector panel displays its attributes. Change the Tint Color to white—now you can see it better.

Next, you need to change the navigation bar background color for the `AddEdit-ViewController`. It's easier this time because the dark brown color is available in the Recently Used Colors drop-down. Select the Navigation Controller between the `Main-ViewController` and the `AddEditViewController`, and, using the Document Outline panel, select the navigation bar again. Select the dark brown color from the recent colors under the Bar Tint attribute drop-down. Make sure the title color shows as white, as well. The Done button on the `AddEditViewController` also needs to change to white, so do it the same way you did the + button earlier.

25.2   Adding an icon

Every app is represented by an icon that appears on your iPhone or iPad, which you tap to launch it. The icon is important—people need to be able to readily recognize the app. The image properties of such icons are spelled out clearly by Apple, and, unfortunately, the icon images aren't handled the same way as the images we've been discussing are. Back in section 1.1.2, you learned that you could either provide the images in all required sizes or provide one single vector PDF graphic. That doesn't apply for icons—you must provide the required sizes for each icon.

Open the Asset library again in Xcode, and at the top of the list, you should see an AppIcon placeholder. Click it, and note that the Standard Editor panel shows all the different sizes of icons that you need to provide. It's handy that Apple tells you exactly what sizes to provide, but what a pain to create all those! Thank goodness a) I've already created them so you don't have to; b) there are plenty of free services out on the web that allow you to upload a single image, and the scripts will provide a zip file for you to download all the different sizes required; and c) there are also Photoshop scripts you can run that create all the required sizes. I chose option c, but you should choose option a.

Open the folder where you saved all the icon files, and drag and drop them into the appropriate icon areas. Each icon file is labeled with the size of the icon so it's easy to know which icon files belong in each area. Run the app again; after it loads, click Hardware > Home to simulate a home button push in the Simulator, or press Command-Shift-H. Doesn't that icon look cute on the desktop? I think so.

25.3   *Updating the launch scene*

The launch image is displayed when the app first launches (big surprise, huh?). Apple recommends that the launch image look similar to the first scene so it appears that the app loads more quickly. Some people like to put an image on the scene to promote their company, their app, or other apps they might have. You'll stick with Apple's best practices and use a launch scene that looks somewhat like the main scene that loads. The only thing you want to do then is change the background color of the launch scene that Apple already created for you.

In the Project Navigator, you'll see a LaunchScreen.storyboard file. Open it, and note the title and copyright information at the bottom of the screen. Delete both of those labels so the scene is completely empty. Now click the empty scene once so the Attributes Inspector opens for the scene. Change the background color to the same color as the background of the table views. This will make the app look like it's loading that much quicker.

25.4   *Summary*

It's surprising how much work it takes to make the app attractive, isn't it? You learned quite a bit in this chapter, and the app looks great. There are many books about designing apps, making them look good, and creating a good user experience and graphics, and they cover these topics in much greater depth than this chapter did.

You learned the basics well enough that you can experiment with the different designs. The best way to learn is to try—so keep practicing and you'll be a master!

In this chapter, you learned about

- Changing background colors
- Adding images
- Updating the launch screen
- Adding icons

You'll learn about Auto Layout, stack views, and constraints in the next chapter, so the app will look good on all different device sizes.

Working with Auto Layout

So far we haven't focused much on ensuring that apps work across all different screen sizes, but we will now!

26.1 Changing the layout to work for all screen sizes

It's important that all of your apps work on the different screen sizes that you're building for, or your end users won't be happy. Apple provides some classes that make it easy to lay out the scenes so they expand and contract based on the size of the screen the apps are running on. *Stack views* are classes that allow you to lay out the scenes in either rows or columns. If you think about the majority of the apps you use, most scenes can be divided by imaginary lines into rows and columns.

Think about stack views like a bookshelf: the bookshelf itself is one stack view, and each stack of books is like a nested stack view. Figure 26.1 would be considered five stack views, because the bookshelf is one and each stack of books (horizontal or vertical) is a stack. You can stack books upright so they're laid out horizontally (as in a library—the books themselves are vertical, but they're arranged horizontally on a shelf), or you can stack them on top of each other so they're stacked vertically but the books themselves are lying horizontally. You can do this as many times as you want on a single shelf, as long as there is plenty of room both horizontally and vertically. You can have the first stack of books lying sideways (so the books are lying on top of each other) and then you can stack them so they are sitting vertically, as in figure 26.1.

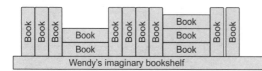

Figure 26.1   Books can be stacked vertically or horizontally, like stack views.

Stack views provide the same type of functionality, but instead of stacking books, you're stacking UI components. You can stack a few components vertically and then a few horizontally, as long as you have space. The neat thing about stack views is that you can set different attributes to tell Apple how to scale the components based on the screen size. You can set the alignment of the items (perpendicular layout), the distribution (along the axis), and the spacing (how far apart the components are), as shown in figure 26.2.

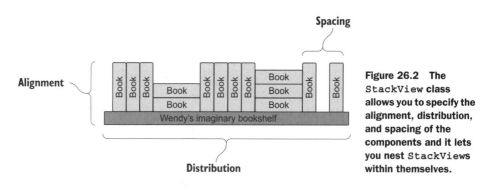

Figure 26.2   The `StackView` class allows you to specify the alignment, distribution, and spacing of the components and it lets you nest `StackViews` within themselves.

Stack views work hand-in-hand with Auto Layout, which provides constraints. *Constraints* constrain how the different components can change based on varying factors, like screen size and orientation (landscape or portrait). You can "pin" a component to the corner of a screen, or you can specify that the component must always be a certain distance from the margin of the scene. It will be easier to explain if you start making changes to the LioN app, so you'll do that now.

26.1.1 Make changes to the AddEditView scene

Open the main storyboard, and make sure the AddEditViewController scene is visible. The first thing you need to do is make sure the Name and Description fields shrink and stretch to the size of the table row, regardless of the screen size. You'll set some constraints to make this happen. Make sure the Document Outline is visible (click the square box on the bottom left of the storyboard panel—see figure 26.3), and then select the lionName text box.

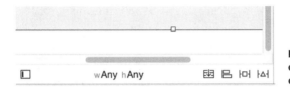

Figure 26.3   Button at the bottom of the main storyboard panel that opens the Document Outline

You can set the constraints in the scene or in the Document Outline; I find it easier to do it in the Document Outline. Again, with the lionName field selected in the Document Outline, hold down the Control button and click and drag between the lionName field and Content View (above it). When Content View above the lionName field is highlighted, let go of the button and the Control button. A black dialog box pops up, as shown in figure 26.4.

Figure 26.4   Control-click the lionName field, and drag and drop it to Content View so this dark dialog box pops up.

As you can see from the resulting pop-up box, there are many constraints you could select. Here are some high-level definitions of the different constraints:

- *Leading Space to Container Margin*—This is the space between the component (in this case, the name text field) and the containing view that it's in (in this case, the content view of the table view cell). This sets the left margin spacing of the component.
- *Trailing Space to Container Margin*—This is the space between the component (again, in this case the name text field) and the right side of the containing

view (still the table view cell's content view). This sets the right margin spacing of the component.

- *Top Space to Container Margin*—If I repeat what this does, it might be getting a bit redundant, don't you think? This sets the top margin.
- *Bottom Space to Container Margin*—Okay, can you guess what this one does? It sets the bottom space.
- *Center Horizontally in Container*—This will center the component horizontally in the container. Aren't you glad I told you that?
- *Center Vertically in Container*—Your turn to guess what this one does. That's right; it centers the component vertically in the container.
- *Equal Widths*—Sets the component to the same width of the container.
- *Equal Heights*—Sets the component to the same height as the container.
- *Aspect Ratio*—Ensures the component has equal width and equal height.

Although these options seem self-explanatory in most cases, I've found them to be tricky at times. That's in part due to ordering—you can set the container to Equal Widths as the component, or the component to Equal Widths as the container. It's a subtle difference, but it does change the layout. It takes practice to learn to use these effectively to get the best layouts, but once you've mastered them, laying out your apps is a breeze.

Come on. I'll show you how.

LAYING OUT THE TEXT FIELDS

You need to set four constraints for each of the text fields—four for the LioN Name and four for the Description. You need to set the LioN Name text field's top margin, bottom margin, trailing space, and leading space equal to the container's top, bottom, trailing, and leading space, respectively. Control-click and drag from the Name text field to Content View (above it), and select Top Space to Container Margin. Do it again for each of the other three constraints (figure 26.5).

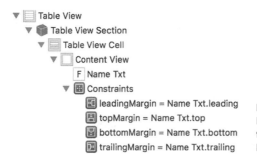

Figure 26.5   Control-click and drag from the Name text field to Content View, and set the four constraints for top margin, bottom margin, leading margin, and trailing margin.

Notice the small arrow at upper right in the outline view of the Storyboard (at left in figure 26.6): click it to open a detailed Misplaced Views tab (at right in figure 26.6).

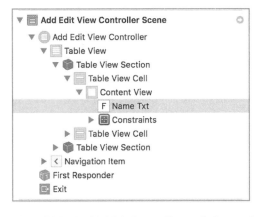

Figure 26.6   (Left) Click the small arrow indicator. (Right) In the Misplaced Views tab that opens, click the small triangle.

Then click the little triangle indicator at right in the Misplaced Views tab. Xcode will open a new Resolve tab, where you can update the frames. Make sure the Update Frames option is selected, as shown in figure 26.7, and then click the Fix Misplacement button.

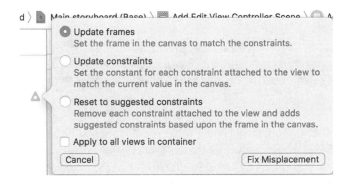

Figure 26.7   Select the Update Frames option, and then click Fix Misplacement to update the size and layout for the component.

Notice now that the Name text field is the same length as the row. Pretty cool, huh? The text field will shrink and grow based on the screen size and the rows, and that's all you had to do.

Do the same thing for the Description text field: set the four constraints, and then update the frames.

SETTING THE ASPECT RATIO FOR THE BUTTONS

The first thing you need to do to the buttons is make sure they don't stretch too far one way or the other and end up skewed. Nobody likes a skewed LioN. You need to set the aspect ratio to 1, meaning it should be as equally tall and wide. Select the Like It button, and then click the Pin button at the bottom of the Standard Editor (the third one from the left). A new dialog box will open. Select the Aspect Ratio check box, and then click Add 1 Constraint at the bottom, as shown in figure 26.8.

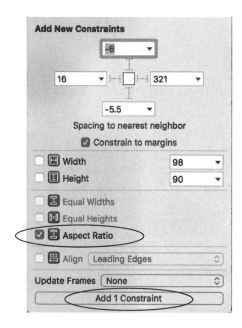

Figure 26.8　Click the Pin button, and then add the Aspect Ratio constraint to the Like button.

The Like It button on the storyboard likely has some red lines across it in several places. This is okay—it's Xcode warning you that you haven't set enough constraints on the button yet so the layout won't look exactly right. You'll fix it, though; never fear. Check the Document Outline panel (with the Like button still selected), and click down so the new constraint is visible (under the Like button). If the constraint doesn't say aspect = 1 (figure 26.9), then the original button wasn't exactly square. Click the Aspect constraint in the Document Outline, and notice that the Attribute panel changes to reflect the aspect constraint. Change the Multiplier field so it's equal to 1 (figure 26.10).

Great job! Now do the exact same thing for the Or Not button.

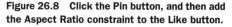

Figure 26.9　The aspect for the Like and Dislike buttons should be 1.

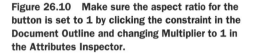

Aspect Ratio Constraint

First Item	Like Button.Width	
Relation	Equal	
Second Item	Like Button.Height	
+ Constant	0	
Priority	1000	
Multiplier	1	

Figure 26.10 Make sure the aspect ratio for the button is set to 1 by clicking the constraint in the Document Outline and changing Multiplier to 1 in the Attributes Inspector.

CREATING STACK VIEWS

Next, you need to lay out the buttons relative to each other and relative to the rest of the view. Click the Like It button in the storyboard; then, while holding down the Command key, click the other button so they're both highlighted. In the menu, click Editor > Embed In > Stack View. The two LioN buttons may have grown incredibly large now. That's okay; you can fix it. You need to set the constraints of the stack view so that its layout is updated relative to the row and surrounding views. Specifically, you need to set the stack view's top and bottom margins relative to the content view's top and bottom margins. I bet you can do this without reading about it, but I'm making some money by writing this book, so I feel it's my duty to tell you how.

In the Document Outline (left panel), select the new Stack View component; with the Control button held down, drag to Content View. When the dialog pops up (figure 26.11), select the Bottom Space to Container Margin setting. Do this again for the top margin.

Figure 26.11 Control-drag from Stack View to Content View to display this dialog. Set each of the top four constraints by clicking them (you'll have to Option-click and drag for each setting).

You may notice that the size of the buttons didn't change. Don't worry; you'll change that in a moment. You need to embed two more stack views in the first stack view, one for each button. You can think of these two new stack views as sections on your book-shelf. With the first stack view selected in the Document Outline, click the Stack button on the bottom of the Standard Editor (the first button). You should see another stack view appear in the Outline. Click it once more so you see a total of three stack views in the Document Outline.

You may have noticed that one of the new stack views look horizontal instead of vertical. Again, you can fix this. With the stack view selected, change the Axis in the Attributes Inspector to Vertical (instead of Horizontal), as shown in figure 26.12.

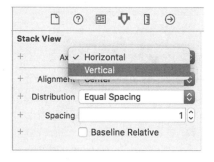

Figure 26.12   Select a stack view in the Document Outline to display the Attributes Inspector panel. You can change the Axis field this way.

Do this for all three stack views if they aren't already vertical. Next, you need to rear-range the stack views so they're stacked correctly (see what I did there?). You can eas-ily drag and drop the views in the Outline, so make sure you have two stack views lined up equally under the topmost stack view. The views will want to nest themselves in each other, but you need to pull them out so two stack views are nested equally under the top stack view. Once you have that set up, drag and drop the Like It button under the second stack view and drag and drop the Or Not button under the second stack view, as shown in figure 26.13.

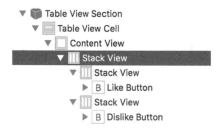

Figure 26.13   Align the stack views so two are nested equally under the top one. Drop the Like button under the first nested stack view and the Dislike button under the second nested view.

Next you'll fix how large the buttons look compared to the row. Open the stack view Constraints for the top and bottom margins in the Document Outline, and check the Attributes Inspector to make sure they look right. Figure 26.14 shows the Constraints for the main Stack View—each Stack View will get its own set of Constraints in the Document Outline.

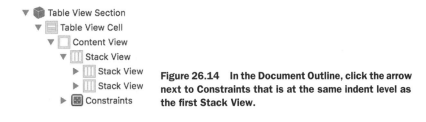

Figure 26.14   In the Document Outline, click the arrow next to Constraints that is at the same indent level as the first Stack View.

My Attributes Inspector shows something crazy: the Constant attribute is 443. This is telling Xcode that I want the buttons to be 443 points larger than the content view. I don't want that—I want the buttons to be the same size—so change the Constant attribute to 0. Do this for both the top and bottom constraint, and the buttons should get back to a normal size.

This is looking better, but the two buttons are huddled together at the left side of the row, and you want them spread out equally. Create the leading and trailing constraints again for the topmost stack view. Control-click and drag from the topmost Stack View to Content View, and select the Leading Space to Container Margin option, as shown in figure 26.15.

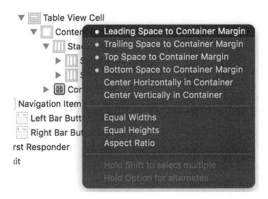

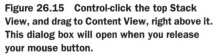

Figure 26.15   Control-click the top Stack View, and drag to Content View, right above it. This dialog box will open when you release your mouse button.

Do it again, but this time, select Trailing Space to Container Margin. This will ensure that the Or Not button stays to the right and the Like It button to the left. This looks better, but I'd rather have the buttons spaced a little more. Select the Trailing Space to Container Margin constraint in the Document Outline (figure 26.16), and change the Constant value to 25 (figure 26.17).

This will push the button out 25 points from the margin. Do the same thing for the leading margin. You're buttons may not look quite right, because you didn't update the frame yet. With the topmost stack view selected, click the Resolve Auto Layout Issues button (at the bottom of the Standard Editor, the rightmost button), and click Update Frames for the Selected View. This should update the frame so the buttons are more equally spaced.

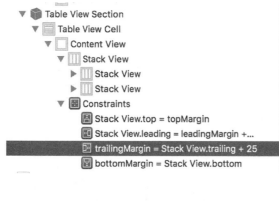

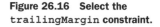

Figure 26.16   **Select the**
`trailingMargin` **constraint.**

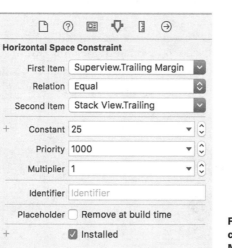

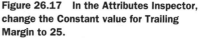

Figure 26.17   **In the Attributes Inspector,**
change the Constant value for Trailing
Margin to 25.

26.1.2 *Changing the color of cells on the main scene*

The final layout changes you need to make for the app are on the main scene, so the
font and the colors look better. Make sure the LioN scene is visible in the storyboard.
Click lionCell so Content View is visible beneath it, and then expand Content View so
the two text labels and the image are visible (see figure 26.18).

Let's start by making the text look better. Back in the storyboard, select the Title
label, open the Attributes Inspector, and make sure Font is set to Helvetica Neue 17.0
and Color is set to black, as shown in figure 26.19.

Next, select the Description label. Set Font to System 13.0 and Color to Dark Gray
Color, as shown in figure 26.20.

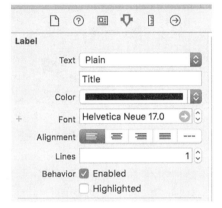

Figure 26.18   Expand lionCell and Content View so the Title label, the Subtitle label, and the likeItCell image are visible.

Figure 26.19   Set the color for the Title label to black and the font to Helvetica Neue 17.0.

Figure 26.20   Set Color for the Description label to Dark Gray Color and Font to System 13.0.

26.2   Summary

Understanding topics like Auto Layout, constraints, and stack views will be key for you as you design your own apps in the future. This chapter was a high-level overview of some of the things you can do with them. The best way to learn is to try. I don't find these topics that intuitive, so it took me a while to figure things out, and it may take you a while, too. Be patient, though, and keep experimenting. It will be worth the effort when you create an awesome app!

You're going to add search functionality in the next chapter so you can find the LioNs that you've added.

Search your LioNs

This chapter covers

- Adding search functionality
- Closures
- Cleaning up the code

Can you believe how far you've come in this book? You're almost finished with the LioN app. It would be really nice if you allowed your users to search for the LioNs they've added—otherwise they'll have to scroll through everything. Let's see how to add that feature!

27.1 Adding the search functionality

The first thing you need to do is add the search bar to the LioN scene. Search the Object Library for *search*, and two different objects will be returned. The first is Search Bar, which is just the visual component, and the second is Search Bar and Search Display Controller. You want the second component, because you can use the controller to capture and manage users' searches. Grab the Search Bar and Search Display Controller, and drop it at the very top of the table view on the `Main-ViewController` scene, above the words *Prototype Cells*. It should automatically take up the entire scene horizontally, as shown in figure 27.1.

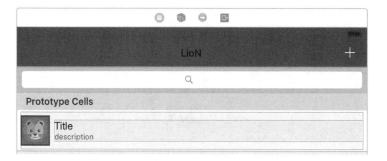

Figure 27.1   The Search Bar and Search Display Controller should be dropped directly above the words *Prototype Cells*. The component will resize itself to span the entire scene horizontally.

Now you need to implement all the functions to make the search bar useable. Thinking back to what you've learned in this book, how do you think the search bar will be added to `MainViewController` so you can use some of the functions the search bar provides? Think back to chapter 22...protocols and delegates! Right! You'll start by having your `MainViewController` conform to the `UISearchControllerDelegate` protocol. Change the `MainViewController` class definition to conform to the `UISearch-ControllerDelegate` protocol and the `UISearchBarDelegate` so it looks like this:

```
class MainViewController: UITableViewController,
    AddEditViewControllerDelegate, UISearchControllerDelegate,
➡ UISearchBarDelegate {
```

Next you need to create a variable for the Search Controller, so add this line at the top of the class with your other class-level definitions:

```
var resultSearchController = UISearchController(searchResultsController: nil)
```

You learned about ViewControllers in chapter 15, but to refresh your memory: they control the flow of the app based in part on the users' interactions on the view they control. So the `MainViewController` is the controller for the LioN scene, and the `UISearch-Controller` is the controller in the same way for the search bar. It controls what happens when the user taps inside the search bar, types a search term, clicks the Search button, and much more.

What you really want to do is have the table view update to just the LioN objects that have the letter or series of letters the user is typing in the search bar. If the user types a *T*, the table view should immediately limit the LioN objects in the table to ones that contain the letter *T* in the title. Then, if the user types the letter *H*, again the table view should limit the objects shown to ones that contain *TH* in the title. The user doesn't have to tap the Search button when they want to search—the app should respond to the letters tapped and filter the results based on their search.

What you need, then, is some way to "listen" for events that happen to the search bar. Guess what? You can. Apple made a way to do this easily—you just need to make sure your class conforms to the `UISearchResultsUpdating` protocol. First add `UISearch-ResultsUpdating` to the class definition so it looks like this:

```
class MainViewController: UITableViewController,
    AddEditViewControllerDelegate, UISearchControllerDelegate,
➡ UISearchBarDelegate, UISearchResultsUpdating {
```

Now you can add the following function to capture every time the search bar becomes the first responder (you learned about first responders in section 13.4.3) or has focus:

```
func updateSearchResults(for searchController: UISearchController){}
```

Add a `print` line in the function so you can see when it's called. It should look like this:

```
print ("update search results called")
```

Run the app, and see what happens. Nothing?! Why is that? You made the class itself conform to the delegates, but you didn't tell the `resultSearchController` that the class would be its delegate. You need to add the following two lines to the `viewDid-Load()` function of the `MainViewController`:

```
resultSearchController.searchResultsUpdater = self
resultSearchController.searchBar.delegate = self
```

Now the `MainViewController` is the delegate for the `resultSearchController`, `searchResultsUpdates`, and `searchBar`. You have to tie in one last piece for this to work, though: the table view needs to know that the `searchBar` is connected to it. Add the following line just under the lines you added earlier:

```
tableView.tableHeaderView = resultSearchController.searchBar
```

Add this line next:

```
self.definesPresentationContext = true
```

This line basically says, "Let the main ViewController be the 'king' of the views," meaning it's the primary presentation layer.

Run the app again, and notice that every time you tap the search bar or type a letter in it, a new line is printed out to the console. This means it's working as expected, and you can respond to those actions! Pretty cool, huh?

27.2 *Filtering LioNs based on user input*

To filter the LioN data, you'll create a new empty array and add LioN objects to that array if they match the letters the user typed in the search bar. Figure 27.2 shows the flow of events from top to bottom when a user initiates a search by tapping the search bar:

1 The Table View uses the original `lionData` array as the data source, which means that by default all LioN objects will appear in the table view.
2 When the user taps the search bar...
3 ...the Search Controller sets itself to *active*, meaning the search bar has focus, and then...
4 ...the Search Controller calls the function that updates the search results.
5 Based on all of these events, you can then call a function to filter the LioN objects based on the search text.
6 Once filtered, you need to set the table view's data source to the filtered LioN objects so only those that matched the search will show up.
7 When the user cancels the search...
8 ...the Search Controller sets the active state to *false*, and...
9 ...you need to set the table view's data source property back to the original `lionData` array so all LioN objects are shown.

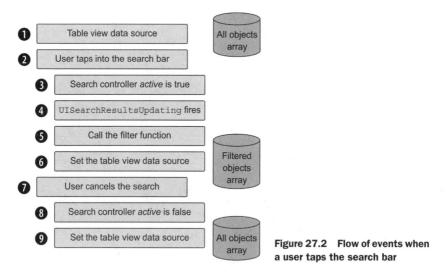

Figure 27.2   Flow of events when a user taps the search bar

Let's think about what you already have in place so you can figure out where to go from here. The table view data source is already set to all LioN objects, so step 1 is complete. Users can tap the search bar by themselves, so nothing to do there—step 2 is complete. The controller sets itself to *active* when the user taps the search bar, so nothing to do there either—step 3 is complete. You've already seen that the results-updating function is called every time you interact with the search bar, so you can count step 4 as complete, too. Step 5: you need to filter the LioN objects based on what the user types in the search bar. Nope—haven't done that yet. Let's get to it!

27.2.1 *Creating the filter function*

You need to create a new function that will be called every time the `updateSearch-Results` function is called. Add the following code to the `MainViewController`:

```
func filterLioNsforSearchText(searchedText: String){}
```

You can tell by looking at the function that it takes a string as an argument. This means when you call this function, you need to pass a string in, and the function will filter the LioN array based on the string that's passed. Where do you think the string comes from? I sure hope you answered the search bar, because it's the string the user typed in! You'll call this new function and pass in the search string. Add the following line of code in the `updateSearchResults` function:

```
filterLioNsforSearchText(searchedText: searchController.searchBar.text!)
```

Next you'll add another `print` line so you can see how the flow of the app works. Add the following line of code in the `filterLioNforSearchText` function:

```
print(searchedText)
```

This will print the value of whatever the user typed in the search bar. Run the app, and see what happens. Notice that the first time you run it, the "update search results called" line prints, but nothing prints after that. Great—the user hasn't had a chance to type in the search bar yet, so the app is working as expected. Now, type a letter: you'll see it appear in the console. Type another one—it appears as well. You're successfully capturing the search text from the search bar, and you need to filter the array based on that search text.

27.2.2 *Filtering the array using a closure*

First of all, you need to create a new array that will hold the results of your search. Add the following line at the top of the `MainViewController` with the other variables:

```
var searchLionData : [Lion] = []
```

Good. Now you have somewhere to store the LioN objects that match the search criteria. Swift arrays have a method called `filter()` that will work just fine! Get ready, though—the `filter()` method doesn't look like anything you've seen before. You'll start adding the `filter()` method to the `filter` function you created so you can see what I'm talking about. Add the following code to the `filterLioNsforSearchText` function:

```
self.searchLionData = self.lionData.filter({})
```

Given what you know now about parameters, what can you infer from this? It looks like you're passing in a function or a block of code as a parameter to the `filter()` call, doesn't it? That's exactly what this is doing. It's called a *closure*, and it looks like this (I'm only showing the filter part, to demonstrate the closure statement):

```
filter({(parameter named passed in: parameter type passed in) -> return type in
        Some statements
        Return statement
})
```

In your case, it will look like this:

```
filter({(lion:Lion) -> Bool in
    evaluation statements
return (true or false)
})
```

The evaluation statements will evaluate whether the search text appears in the LioN name, and then the closure will return the Boolean `true` (if the text did appear) or `false` (if it didn't appear). The `in` at the end of the first line lets you know that you're looking through the entire `lionData` array—in other words, you're iterating through each LioN to evaluate the search string against the LioN name. Now add the entire function so you can see it:

```
func filterLioNsforSearchText(searchedText: String) {
    print(searchedText)
    self.searchLionData = self.lionData.filter({(lion: Lion) -> Bool in
        let stringMatch = lion.lionName.range(of: searchedText)
        return stringMatch != nil
    })
}
```

To recap, in this code you do the following:

1   Set the new `SearchLionData` array equal to the `lionData` array (`self.search-LionData = self.lionData`).

2   Add the `filter()` method to the `lionData`, with a closure expression as the parameter (as indicated by the opening and closing curly brackets, `{ }`).

3   The closure expression takes the `lion` object from the `lionData` array as a parameter (`lion:Lion`)...

4   ...and returns a Boolean (`-> Bool`).

5   The keyword `in` is the start of a *closure* (the next two lines). Closures are a more advanced topic than is suitable for this book, but at a high level, they're blocks of code that can be passed around..

6   You create a string called `stringMatch` that checks to see whether the `lionName` of the `lion` passed in (`lion.lionName`) includes the searched text (`searched-Text`) in any range of its name (`rangeOfString`).

7   If `searchedText` was found in `lionName`, `true` is returned from the closure, and the `lion` object that was passed in will be added to the `searchLionData` array. If

the searchedText didn't match the lion name, the stringMatch object will be nil, so false will be returned, and the lion object won't be added to the searchLionData array.

You've successfully filtered the array based on the search term, but you can't see the results yet. If you look back to figure 27.2, you've now completed steps 1–5, but you need to complete step 6 before you can see what was filtered.

27.2.3 Changing the table view data source

When the user taps in the search bar to search on text, you want the table view to only show the rows that have that text in the name of the LioN object. This means you need to change the table view's data source property to the searchLionData array instead of the lionData array. The best place to do this in the cellForRowAtIndex-Path function, so you're going to add some code there to change the data source property. Why is this is the best place? Because I said so. No, really, cellForRowAt-IndexPath is grabbing data from your array, so if you want to display a different array, you can do it here easily.

How do you think you can find out whether the search is active? (See what I did there? I threw in the word *active* to give you a hint.) That's right! You can check the resultSearchController active property to see if it's set to true or false.

At the top (but inside) your cellForRowAtIndexPath function, add a new variable called lion of type Lion:

```
var lion : Lion
```

Just under that new line, add an if statement to check the active parameter of the resultSearchController. If it's active (meaning the searchBar has focus), set the lion variable equal to the right searchLionData object:

```
if self.resultSearchController.isActive {
    lion = searchLionData[indexPath.row]
}
```

If the resultSearchController isn't active, set the lion object equal to the appropriate lionData object:

```
else {
    lion = lionData[indexPath.row]
}
```

Now you can change the rest of the code in the function to use the lion object instead of the lionData[indexPath.row] object, because this will be correct only when the searchBar doesn't have focus. If you change everything, your full function should look like this:

```
override func tableView(_ tableView: UITableView, cellForRowAt indexPath:
➥ IndexPath) -> UITableViewCell {
```

```
        var lion : Lion
        if self.resultSearchController.isActive {
            lion = searchLionData[indexPath.row]
        { else }
            lion = lionData[indexPath.row]
        }
        let cell = tableView.dequeueReusableCell(withIdentifier:
    "lionCell", for: indexPath);

        cell.textLabel?.text = lion.lionName
        cell.detailTextLabel?.text = lion.lionDescription
        if lion.like == true {
            cell.imageView?.image =   UIImage(named: "likeItCell")
        }else{
            cell.imageView?.image =   UIImage(named: "orNotCell")
        }
        return cell
    }
```

Now you need to return the right number of rows in the `numberOfRowsInSection` function:

```
override func tableView(_ tableView: UITableView, numberOfRowsInSection
    section: Int) -> Int {
        if self.resultSearchController.isActive {
            return searchLionData.count
        { else }
            return lionData.count
        }
    }
```

Next, let's look at your segue function. When the user taps a row to edit that cell, that `lion` object is passed into the `AddEditViewController`. If your table view data source is pointing to the wrong array here, you could pass the wrong `lion` object. You'll fix that now, too. Change the segue code for the `Edit` segue so it looks like this:

```
else if segue.identifier == "Edit" {
        let navigationController = segue.destination as!
    UINavigationController
        let controller = navigationController.topViewController as!
    AddEditViewController
        if let indexPath = tableView.indexPath(for: sender as!
    UITableViewCell) {
            if resultSearchController.isActive {
                controller.lionToEdit = searchLionData[indexPath.row]
                editIndexPath = indexPath as NSIndexPath?
            { else }
                controller.lionToEdit = lionData[indexPath.row]
                editIndexPath = indexPath as NSIndexPath?
            }
        }
        controller.delegate = self
    }
}
```

The last thing you need to do to make sure your table view is updated appropriately when the searchBar has focus is to reload the table data. The best place to do this is in the updateSearchResults function that's called each time the search bar gets focus. Add the following line just under the print line:

```
self.tableView.reloadData()
```

Run the app, and notice that as soon as you tap in the search bar, the existing table view cells disappear. This makes sense because you're setting the data source to the search array, which doesn't have anything in it yet. Once you search on text that exists in a lion name field, you'll see the cells appear. Pretty cool, huh?

One thing I don't like right now is that when you tap in the search bar field, the table view turns a greyish color in the background. I'd rather it stayed nice and bright, wouldn't you? Add the following line to the viewDidLoad function:

```
resultSearchController.dimsBackgroundDuringPresentation = false
```

That looks much better, doesn't it?

You may have noticed that the search field is case-sensitive, meaning you have to type the right case in to get a search match. If you search on *T*, you don't get any results back; but if you search on *t*, you do. That isn't a very nice experience for your users, so you'll fix that, too. Go back to the filter Lions function (filterLioNs-forSearchText) that you wrote, and change the search string line to this:

```
let stringMatch = lion.lionName.uppercased().range(of:
    searchedText.uppercased())
```

This changes the lion name text to all uppercase (capital) letters and compares it to the searched text in all uppercase. Now the user can type in lowercase or uppercase and still get search results.

You may be wondering when you'll get around to steps 7, 8, and 9 from figure 27.2. You already changed the data source back to the main lion array in the if statement in the cellForRowAtIndexPath function. You finished the steps without knowing it!

27.2.4 *Polishing the app*

If you start testing the app by entering search terms, clicking a cell, and then returning to the main view, you'll notice that your search stays active. I don't like this functionality. I want the table view to reset to the lionData array when I return to the mainView. Let's see how to add the following new function to your code to reset the search bar when you return from the AddEditViewController:

```
func resetSearchBar() {
    resultSearchController.isActive = false
    resultSearchController.searchBar.text = ""
}
```

This code sets the active property of the `resultSearchController` to false and clears the text from the search bar. Make sure to set the search bar text to `""` and not `" "` (no space between the quotes), or you'll have a space in your search bar that will drive you crazy (I've never done this—really—a friend told me it happened to her one time).

Where do you think you should call the new `resetSearchBar()` function from? I'll give you a hint—you want to call it from two places:

- When the user finishes editing an item (at the end of `didFinishEditingItem`)
- When the user cancels out of editing an item (`addItemViewControllerDid-Cancel`)

Add the `resetSearchBar()` call at the end of each of these functions, and you should be set on the Search Bar functionality.

27.3   *Searching other fields*

Thinking about your app users, wouldn't it be nice if they could search both the name and description fields instead of just the name field? You can do that pretty easily, so you'll add that functionality next.

The search bar changes the *scope* of the search, meaning which fields you want to search. Add the following line in the `viewDidLoad()` function:

```
resultSearchController.searchBar.scopeButtonTitles = ["LioN: Name",
➥ "Description"]
```

As you can see, you're adding two strings into the `scopeButtonTitles` property. Run the app, and you can see the two new scope buttons once you tap in the search field. That was easy! Now you need to change your filter function based on the scope. The `scopeButtonTitles` property is expecting an array of strings, which means the strings themselves will be part of an index. Change the filter function so it looks like this:

```
func filterLioNsforSearchText(searchedText: String) {
        self.searchLionData = self.lionData.filter({(lion: Lion) -> Bool in
            if resultSearchController.searchBar.selectedScopeButtonIndex == 0 {
                let stringMatch = lion.lionName.uppercased().range(of:
➥ searchedText.uppercased())
                return stringMatch != nil
            { else }
                let stringMatch = lion.lionDescription.uppercased().range(of:
    searchedText.uppercased())
                return stringMatch != nil
            }
        })
    }
```

The last thing you need to add is a way to capture the new index when the user taps the different scope buttons. Add this new function:

```
func searchBar(_ searchBar: UISearchBar, selectedScopeButtonIndexDidChange
➥ selectedScope: Int) {
    updateSearchResults(for: resultSearchController)
}
```

This function is called each time the user changes the scope of the search, and the function in turn calls the `updateSearchResults` function. Run the app, and you can search both the Lion Name and Lion Description fields. Awesome!

27.4 *Summary*

Can you believe it? You created the LioN app all by yourself. The only differences between the version you created and the version in the App Store are

- The version in the App Store includes a Notes field, which the user can add, edit, and search on.
- The App Store version includes ads that display to the user.

You now have all the basic tools you need to create an app. I challenge you to add the Notes field yourself—you can absolutely do it. Here are a few hints to get you started:

- Use a `UITextView` instead of a `UITextField`.
- Update the LioN object definition—add the `lionNotes` to the object, and update the encode and decode functions
- You'll need to delete the old version of the LioN app from the Simulator and your iPhone before you run the version with the notes. Otherwise the `decode` function will look for a Notes field that doesn't exist.

I hope you enjoyed reading this book as much as I enjoyed writing it! Hopefully you realize now that programming isn't some mysterious science that only some people can learn—it's for everyone.

27.5 *Where do you go from here?*

As I've said before, you have all the basic tools you need to program. You can watch tutorials online, search for subjects you want to know more about, and join a local programming club to keep learning. I'm already working on the follow-up book to this one, which will teach you the next level of programming—I hope you can wait! The next book will teach you about the following:

- *Categories*—Adding categories to the LioN app (like a Beer category, a Wine category, and a Household category—for my toothpaste)
- *Photos*—Taking pictures and saving them to a LioN object; working with the Camera framework

- *iCloud*—Syncing the data to the cloud so it will be available across all your devices
- *MapKit*—Tagging locations on the map for the LioN objects so you can save the location (think restaurants and shops)

And much more!

Thank you again for reading this far. If you really did read this far, drop me a note on Twitter, Facebook, or the Manning Author Forum (which you can access at www.manning.com/books/anyone-can-create-an-app) to let me know your thoughts. (I don't think people even read the Summary, so I want to know if you read this far!)

appendix A
Installing Xcode
and Apple developer
registration

This appendix explains how to download and install Xcode, your primary iPhone and iPad development tool. It also explains how to register for the Apple Developer Program, which is a requirement for developing apps for iPhones and iPads.

A.1 Downloading and installing Xcode

You can download the latest version of Xcode from the App Store on your Mac. Open the Store, search for Xcode, and there should be a free download in the top spot. If you're new to Macs and you don't know where the App Store icon is, you can find it easily using Spotlight Search. Press the Command key (⌘) and the space-bar at the same time, and a search window will appear, as shown in figure A.1.

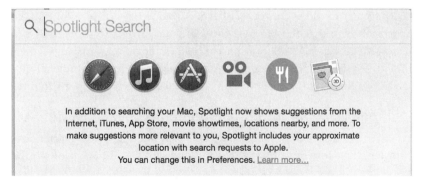

Figure A.1 Spotlight Search—press Command (⌘) and spacebar to launch it.

Now begin typing what you're looking for. In this case, you want to search for the App Store, so type *app* and it should be the first item to appear in the search results (shown on the left side of figure A.2). Once the App Store launches, search for *Xcode* (results shown at the bottom of figure A.2) and start your download.

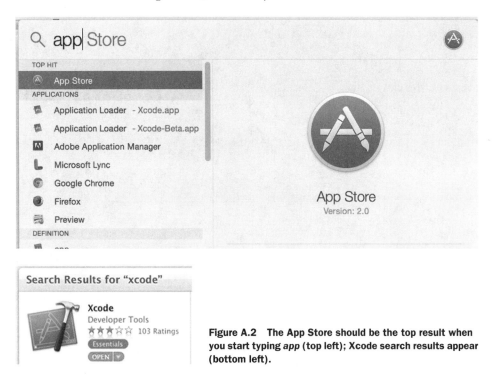

Figure A.2   The App Store should be the top result when you start typing *app* (top left); Xcode search results appear (bottom left).

Sit back or have a glass of wine now, because the download size is over 2.4 GB, so it takes quite a while. Once it's downloaded, go ahead and install it. It's easiest to accept the default settings, but read through them and decide if you want to change something.

If you have an older computer that has Xcode already installed, make sure it's at least version 8 so that the basic features are similar to the screen shots and features depicted in this book. It's okay to have a version that is newer than 8—the screens may look slightly different, but the main features and functions should still be okay.

Next you'll need to register to be part of the Apple Developer Program.

A.2   *Apple requirements for iPhone and iPad development*

The Apple Developer Program is like your driver's license for Apple development—you have to have it to develop for iPhones and iPads. You have two options for this:

- You can register for a free account, and this will let you simulate your applications on your Mac and install them only on your phone.
- You can register for the paid license ($99) which will allow you to install your applications on your iPhone and submit them to the App Store when you're ready.

It's up to you to decide which one you want to register for—if you just want to learn programming, then the free license is for you. The free license will let you program your apps and see them running on your Mac and your iPhone, but you can't submit them to the App Store. If you know you want to program and put the apps on the Store, you will need the $99 license. The license is good for one year, so you'll need to pay each year if you choose this option. You learn to run your apps on the Mac using the Simulator. Appendix B will help you install them on your phone.

You have to be part of the program (paid or free) in order to develop iOS apps. You can always start with the free account and then upgrade in the future if you want, but you can't "return" your paid $99 membership. I suggest you start with the free version and then upgrade when you're ready. Consider the Apple Development Program registration as a membership card into the cool kids' club. Registering for the membership isn't hard. Go to https://developer.apple.com/programs/ios and make sure you select the iOS Developer Program. There are other programs available that you don't need, such as Mac and Safari development. You'll have the choice to enroll as an individual or a company/organization. The easiest thing is to register as an individual for now, even if you think you may want to start a company in the future.

You'll need an Apple ID to register—and you should have one if you already have an iPhone, iPad, or Mac. You can use the same Apple ID here without a problem. If you don't already have one, you'll need to create one now:

- Enter your credit card information, if required.
- Select the program (remember, select the iOS Developer Program, not the macOS Program).
- Review and submit your information.
- Agree to the licenses.
- Purchase.
- Activate your program.

Can you believe it? You're now part of the Apple Developer Program—your first step. I hope you're excited. I know I was!

appendix B
Running the app
on your device

Do you want to see what your app looks like on your iPhone or iPad? Great—you're definitely in the right place. The first thing to do is open Xcode Preferences and go to the Account tab. Sign in with your Apple ID (use the + button on the bottom left of the window). Once you sign in, Apple will retrieve your associated developer account(s) and display them on the right pane, as shown in figure B.1.

Team Name	iOS	Mac
Wendy Wise	Agent	Agent
Wendy Wise (Personal Team)	Free	Free

Figure B.1 Adding your account information into the Xcode Preferences > Account panel will show you which development teams are associated to your Apple ID.

If you signed up for a paid developer account, you'll see that you are an agent for that team; if not, you'll see that you have a free account. Click the team name for which you are an agent (the paid team) and then click the View Details button to see the list of what you can create apps for, as shown in figure B.2.

Click the Create button for the iOS Development identity and then click Done. Although you can't tell, Apple has just done some magic in the background. Close the Preferences window and go back to the main Xcode window now. Open the Project Navigator (the leftmost panel, first button) so your project files are visible. Now click the very first object in that group (for me, it's the LioN app).

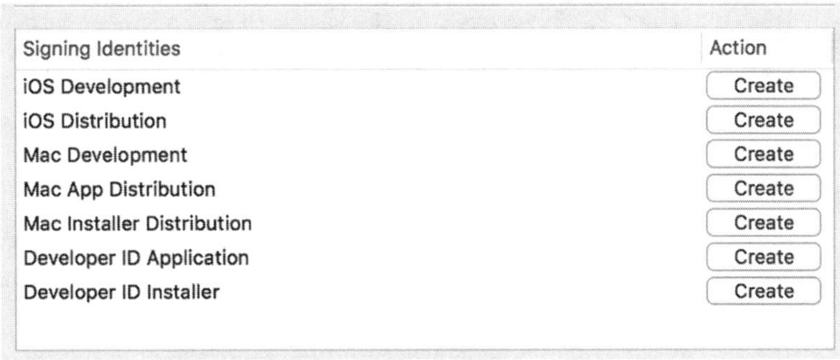

Signing Identities	Action
iOS Development	Create
iOS Distribution	Create
Mac Development	Create
Mac App Distribution	Create
Mac Installer Distribution	Create
Developer ID Application	Create
Developer ID Installer	Create

Figure B.2 Clicking the View Details button for your paid account will show you the Signing Identities you can create apps for.

The General tab for your Project will now show in the Standard Editor (the center pane). The Bundle Identifier should look familiar—you entered this into the Project detail pane when you first created your project. If your team name isn't already selected in the Team drop-down, select it. Xcode will now show an error code that states that no provisioning profiles were found and will display a Fix Issues button, as shown in figure B.3. Click that.

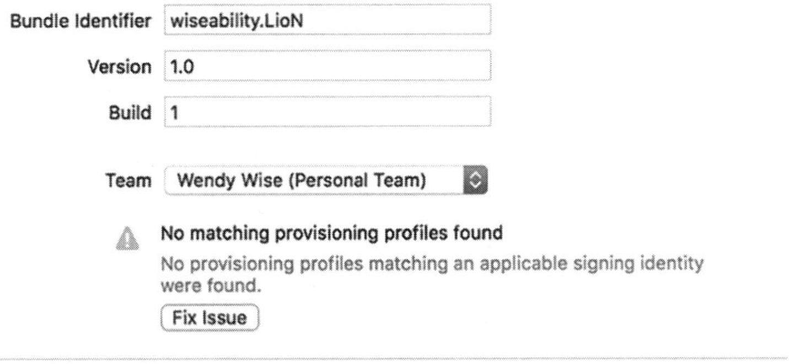

Bundle Identifier	wiseability.LioN
Version	1.0
Build	1
Team	Wendy Wise (Personal Team)

⚠ **No matching provisioning profiles found**
No provisioning profiles matching an applicable signing identity were found.

Fix Issue

Figure B.3 The General tab of your project allows you to select the team profile in the drop-down box.

As you soon as you click the Fix Issues button, Xcode communicates with Apple and then displays another message stating that you must have a device registered with your team. In other words, Apple wants to know which iPhone or iPad you'll be using. Go ahead and connect your device to your Mac. iTunes and iPhoto will most likely open to sync your device to your computer, but you can ignore those for now.

In Xcode, the schema selector displays all the Simulator devices that are available for to test the app on, as shown in figure B.4.

Figure B.4   The schema selector shows all the devices you can run your app on—some are Simulators, like this iPhone 5.

Select your device from the drop-down in the schema. In figure B.5, I selected my iPhone—which happens to have the name Wonderwoman (I'm a fan, aren't you?).

Figure B.5   Select your device name from the drop-down, and the icon will change to the appropriate device—an iPhone or iPad.

Click the Fix Issue button again, and the error message in Xcode should go away. Now run the app again in Xcode, making sure your device is unlocked, and the files should be installed on your device so you can see your app run.

If you get an error message that says you cannot run your app and the reason is "Security," don't despair—you can fix that! On your device, tap the app that you just installed (in my case, I just installed the LioN app to test it), and a new dialog box will open asking whether you want to allow the app to run since it's written by an untrusted developer (can you believe Apple doesn't trust you yet?). It's okay—you're going to fix this.

On your device, open the Settings app and tap General. Scroll nearly to the bottom and you'll see an option for Profiles and Device Management. When you tap this, you should see a screen that has your Apple ID under the Developer App section. Tap your Apple ID and a new screen will open giving you the option to tap the "Trust <your developer account>" message. Tap that and you'll receive another message asking if you want to allow any apps from this developer account to be run on your phone. Tap Trust and then rerun your app from Xcode.

Behold! Your app is now running on your device so you can show all your family and friends just how cool you are! I can remember how excited I was the first time I ran one of my very own apps on my iPhone. It didn't do much but I was proud of it— and you should be too!

index

MORE TITLES FROM MANNING

Hello World! Second Edition
Computer Programming for Kids and Other Beginners
by Warren Sande and Carter Sande

ISBN: 9781617290923
464 pages
$39.99
December 2013

Hello App Inventor!
Android programming for kids and the rest of us
by Paula Beer and Carl Simmons

ISBN: 9781617291432
360 pages
$39.99
October 2014

Hello Raspberry Pi!
Python programming for kids and other beginners
by Ryan Heitz

ISBN: 9781617292453
320 pages
$24.99
January 2016

For ordering information go to www.manning.com